D0070726

Creation and Complexity
Interdisciplinary Issues in Science and Religion

edited by Christine Ledger and Stephen Pickard

The ATF Science and Theology Series is a publication of the Australian Theological Forum. Each volume is a collection of essays by one or a number of authors in the area of science and theology. The Series addresses particular themes in the nexus between the two disciplines, and draws upon the expertise of both scientists and theologians.

Series Editor: Mark Wm Worthing

ATF Press
Adelaide

ATF Series in Science and Theology
Series Editor: Mark Wm Worthing,

1. *God, Life Intelligence and the Universe*, Terrence J Kelly SJ and Hilary D Regan, editors 2002.

2. *Habitat of Grace*, Carolyn M King, 2002.

3. *Interdisciplinary Perspectives on Cosmology and Biological Evolution*, Hilary D Regan and Mark Wm Worthing, editors, 2002.

4. *Beyond Determinism: Genetic Science and the Person*, Mark Chan and Roland Chia, editors, 2003

Creation and Complexity:

Interdisciplinary Issues in Science and Religion

edited by

Christine Ledger

and

Stephen Pickard

ATF Press
Adelaide

First published 2004

National Library of Australia
Cataloguing-in-Publication data

Creation and complexity.

ISBN 1 920691 02 2.

1. Creation. 2. Religion and Science. I. Pickard, Stephen K. II. Ledger, Christine. (Series : ATF science and theology series ; 5).

231.765

Published by
ATF Press
An imprint of the Australian Theological Forum
P O Box 504
Hindmarsh
SA 5007
ABN 68 314 074 034
www.atfpress.com

Cover design and printed by Openbook Print, Adelaide, Australia

Foreword

Many discussions of creation in the context of the science and theology dialogue come back to the question of the debate between a particular understanding of creation and the theory of evolution. This is unfortunate for some of the most fertile possibilities for genuine dialogue are often obscured when this occurs. It was refreshing, therefore, to have the privilege to be involved with a science-theology dialogue that focused on the topic of creation and complexity. Without getting bogged down in the distractions of how God may have created, the link to the theme of complexity allowed for much fruitful discussion about the nature of creation in light of the natural sciences. Related to the newly popular concept of emergence in the sciences, the concept of complexity is certainly not new. Yet in recent times it has taken on increased significance as the levels and depth of complexity within physical processes and systems has become more fully appreciated. A particular level of complexity is not so much the trigger for emergence as its prerequisite corollary. When matter unfolds its complexity through self-organisation, emergence appears as what some have called an epiphenomenon of this process. The complexity inherent in many systems, especially in living organisms, presents the scientific program of reduction with what may well be its limits: irreducible complexity that is not explicable on the basis of known laws of physics, and likely will not be explained by the discovery of any future laws.

The concept of creation is also understood broadly by the contributors to this volume. While some focus on issues related to the beginning, others look at time and eschatology. Still others are concerned with creation as the physical world in which we live and the processes which characterise this world. That is to say, creation is viewed both as becoming and as being.

For many within the sciences the concept of complexity lays at the very heart of the nature of physical reality. For those within the Christian tradition this means that complexity is also significant for an understanding of the nature of creation as well as the One who calls all things into being. The papers assembled here reflect some of the best current thinking, both from Australia and overseas, from scientists and theologians working together to better understand the nature of creation and Creator in light of the complexity inherent within every aspect of the physical processes of the world around us.

What the present volume achieves is a wide-ranging and nuanced look at the Christian idea of creation (both as process and material reality) in the light of scientific understandings of complexity. The result, which comes through the various approaches to the theme, is an underscoring of the idea that complexity is not merely a point of contact in the dialogue between theology and the sciences, it is an integral and necessary component of an adequate understanding of both creation and Creator.

Mark Worthing
Dean of Theology
Tabor College, Adelaide

Contents

Contents

Part Three: Cosmolgy

Contributors

At the time of writing, Richard Campbell was the Head of the School of Humanities of the Australian National University, Canberra, Australia. He is now an Emeritus Professor of Philosophy and Visiting Fellow of the School of Humanities of the Australian National University. He has also served as Dean of Arts, as Pro Vice-Chancellor and Chair of the Board of Faculties of the Australian National University.

At the time of writing, Niels Henrik Gregersen was Research Professor in Science and Theology in the Department of Systematic Theology of the Faculty of Theology of the University of Aarhus, Denmark. He is now Chair of Systematic Theology (Doctrine) at the University of Copenhagen, Denmark. He is a founding member and trustee of the International Society for Science and Religion.

Carolyn King is a Member of the Centre for Biodiversity and Ecology Research in the Department of Biological Sciences of the University of Waikate, Hamilton, New Zealand.

Christine Ledger was Workshop Site Director of the Creation and Complexity workshop while a PhD student at St Mark's National Theological Centre, Charles Sturt University, Canberra, Australia. She is now Centre Manager of the Australian Centre for Christianity and Culture in Canberra.

Stephen Pickard was Convenor of the Creation and Complexity workshop. He is Associate Professor and the Head of the School of Theology of Charles Sturt University and Director of St Mark's National Theological Centre, Canberra, Australia.

John White is Professor of Physical and Theoretical Chemistry in the Institute of Advanced Studies of the Australian National University and the Science Policy Secretary of the Australian Academy of Science, Canberra, Australia.

Contributors

At the time of writing, David Wilkinson was a Fellow in Christian Apologetics and the Associate Director of the Centre for Christian Communication, St Johns College in the University of Durham, United Kingdom. He is now Wesley Research Lecturer in Theology and Science in the University of Durham.

Mark Worthing was Regional Director of the Science and Religion Course Program for Australia and New Zealand and is Dean of Studies of Tabor College, Adelaide, Australia.

Introduction

Christine Ledger and Stephen Pickard

Over the Australia Day long weekend in January 2002, over 100 people gathered in Canberra for an international workshop on 'Creation and complexity: interdisciplinary issues in science and religion'. They came from all states and territories of Australia and from Denmark, Fiji, Indonesia, New Zealand, the Philippines, the UK and the USA. Most participants belonged to the Christian faith, however, Judaism and Buddhism were also represented.

The workshop was part of a Science and Religion Course Program funded by the Center for Theology and the Natural Sciences in Berkeley (CTNS) with a grant from the John Templeton Foundation. It was hosted by St Mark's National Theological Centre in association with the School of Theology of Charles Sturt University and the Flinders Centre for Theology, Science and Culture, Adelaide. As well as receiving papers, most of which are published here, the workshop participants met with botanists from the Australian National Botanic Gardens and with astronomers at Mt Stromlo Observatory. Little did we know that, one year later, that same observatory would be destroyed by bushfire.

The workshop addressed its theme, 'Creation and complexity', through the eyes of theology, philosophy and science. It did so, not setting one discipline against another, but in a spirit of dialogue and combined wisdom. Consistent with its theme, participants did not seek simplistic answers or draw upon literal readings of the Bible. Rather, they embraced the enormity, majesty, mystery and complexity of God's creation and sought to understand so as to praise God more.

Creation and complexity

'Creation' is a word theologians are generally more comfortable with while 'complexity' is more common in scientific circles. In bringing these two concepts together, the workshop stimulated discussion about our understandings of God's activity in the world and the expressions of that activity. Is God's creation necessarily complex?

Can human comprehension, through science, grasp a theory of everything? How is the complexity of the world related to the complexity of God?

Welten suggests that science, after spending centuries searching for simple explanations of the world's phenomena, is now coming to terms with complexity. He cites a wide variety of systems through which complexity is considered: 'ecological systems, neural networks, oceanography, atmospheric circulation, meteorology, turbulences and vortices, fractals, the dynamic of natural populations, the evolution of proteins, genetic fluxes, in populations, etc.'[1] Complexity, in this scientific understanding, is often associated with mathematical models. However, Schmitz-Moorma argues that to fully understand complexity, we need to 'engage in a qualitative, and not only a quantitative analysis of reality'[2] and that we 'most probably will not be able to understand complexity reduced to digits any more than trying to understand Beethoven's ninth symphony when we see a digitalised transcript of the music'.[3] Complexity cannot be reduced to formulae but requires us 'to describe the wholeness experienced',[4] a complex unity held together in relation.

Complexity, then, may be another way of expressing the old problem of the one and the many, a problem addressed by Greek philosophers.[5] How might we understand an organism, a phenomenon, a system made up of many interacting parts yet comprehensible as an identity, a unity, a whole? It is here that we find an intersection between the theology of creation and our

---

1. W Welten, 'Questions and Remarks Concerning Origins, Time and Complexity', in *Origins, Time and Complexity*, volume 1, part 1, edited by George V Coyne *et al* (Geneva: Labor et Fides, 1993), 170–171.
2. K Schmitz-Moorman, 'The Concept of Complexity Seen in the Light of the Evolution of Complexes', in *Origins, Time and Complexity*, volume 2, part 2, edited by George V Coyne et al (Geneva: Labor et Fides, 1994), 241.
3. *Ibid*, 239.
4. *Ibid*, 240.
5. W Welten, 'Questions and Remarks Concerning Origins, Time and Complexity', *op cit*, 172.

understanding of complexity, for theology of creation also grapples with the questions of the one and the many.

Contemporary theology of creation arises from a Trinitarian understanding of God. The doctrine of the Trinity is profoundly relational, speaking as it does of God as three-in-one, and the unity and diversity of the being of God. The relations between the persons of the Trinity is known as 'perichoresis' and corres-ponding understandings of the trinitarian God's interaction with and in the world is known as 'divine economy'.[6] Perichoresis is a highly speculative concept to address ultimate mysteries. It is from human understandings of the divine economy of God, ie the ways in which God's creative, redeeming and sustaining actions are experienced in the world, that perichoresis, the interrelations between the divine persons of the Trinity, is normally inferred. Gunton suggests, however, that the 'conceptual mapping' may be reversed.[7] That is, the perichoresis, the unity and diversity of the Godhead, may inform us about the fundamental relatedness of reality. In this understanding, perichoresis, or relatedness, is itself a 'transcendental' In Gunton's words, 'If . . . the concept of perichoresis is of transcendental status . . . it must enable us . . . to explore whether reality is on all levels perichoretic, a dynamic of relatedness. Do we live in a world that can be understood relationally on all its levels?'[8]

A key, then, for a theological understanding of complexity is to be found in the concept of trinitarian relationality, for it is there that theological debates about the one and the many, unity and diversity, are located. Just as complexity, in the scientific sense, requires us to hold together both the specificity of an identity—whether it be an organism, an meteorological phenomenon or an ecosystem—with the intricate interrelationships of events and particles, so too does trinitarian relationality require us to grapple with the oneness of God, who is known and acts together as Father, Son and Holy Spirit. God cannot be divided or reduced to component parts. God's very nature is relational and complex and it follows that God's creation is characterised by this same relationality and complexity.

---

6. Colin Gunton, *The One, the Three and the Many: God, Creation and the Culture of Modernity* (Cambridge: Cambridge University Press, 1993).
7. *Ibid*, 165.
8. *Ibid*.

There is a growing consensus among theologians that relationality is key to understanding creation. Moltmann bases his ecological doctrine of creation on trinitarian relations, arguing that a trinitarian understanding of God leads us to understand God's relationship with the world as one of community rather than domination. He states, 'Our starting point is that all relationships which are analogous to God reflect the primal, reciprocal indwelling and mutual interpenetration of the trinitarian perichoresis: God in the world and the world in God . . . All living things . . . live in one another and with one another, from one another and for one another.'[9] According to Johnson, 'The Trinity as pure relationality . . . epitomises the connectedness of all that exists in the universe. Relation encompasses and constitutes the web of reality and, when rightly ordered, forms the matrix for the flourishing of all creatures.'[10]

Cunningham suggests that relationality is being embraced as an alternative to the metaphysics of substance. Instead of the world—and God—being understood as a collection of independent entities each known by its specific essence, the concept of relationality gives emphasis to 'both God's internal relationality and God's loving relationship with the world'.[11] Relationality and, therefore, complexity, is a quality that comes from God and speaks of God's way of being with the created world. A trinitarian understanding of the doctrine of creation speaks of the complex and loving interrelatedness that suffuses reality, of 'being in communion'.[12]

, According to this understanding, the complexity of the world is entirely natural and God-given. A dynamic of relatedness marks

---

9.   Jurgen Moltmann, *God in Creation: An Ecological Doctrine of Creation*, translated by Margaret Kohl (London: SCM Press, 1985), 17.

10. Elizabeth Johnson, *She Who Is: The Mystery of God in Feminist Theological Discourse* (New York: Crossroad, 1992), 222.

11. David Cunningham, *The Three Are One: The Practice of Trinitarian Theology* (Oxford: Blackwell Publishers, 1998), 25.

12. Colin Gunton, *The Promise of Trinitarian Theology* (Edinburgh: T&T Clark, 1991), 10.

God's creative activity in the world. Creatures and all created things cannot exist, nor be understood, in isolation from each other and God. As Edwards puts it, 'Once the nature of God is understood as relational, then this suggests that the fundamental nature of all reality is relational.'[13] The complexity of the world, therefore, cannot be entirely disentangled any more than the trinitarian nature of God can be divided into neat categories.

Gunton argues that God is a being-in-relation and that a dynamic of relatedness marks God's creative activity in the world.[14] The network of relations between God and humankind, among humankind and between humankind and the rest of the universe find their basis in the relational nature of God's creative being. The world's unity and diversity are born of God. The complexity of the world and its interrelations, according to a trinitarian understanding of creation, is natural and is manifested in the relations between the smallest physical particles as well as in ecosystems and human social structures.

Yet the correspondences between the inner complexities of the world and the complexity appropriate to God's being and action, while related, are not isomorphic. Thus, when one theologian considers the 'postmodern' situation he suggests 'it is a picture of plenitude, consisting of an endless complexity and dynamism of meaning at every level'.[15] What emerges is a continuous 'complexity of interrelations' that radically undermines all simple notions of correspondence between concepts and realities and at the same time opens up many new possibilities for understanding the created order. Layers of complexity reveal themselves through attentive discernment. For example the organised complexity of human life and behaviour is of a higher order in relation to animals, though no absolute boundary can be fixed.[16] The structuring of human beings

---

13. Denis Edwards, *The God of Evolution: A Trinitarian Theology* (New Jersey: Paulist Press, 1999).

14. Colin Gunton, *The One, the Three and the Many: God, Creation and the Culture of Modernity, op cit.*

15. Daniel Hardy, *God's Ways with the World: Thinking and Practising Christian Faith* (Edinburgh: T&T Clark, 1996), 259.

16. *Ibid*, 104.

and societies is generative of increasing complexity though this is often interpreted as alien and unwelcome. The world can seem too complex for us and makes too great a claim upon us. For one thing recognition of such complexity 'is incapable of being known without comparable complexities in the structure of knowledge . . . and in the relation between knowledge and other aspects of the wellbeing of mankind such as goodness and beauty'.[17] We would prefer the world and ourselves to be simple. This, in Karl Barth's view, was the fundamental sin of human beings: 'It is very understandable that, complex as he [sic] is and suffering from his own complexity as he does, man would like to be different, ie simple.'[18] The appeal of simplicity in a complex world was natural enough but a distortion of the structure and energy of human life, society and, ultimately, God.

The inability of human beings to deal with the deep complexities of the world, and the movement toward simpler social structures 'reflects an inability to comprehend the complexity of God's own life and relation with the world'.[19] The default is a notion of God as the absolute and simple being lacking inner differentiation and dynamism. Under these conditions 'the *monarche* of God is transferred to states and individuals'.[20] The result is various forms of domination in the political, social and biological worlds. The issue of complexity is thus a highly charged matter that involves many disciplines and peoples. How it is recognised, understood and allowed to influence our thinking and practices becomes a litmus test of our moral vision and courage.

However the supposition of the complexity in the world and God is only part of the story. Specifying the nature of the complexities and their relations is another part. Though even here we can miss the fundamentally dynamic nature of the world as a place of ever-expanding complexity. In the Christian tradition this expansive and deepening quality of the nature of creation and human social life provides clues and hints of the rich complexity of God's own life.

---

17. *Ibid*, 237.
18. Karl Barth, *Church Dogmatics*, volume 2, part 1 (Edinburgh: T&T Clark, 1964 reprint), 449.
19. Daniel Hardy, *God's Ways with the World, op cit*, 184.
20. *Ibid*.

The language of relationality and communion is an important attempt to articulate that complex dynamic that inheres in God's life. But the problem is how might this relational life be further specified? This is necessary in order to avoid abstraction. It is one of the most important projects in contemporary theology and the supposition is that as theology undertakes this inquiry it will necessarily interact with other disciplines and modes of thought. The reason for this is that God and creation are deeply related, and coming to an understanding of the nature of this relationship and its dynamism requires a wisdom not held by any one discipline but only found in relation. This is indeed an exciting prospect, for it means that the future of theology is bound up with a deeper search for knowledge and wisdom in concert with other disciplines. But in this activity theology ought to be able to make its contribution as it faithfully reasons from the presence and action of God's ways in the world.

What shall we find in such an inquiry? A Christian trinitarianism points to an understanding of God 'as a dynamic structured relationality in whom there is an infinite possibility of life'.[21] But this requires far more unravelling than space allows here. Minimally it will require attention to the event of Jesus Christ as a life mediating in maximal form and information to economy of the Trinity in the created order.[22] Working with such an insight ought to give confidence that a trinitarian understanding of God with creation is key to a theological understanding of complexity. Just as our understanding of the triune God is not reducible to a mathematical principle but is bound up with the quality of loving relations, so too must our understanding of God's creation be informed by its complex interrelatedness.

Conference papers
The papers published here explore the themes of creation and complexity from a variety of angles. The book is divided into three parts. The first, 'A complex world', explores the nature of complexity and creation. The second, 'Evolutionary biology', elaborates the theme through the lens of the biological sciences, and the third part,

---

21.   *Ibid*, 186.
22.   *Ibid*, 130f.

'Cosmology', explores the origins of the universe and eschatological questions.

In chapter 1, Niels Gregersen offers his understanding of complexity by addressing the basic question, 'How does nature work?' He notes that complexity research is intrinsically interdisciplinary as it bridges 'the inorganic and the organic, the natural and the cultural' and even science and religion. He elaborates various definitions of complexity from the mathematical to the informal and suggests ten ways in which complexity is relevant so the science and religion dialogue.

In chapter 2, Carolyn King examines the nature of dialogues and debates between science and theology. After illustrating how these debates and dialogues often fail through miscommunication, she argues that a new model is needed for the way science and theology understand and regard each other. She suggests that this new model would need to begin with a celebration of what science and theology have in common, for example, the use of models and metaphors.

In chapter 3, Carolyn King brings her biological expertise to exploring whether contemporary theology and science are consistent in their understandings of the complexity of the natural world. She concludes that it is imperative that we 'integrate the unlimited freedom of nature with the unlimited love of God'.

In chapter 4, Niels Gregersen engages in a dialogue between creation theology and evolutionary biology, tracing the trend towards complexification of the universe, from simpler to more complex lifeforms. He argues that self-organisation is not a threat to religion but is a manifestation of God's continuous creation of the world through such processes.

In chapter 5, John White and others present the findings of a committee of the Anglican Synod of the Canberra and Goulburn Diocese regarding current biomedical research into the cloning of human cells. This committee, while rejecting the cloning of people, supported the exploration of cloning techniques for therapeutic purposes.

In chapter 6, Richard Campbell 'proposes a process-based model for an ontology that encompasses the emergence of increasing complex systems'. In so doing, he provides 'a non-reductive model for understanding human beings as both emergent and yet embodied'. We are interrelated to our environment and to our societies and cannot simply be reduced to cellular components.

In chapter 7, David Wilkinson, introduces the theme of the conference by considering how questions of science and religion are expressed in popular culture. He does so by focusing on scientific and theological understandings of the origin of the universe. He concludes that questions of the origin of the universe are not about the absence of God or a surer path to God but rather these questions stimulate the interaction between science and theology.

In chapter 8, Mark Worthing grapples with the concepts of time and eternity as both scientific and theological problems. He argues that time itself is open to transformation and that if we are able to think differently about time theologically, as well as scientifically, new theological horizons would open up.

In chapter 9, David Wilkinson shifts his attention from the origins of the universe to eschatology. He argues that whereas much debate has taken place between science and theology about the beginning of life, little has taken place about the future of the universe. Contemporary science tends to have a pessimistic view and this raises theological questions regarding creation, new creation, providence, hope and ethics.

All these contributions provide a rich meal of ideas to digest. What then, are their implications for our living ethically and creatively in God's complex world?

Complexity, creativity and culture

In contemporary technological culture there is a tendency to ignore or deny the natural relationality and complexity of creation. We seek to simplify and reduce so as to control. In our denial of our relatedness to God, each other and the rest of the universe, we often damage or destroy fragile ecosystems and human societies. Our relationship with God from whom all creativity flows is also damaged. True creativity arises from our acknowledgment and our nourishing of the complexity, of the interrelatedness, of all life and its sustenance from the life-giving energy of God.[23]

---

23. *Ibid*, 82.

According to the doctrine of creation, human beings are the *imago dei*, the image of God. What are the implications of our being created the *imago dei* for the way we act in the world and for our creativity?

There are several theological traditions regarding the *imago dei*. One tradition sees human beings as being like God in the rational sense—our mind mirrors God's. Another sees human beings as being like God in the moral sense—we share in God's dominion over nature. The third sees human beings' participation in God's capacity for relationship—we live in relationship. The fourth sees human beings as being like God in the creative sense—we are partners with God in ongoing creative processes.[24]

Gunton argues that the primary quality of the *imago dei* is relational, that 'to be in the image of God is to be placed in a dynamic of relationships: first of all with other human beings and second with the created order'.[25] He challenges the understanding of the *imago dei* that locates it in the human capacity for reason, arguing that this results in a lack of appreciation of humankind's intrinsic relationships with the world. This in turn leads to an individualistic understanding of the *imago dei* and a lack of ecological sensitivity. Gunton suggests that it is also mistaken to understand creativity as defining the *imago dei* as creativity is not a defining characteristic of God because God is not bound to create.[26] However, relationality does have profound implications for humankind's creativity. While God may not need to create, God has created and does create. Human beings, as the *imago dei*, are called to live in communion, echoing God's being-in-communion. We are called to exercise our creative talents fully cognisant of and while nurturing loving relationships. True creativity is defined by relationality.

Berdyaev argues that creativeness 'is only possible because the world is created, because there is a creator' and that 'nothing can be more pitiful and absurd that to pride oneself on one's genius' for all our gifts and our genius are received from God and not of our own

---

24. Ted Peters, *God—The World's Future*, 2nd edition (Burlington: Ashgate, 2000), 153–155.
25. Colin Gunton, *Christ and Creation* (Carlisle: The Paternoster Press, 1992), 102.
26. *Ibid*, 121.

making.[27] The love of others, not power over others, is the motivation of true creativity. He speaks of creative acts arising from our standing face to face, first with God and then with each other and the world. In facing God we acknowledge the mystery of existence and are inspired by 'creative fire' and, in facing each other and the world, we seek to give expression to this inspiration, albeit in a limited way.[28]

Heidegger's insistence that 'building' arises from 'dwelling' is a comment on human creativity being inseparable from recognising the fundamental relationships that make this world our home. He maintains, 'Only if we are capable of dwelling, only then can we build.'[29] This might be paraphrased as, 'Only if we are mindful of, and foster, our relatedness, only then can we be creative.' This is the true nature of creativity. It is formed by an awareness of dwelling in a complex network of living relationships.

Technological culture is profoundly instrumental. It rests on a worldview of understanding, organising and using the world as a resource. A trinitarian doctrine of creation is profoundly relational. It speaks of the otherness-in-relation of the triune God and of the relatedness of God with the created world. Our cultural instincts, therefore, encourage us to disregard or dismember the innate complexity of our world and its interrelatedness, whereas a trinitarian theology of creation honours complexity and relatedness as a defining feature of all that is, including God. An instrumentalist attitude towards the world results in a distancing, a disengagement from the world, which in turn develops into alienation.[30] In contrast, a trinitarian understanding of creation calls us to be in communion with God, the world and each other.

---

27. Nicolas Berdyaev, *The Destiny of Man* (London: Geoffrey Bles, 1937), 127.
28. *Ibid*, 128–129.
29. Martin Heidegger, 'Building Dwelling Thinking', in *Basic Writings from Being and Time (1927) to The Task of Thinking (1964)*, edited by David Farrell Krell, 2nd edition (San Francisco: HarperCollins, 1993), 361.
30. Colin Gunton, *The One, the Three and the Many: God, Creation and the Culture of Modernity, op cit*, 13–14.

Buber describes an instrumental attitude to the world as an I-It stance. He warns about the danger of a human culture becoming overly preoccupied with this I-It stance and losing its grounding in relations. 'Only as long as [man] himself enters into relations is he free and thus creative. When a culture is no longer centered in a living and continually relational process, it freezes into the It-world... From that point on, common causality . . . grows into an oppressive and crushing doom.'[31]

Borgmann describes the distinction between instrumental and relational ways of living in terms of 'regardless power' and 'careful power.'[32] 'Regardless power' is reflected in the contemporary obsession with the commodities of daily life and self-indulgent attitudes. 'Careful power' gives honour to the other and values the interrelatedness of God with all things. It does not seek to use or control but rather to relate in love. Hefner argues that the purpose of human beings is 'to birth the future that is most wholesome for the nature that has birthed us'.[33] For human beings to take seriously both their inescapable relatedness to God and the world means to honour and nurture that relatedness by caring for the 'wholesomeness' or, as the World Council of Churches calls it, the 'integrity' of God's creation.[34]

A crisis in technological culture has arisen as we have become alienated, not only from the world of which we are a part, but also from our very nature as human beings, as the *imago dei*. Either we deny our createdness and our ultimate dependency on God, and so lapse into arrogance, or we relinquish our creative freedom and lapse into an irresponsible apathy of disengagement from the world and community and act out of isolated selfishness. As Gunton maintains,

---

31. Martin Buber, *I and Thou,* translated by Walter Kaufmann (Edinburgh: T&T Clark, 1970), 103.

32. Albert Borgmann, 'Prospects for the Theology of Technology', in *Theology and Technology,* edited by Carl Mitcham and Jim Grote (Lanham, Maryland: University Press of America), 315.

33. Philip Hefner, *The Human Factor: Evolution, Culture, and Religion* (Minneapolis: Fortress Press, 1993), 264.

34. Preman Niles, *Resisting the Threats to Life: Covenanting Justice, Peace and the Integrity of Creation* (Geneva: WCC Publications).

'We shall not understand our place in the world unless we face up to the way in which we are internally related to the rest of the world.'[35]

Through the theme of creation and complexity we can discern an interesting convergence of contemporary scientific and theological thought. Science is acknowledging that its earlier quest to simplify and reduce so as to understand is inherently limited. The world and its systems are complex. There are thresholds to quantitative analysis, which are characterised by complex interrelationships. The trinitarian doctrine of creation affirms this insight, suggesting that, just as God must be understood in terms of loving relationships, of being-in-communion, so too must all creation be understood as complex and its relatedness respected and nurtured.

Our enquiries into the complexity of creation can never reach a conclusion through our cosmological and scientific questioning. The world continues to change and evolve. God and God's creation are infinitely rich and complex, as evidenced by the very nature of the triune God we worship. True human creativity, which arises from our knowledge of God's love of the world in all the world's specificity and intricacy, is part of the expanding richness and complexity of creation. As the *imago dei*, we participate in God's creation, not only through our discovery of ever more dimensions of complexity. Our creativity, if mindful of the unity in diversity of creation and respectful of the beauty and integrity of God's continuing loving actions in the world, contributes to the increasing richness and complexity of the world. Yet this increasing complexity 'is itself the manifestation of the ongoingly energetic involvement and participation of God, whereby he intends to move toward fuller and fuller relationship with his people and their societies'.[36]

These insights raise a challenge to us for the way we live in God's beautifully complex world. How might we honour the complex interrelatedness of this world, not as a problem to be solved, but as a gift to be celebrated?

---

35. Colin Gunton, *The One, The Three and the Many: God, Creation and the Culture of Modernity, op cit,* 15.
36. Daniel Hardy, *God's Ways with the World, op cit,* 30.

interrelatedness of this world, not as a problem to be solved, but as a gift to be celebrated?

Part One

A Complex World

A primer on Complexity: Definitions, Theories, and Theological Perspectives[1]

Niels Henrik Gregersen

Whereas cosmology explores the boundaries of the very large and quantum theory the nature of the very small, complexity theory aims to understand the emergence and development of orders at every level, including the medium-size world. To the riddles of the macroscopic and the microscopic are added the puzzles of complex pattern formation in semistable dynamical systems known from everyday life.

Semistable systems are usually nonlinear, so small inputs may trigger dramatic changes. Examples are volcanoes and tornadoes, embryologic and ecological evolution, traffic systems and stock markets. These are not new areas of research, but the computerisation of science since the 1970s has made possible new formalistic approaches to the study of dynamical systems. The question is hereby not so much 'What are the constituents of nature (quarks, protons, electrons etc.)?' but rather 'How does nature work?'

Complexity theory, however, is not the name of a single theory comparable to, say, Albert Einstein's Theory of Relativity. There hardly exists one overarching 'law of complexity' waiting to be discovered. Rather, complexity research is an umbrella term for a wide variety of studies on pattern formation, some more general, some arising under specific organisational conditions. The field builds in particular on thermodynamics, information theory, cybernetics and evolutionary biology, but also on economics, systems theory, and other disciplines.

Since complexity research consistently crosses the boundaries between the inorganic and the organic, the natural and the cultural, the field is likely to influence the future science-religion dialogue significantly. What follows here is an attempt to provide an overview

---

1. This article is an extended version of my entry 'Complexity', written for the *Encyclopedia of Science and Religion* (New York: Macmillan, 2003). Used with permission.

of a relatively new theoretical field. I start out by presenting different definitions of complexity, some of which are mathematical, while others are more informal (sections 1 and 2). I continue to discuss the relation between computational approaches to complexity in the tradition of information theory and cybernetics and the more conceptual approaches that we find in organicism, emergentism and systems theory (sections 3 and 4). Fundamental is here the distinction between computational complexity and real-world complexity, a distinction that is often missing in recent discussions (section 5). I end by pointing to ten areas of contact, where I believe that theology has particularly much to learn from an engagement with the new sciences of complexity.

Algorithmic complexity
There is no consensus on a general definition of complexity. The complex is usually defined in contrast to the simple, but the distinction between simple and complex is a relative one. What is simple in one frame of reference may be complex in another. Walking downstairs, for example, is simple from the perspective of a healthy person, but physiologically highly complex. On the other hand, chaos theory shows that complex phenomena can be described by simple non-linear equations.

An exact measure of *algorithmic complexity* has been available since the 1960s. In the Kolmogorov-Chaitin model, the complexity of a digital code consisting of 0s and 1s is measured by the length of the computer program needed to describe it. Even a long series of digits (eg '01010101010101010101 . . . ') can be compressed into a compact description: 'write '01' x times'. By contrast, a complex code is a series without a discernable pattern; in the worst case, the series would simply need to be repeated by the computer program (eg '1001110010011000011 . . . '). Such systems are by definition random. However, one can never know with certainty whether a series that one sees as random could be further compressed. This is an information-theoretical version of Gödel's incompleteness theorem discovered by Gregory Chaitin[2].

---

2.   Gregory Chaitin, *Algorithmic Information Theory* (Cambridge: Cambridge University Press, 1975).

Similarly, CH Bennett[3] has suggested a measure for a structure's degree of complexity by referring to its *logical depth*, defined as the time needed (measured by the number of computational steps) for the shortest possible program to generate that structure. Both Chaitin and Bennett presuppose Claude Shannon's mathematical concept of information: The more disordered a message is, the higher is its informational content. While Chaitin's basic definition has the advantage of being extremely economic, Bennett's definition is capable of measuring the discrete operational steps involved in problem solutions. However, none of these formal definitions of complexity can distinguish organised complexity from pure randomness. The main interest of complexity studies, though, is to understand the self-organised complexity that arises in the creative zones between pure order and pure randomness. It seems that a more qualitative approach is helpful in supplementing the pure algorithmic definitions of complexity

Real-world complexity
To catch the idea of organised complexity, it may be useful to distinguish between descriptive, causal and ontological aspects of complexity of natural and social systems.

Systems that require different sorts of analyses can be called *descriptively complex*.[4] Fruit flies, for example, require a variety of descriptions, such as physical descriptions of their thermal conductivity; biochemical descriptions of their constitution; morphological descriptions of their anatomical organs; functional descriptions and so on. This idea of descriptive complexity lends support to an explanatory pluralism, which emphasises the need for different types of explanation at different levels. There might be a natural complexity provided by the simple fact that the world can be

---

3.   CH Bennett, 'Logical Depth and Physical Complexity', in *The Universal Turing Maschine: A Half-Century Survey*, edited by R Herken (Oxford: Oxford University Press, 1987), 227–257.
4.   William C Wimsatt, 'Complexity and Organisation', in *Topics in the Philosophy of Biology*, edited by M Grene and E Mendelsohn, *Boston Studies in the Philosophy of Science*, volume 27 (Dordrecht: Kluwer, 1986), 174–193.

described from endlessly many perspectives, and still have a truth-relation to the real-world complexity.[5]

Systems, however, can also be *pathway complex* while simple in structure, if their causal effects are highly sensitive to environmental conditions. A hormone is a natural-kind entity with an easily specifiable molecular composition, but since the effects of the hormone depend on a variety of bodily constellations (which cannot be finitely determined), the causal trajectory of the hormone is complex. Systems theory and organicist proposals in biology have focused on this aspect of complexity. The causal complexity comes to the fore when we are dealing with large-scale systems that constantly interact with one another, without being reducible to one another. One example is ecology, where Susan Oyama has called for a 'shift from "genes and environment" to a multiplicity of entities, influences, and environments'.[6] The point is here that complex systems may exhibit an ongoing 'constructivist interaction' in which the different actors are changed in the process of walking. A similar approach is used by the German sociologist Niklas Luhmann[7] to investigate the ongoing interpenetration between psychological systems and social systems. The autopoietic systems theory[8] is also standing in this constructionist tradition (without needing, I would argue, to be anti-realistic). In large-scale systems there are at least two limits to computability: one is the well-known problem of infinite regress that the environments of systems cannot be compressed because of the steady influx from the ever-expanding horizon of boundary conditions. The other limit is the fact that causal influences can be different in type, so that one cannot translate, say, the influence of cognitive processes on brain processes, and vice versa.

---

5. Nicholas Rescher, *Complexity: A Philosophical Overview* (New Brunswick, NJ/London, UK: Transaction Publishers, 1998).
6. Susan Oyama, 'Evolution's Eye. A Systems View of the Biology-Culture Divide' (2000), 4.
7. Niklas Luhmann, *Social Systems*, translated by John Bednarz Jr with Dirk Baecker (Stanford: Stanford University Press, 1995).
8. Niels Henrik Gregersen, 'The Idea of Creation and the Theory of Autopoetic Processes', in *Zygon*, 33:3 (1998): 333–367.

The most difficult thing to define is *ontological complexity*. An element-based definition of complexity defines complexity by its large number of *variegated elements*.[9] This definition centres on the fact that many large-scale systems (mountains, geological plates etc.) do not allow for an analytical approach of their micro-physical states. A relation-based definition of complexity will rather focus on the *multiple couplings* of a system in relation to its environments.[10] The human brain with its high number of flexible neurons exemplifies that more possibilities of couplings exist than can be actualised in a life-history. Since the capacity for complex interactions with the environment is usually increased by operational subsystems, organisational features can be added to the definition of complexity. An organisation-based definition of complexity thus emphasises the *hierarchical structure* of interacting levels. Analogously, a performance-based definition focuses on the *capacity for self-organising activity*. Systems are thus ontologically complex if they (1) consist of many variegated elements (in terms of sizes and types), (2) have a high capacity for relating to themselves and their environments, (3) are highly organised in subsystems, multilevel structures and internal programs, and (4) can perform self-organised activities by flexible couplings to the environment. On this scheme it is possible to evaluate different aspects of complexity. A volcano will be more complex than an amoeba on (1) elements and perhaps on (2) relations, but far less complex on the score of (3) hierarchical order and (4) self-organising activity.

On this scheme, the complex can also be distinguished from the merely complicated.[11] Even 'primitive' natural entities such as genes may be ontologically more complex than sophisticated artificial systems such as airplanes. A Boeing 747 jet consists of highly specified elements, related to one another in pre-described way, and there exists a clear recipe for how to assemble the elements into a unified system, which again has a pre-designed purpose: being able

---

9. Per Bak, *How Nature Works: The Science of Self-Organised Criticality* (Oxford: Oxford University Press, 1997), 5.
10. Niklas Luhmann, *Social Systems, op cit*, 23–28.
11. Paul Cilliers, *Complexity and Postmodernism: Understanding Complex Systems* (London: Routledge, 1998).

to take off, fly and land safely. The Boeing is a highly complicated machine, but not terribly complex. In this sense, the complex is more than the simple, but also more than the complicated.

Non-computational complexity

Complexity studies fall into two main families of research, one more conceptual (organicism, emergentism and systems theory) and another more formalistic (information theory, cybernetics and computational complexity). Both types of research continue to interact in understanding complex phenomena. While a conceptual pre-understanding of complex phenomena guides the construction of computational models, these will afterwards have to be tested on real-world situations.

Complexity studies did not start with the computers. The idea that the whole is more than the sum of the parts goes back to Plato's notion of divine providence (*Laws* 903 BC), and in Kant we find a naturalised version of the same idea of self-adjustment: 'parts bind themselves mutually into the unity of a whole in such a way that they are mutually cause and effect of one another' (*Critique of Judgment* B 292). At least this is how human observers are bound to see it.

Embryologists from Karl-Ernst von Baer and Hans Spemann up to C H Waddington embraced *organicism* as the middle course between vitalism and reductionism. In organicism a materialist ontology ('there exists nothing but matter') was combined with the observation that new properties are causally effective within higher-order wholes. Molecules are not semipermeable, but cell membranes are, and without this capacity organisms cannot survive. In the 1920s writers such as C Lloyd Morgan, CD Broad and Samuel Alexander developed organicism from an empirical research program into a meta-physical program of *emergent evolutionism*. The point here was that in the course of evolution higher-order levels are formed in which new properties emerge. Whereas the solidity of a table is a mere 'resultant' of solid state physics, the evolution of life is ripe with 'emergent' properties (for example, metabolism) that require new forms of description and eventually will have real causal feedback effects on the physical system (the atmosphere) that nourished life in the first place.

8

After World War II the *general systems theory* combined organicistic intuitions with cybernetics. Ludwig von Bertalanffy replaced the traditional whole/part difference by the difference between systems and environments. Systems are constitutionally open for environmental inputs and are bound to develop beyond equilibrium under selective pressures. Thereby systems theory established itself as a theory combining thermodynamics and evolutionary theory. Systems are structures of dynamic relations, not frozen objects. In the 1960s Heinz von Foerster and others introduced the theory of self-referential systems according to which all systems relate to their environments by relating to their own internal codes or programs. Brains don't respond to cats in the world, but only to the internal firings of its neurons within the brain. 'Click, click is the vocabulary of neural language' (von Foerster). In this perspective, closure is the precondition of openness, not its preclusion. In this vein, biologists Fransisco J Varela and Humberto Maturana developed a constructionist research program of autopoietic (self-productive) systems. The sociologist Niklas Luhmann has further emphasised how systems proceed by self-differentiation and can no longer be analysed by reference to global physical features of the-world-as-a-whole.

In this perspective, each system needs to reduce, by its own internal operations, the complexities produced by other systems. Different systems (for example, biological, social, psychic) operate with different codes (energy, communication, consciousness), and even though they co-evolve they cannot communicate with one another on neutral ground. They are type different processes. The fleeting experience of consciousness, for example, remains coupled to physiological processes and to social communication, yet has its own irreducible life.

Computational complexity (CC)
CC presupposes the idea of algorithmic compression and embodies the spirit of cybernetics. The dictum of Norbert Wiener that

'Cybernetics is nothing if it is not mathematical',[12] could also be said of CC.

The field of *cybernetics* was developed after World War II by J von Neumann, Ross Ashby, Wiener and others. Central to cybernetics is the concept of automata, defined as machines open for information input but leading to an output modified by an internal program. In cybernetic learning machines, the output functions are reintroduced into the input function, so that the internal program can be tested via trial and error processes. However, the measure for success or failure is still fixed by pre-set criteria.

The cybernetic automata were the direct precursors of *cellular automata*, used in the artificial life models designed by John Conway in and Chris Langton in the 1970s. Cellular automata use individual based modelling: 'organisms' are placed in cubic cells in a two-dimensional grid, and their 'actions' ('die' or 'divide') are specified by the number of living cells in their immediate neighbourhood. In this way, the positive feedback of breeding can be modelled as well as the negative feedback of competition. The result is self-reproducing loops generated by very simple rules.

With the establishment of the Santa Fe Institute in 1984 a multidisciplinary centre for CC was formed. Physicist Murray Gell-Mann, computer scientist John Holland and others introduced the idea of *complex adaptive systems* (CAS). As opposed to simple adaptation (as in a thermostat), there are no pre-set goals for CAS. Like cellular automata CAS are individually modelled systems, but CAS also involve 'cognition'. CAS are thus able to identify perceived regularities, and to compress regular inputs into various 'schemata'. Unlike cybernetic learning machines, there may be several different schemata competing simultaneously, thus simulating cognitive selection processes. In this manner self-adaptation co-evolves with adaptation beyond a pre-set design. Whereas Gell-Mann uses CAS as a general concept, Holland uses the term only about interacting individual agents. CAS agents thus proceed by a limited set of interaction rules, governed by simple stimulus-response mechanisms

---

12. Norbet Wiener, *God and Golem, Inc: A Comment on Certain Points where Cybernetics Impinges on Religion* (Cambridge, Mass: MIT Press, 1964, 1990), 88.

such as (1) *tags* (eg if 'something big', then 'flee'; if 'something small', then 'approach'), (2) *internal models* (or schemata), and (3) *rules for connecting building blocks* to one another (eg 'eyes' and 'mouth' to facial recognition). The result of these local mechanisms, however, is the emergence of global properties such as non-linearity, flow, diversity, and recognition.

In so far as complex patterns are generated by simple mechanisms, CC can be seen as a reductionist research paradigm; in contradistinction to physical reductionism, however, the reduction is to 'interaction rules', not to 'physical entities'. But in so far as higher-level systems can be shown to exert a 'downwards' feedback influence on lower-level interaction-rules, CC may also count as an anti-reductionist research program. The issues of reductionism versus anti-reductionism, bottom-up versus top-down causality are still debated within the CC community. But anyway, it is information and not physics that matters.

CC and real-world complexity

The spirit of CC is not to collect empirical evidence and 'reflect' reality, but to 'generate' reality and explore virtual worlds of possibility. CC is nonetheless empirically motivated and aims to understand real-world complexity by computer modelling. The aspiration is to uncover 'deep' mathematical structures common to virtual worlds and real-world dynamical systems.

The mathematical *chaos theory* is an example of a computer-generated science that has succeeded in explaining many dynamical patterns in nature. Yet the relation between chaos theory and CC is disputed. While chaotic systems (in the technical sense) are extremely sensitive to the initial conditions, complex systems are more robust (that is, they can start from different conditions, and still end up in almost the same states). Accordingly, chaos theory can predict the immediate next states, but not long-term developments, whereas complex systems can reliably describe long-term prospects, but cannot predict the immediate following steps. Moreover, chaotic systems do not display the kind of evolutionary ascent and learning characteristic of CAS, but oscillate or bifurcate endlessly. It therefore seems fair to say that chaos theory is only a small pane in the much larger window of complexity studies. Chaos, in the colloquial sense of disorder, is everywhere in complex systems (and so are fractals and strange attractors), but the equations of chaos in the technical sense (the specific Lyapunov-exponent etc) cannot explain self-organised complexity.

There are also connections between thermodynamics and complexity theory. Beginning in the 1960s, the chemist Ilya Prigogine studied the so-called *dissipative structures* that arise spontaneously in systems dissipated by energy. While classical thermodynamics described isolated systems where nonhomogeneities tend to even out over time, Prigogine studied non-equilibrium processes of 'order out of chaos' ('chaos' in the nontechnical sense). Famous examples are the convection patterns of 'Bénards cells' formed spontaneously under heating, or the beautiful chemical clocks of the 'Belousov-Zhabotinski reaction'. While Ludwig Boltzmann's law of entropy from 1865 still holds for the universe as a whole, the formation of local orders is produced by non-equilibrium thermodynamics. The averaging laws of statistical mechanics are not contradicted, but they simply do not explain the specific trajectories that develop beyond thermodynamical equilibrium.

In the wake of Prigogine a new search for the thermodynamical basis of evolution began.[13] The bifurcation diagrams of Prigogine showed amazing similarities to evolutionary trees. Reaching back to the seminal work of D'Arcy Wentworth Thompson in *On Growth and Form* (1916), many began to think that the interplay of selection and mutation is not self-sufficient for explaining the evolutionary tendency towards complexification. Evolution may be driven by gene selection *and* pre-biotic laws of physical economy.

Since the 1970s theoretical biologist Stuart Kauffman has constructed computational models of self-organising principles at many levels. Motivated by the almost ubiquitous tendency of chemical systems to produce autocatalytic systems, Kauffman theorises that life may have emerged quite suddenly, through phase transitions where chemical reactions function as catalysts for one another far below the threshold of the RNA-DNA cyclus. Kauffman uses a similar model for simulating the empirical findings of Francois

---

13.   JS Wicken, *Evolution, Information and Thermodynamics: Extending the Darwinian Paradigm* (New York: Oxford University Press, 1987).

Jacob and Jacques Monod who showed that genes switch on and off depending on the network in which they are situated. In the simplest model of 'Boolean networks', each 'gene' is coupled randomly to two other 'genes' with only two possible states, 'on' or 'off' (states that are determined by the states of the two other genes). Running this small system with only three genes and two activities recurrently (and later with much larger networks) Kauffman was able to show that the number of state cycles (attractors) increase with the number of 'genes'. Moreover, their relation is constant so that the number of state cycles is roughly the square root of the number of 'genes'. Already in *The Origins of Order* (1993) Kauffman points out in that in real-world species one finds roughly the same relation between the number of genes and the number of cell types in a given species.[14] These mathematical proportions may not be accidental. Agents in coupled systems seem to tune themselves to the optimal number of couplings with other agents. In addition, when investigating fitness landscapes of interacting species at the ecological level, Kauffman finds the principle of 'order for free'. Evolutionary innovations tend to happen 'at the edge of chaos', between the strategy of evolutionarily stable orders and the strategy of the constant evolutionary arms race. In *Investigations*,[15] Kauffman pursues a search for laws by which the biosphere is co-constructed by 'autonomous agents' who are able run up against the stream of entropy. Kauffman hereby acknowledges the impossibility of pre-stating finitely what will come to be within the vast configuration space of the biosphere.

The theory of *Self-organised Criticality* (SOC) formulated by Per Bak and his colleagues takes its point of departure in empirically confirmed regularities (such as the Gutenberg-Richter law of earthquakes). Many systems show slow variation over long periods, rare catastrophic activities over short time, and some critical phases in between. The building up of sandpiles shows these phase

---

14. Stuart Kauffman, *The Origins of Order: Self-Organisation and Selection in Evolution* (New York: Oxford University Press, 1993), chapter 12.

15. Stuart Kauffman, *Investigations* (New York: Oxford University Press, 2000).

transitions, but so do also earthquakes, extinction rates and light from quasars. Bak's point is that SOC systems are self-organising, since they (1) are robust and do not depend on specific initial conditions, (2) emerge spontaneously over time (with no external designer) and (3) are governed by the same mathematical principles in stationary, critical, and catastrophic states. Bak has made both real-world experiments and simplified computer models of SOC systems, but he believes that SOC is only a first approximation to stronger explanations of nature's tendency to build up balances between order and disorder.

Relevance for the science-religion discussion

While organicist programs of non-computational complexity have played a major role in the science-religion dialogue since the seminal works of Ian Barbour, Arthur Peacocke and others, the relevance of CC for theology largely remains to be explored. The following issues are therefore to be taken more as pointers than as conclusions:

(1) The sciences of complexity study pattern formations in the midst of the world rather than in a hidden world beyond imagination. The everyday life so important for religion have regained their status also within the sciences. Moreover, the features of organised complexity resonates with the experiences of being-part-of-a-whole, experiences that since Friedrich Schleiermacher's *On Religion* (1799) have been taken to be essential to religious intuition.

(2) While presupposing a robust naturalism, complexity theory suggests that 'information' is as seminal to nature as are the substance and energy aspects of matter. Complexity theory may thus give further impetus to the de-materialisation of the scientific idea of matter that already started in the wake of relativity theory.

(3) By focusing on relations and interactions rather than on particular objects, complexity theory supports a shift in world-view from a mechanical clockwork view of the world into an emergentist view of the world as an interconnected network, where flows of information take precedence over localised entities. Complexity theory also offers a road for understanding the evolution of co-evolution. By balancing the principle of individual selection by principles of self-organisation, the focus on individual genes is supplemented by the importance of interconnected living organisms,

a view closer to ethical and religious sentiments than the inherited view of the omnipotence of selection.

(4) Even though natural evils (from earthquakes to selection) remain a challenge to religions that presuppose a loving almighty God, the costs of evolutionary creativity are now being placed in a wider framework of evolution. If the same underlying dynamics of SOC produces both stability, criticality and catastrophes, and the constructive aspects of nature cannot exist without the destructive aspects, a theodicy of natural evils may be facilitated.

(5) The idea of CAS gives biological learning and human culture (including science, ethics and religion) a pivotal role in the understanding of what nature is, and what makes human and animal life grow and flourish. In addition, since complexity theory consistently crosses the boundaries between physics, biology, and the cultural sciences, theologians and human scientists may be prompted to rethink human culture (including religion) in terms of the creative interactions between the inorganic, the organic, and the cultural.

(6) From an external scientific perspective, CC may be used to explain a variety of religious phenomena that arise at the critical interface between adaptation and self-adaptation, such as the interaction between religious groups, individual conversion experiences, and so on. The first computer models in this area have already been completed (see www.evalife.au.dk).

(7) From an internal religious perspective, complexity theory offers religious thought a new set of thought models and metaphors, which (when adopted) can stimulate the heuristics of theology when complex phenomena are redescribed from the perspective of religious symbolics. 'Self-organisation', 'coupled networks' and 'adaptation by self-adaption' are candidates for such religious self-interpretation. The principles of complexity are in particular consonant with the idea that a divine Logos is creatively at work in the pattern formations of nature and drives nature towards further complexification.

(8) The CC idea of self-organisation is a challenge to the Enlightenment idea of a divine designer of all natural processes, from to amoebas and eyes. Self-organisation is also a challenge to the creationist 'Intelligent Design' movement, which gives priority to the idea of 'original creation' and tends to perceive novelties as

perversions of pre-established designs. However, self-organisational processes never happen from scratch, but always presuppose a framework of laws and natural tendencies that could well be said to be 'designed' by God. While a design of specific evolutionary outcomes is obsolete in light of self-organised complexity, the coordination of laws leading towards self-organisation and co-evolution may be explained by a divine meta-design.

(9) Since emergence takes place in the merging of coupled systems, theology may escape the alternative between an interventionist God, who acts by breaking natural laws, and a God who only sustains the laws of nature uniformly over time. In higher-organised systems, new informational pathways are continuously tried out in adventure-like processes. If the local interaction rules and the over-all probability patterns are constantly changed over time, the actual pathways of large-scale coupled systems are not reducible to the general laws of physics. Special divine interaction with the evolving world can thus no longer be said to 'break laws' in an interventionist manner; there are simply no fixed laws for interactions in coupled systems to break.

(10) The seminal idea of self-organisation may help overcome the idea that God and nature are contraries, so that God is powerless, if nature is powerful, and vice versa. A more adequate view may be to understand God as the creator who continuously hands over creativity to nature so that natural processes are the signs of a divine self-divestment into the very heart of nature's creativity. On this view, God is at work 'in, with and under' natural and social processes, and self-organisation takes place within a world already created and continuously gifted by God.

Models of Invisible Realities: The Common Thread in Science and Theology

Carolyn M King

Introduction

There is a story, supposedly true, about a bishop who was invited to take part in the consecration of a very new and modern chapel. They handed him a clip-on microphone, and told him that it was an improved type that would not pick up mechanical interference such as the movements of his robes, but would still be very sensitive to his voice. When the time came, he stepped up to the altar, and out of habit, tapped the top of the microphone to check that it was switched on. When nothing happened, he said quietly to the Dean, 'There's something wrong with this thing.' With one voice, the entire congregation replied, 'And also with you.'

I like that story because it encapsulates in a few lines one of the central problems of the science-religion debate. There is something wrong with the debate between science and theology, because listeners on both sides so often hear something different from what the speaker intended to convey. In this paper, I want to suggest that this problem, though real, is soluble.

The nature of knowledge

One day several years ago, I answered a knock at the door and found an earnest young couple wanting to convert me to their particular brand of Christianity. They were not convinced when I said I was a happy Anglican, and they wanted to debate the differences between my beliefs and theirs. Among the most important of those differences were our attitudes to evolution, particularly the origins of humankind. After an hour of completely fruitless arguing, both parties came to the unspoken conclusion, lampooning both God and the ape: 'How could any normal, intelligent, rational human being believe we came from *that*?'

The trouble is, of course, that mutual misunderstanding was inevitable: neither party could actually grasp what the other really believed. My visitors could not understand life as described through the assumptions of evolutionary biology, and I could not understand life without them, so both sides ended up seeing only a caricature of the other's position. Worse, each party was convinced that its own view was right, and each earnestly wanted the other to see why. Such a conversation is far too often typical of at least the casual level of the science-religion debate.

Why is this sort of misunderstanding so common? My contention is that mutual fog is inevitable when the science-religion debate concentrates on *the differences* between what the two sides believe, rather than on what they have *in common*. For example, people with training in biology find it difficult to accept the idea of a hands-on, patriarchal Creator as traditionally understood from Old Testament texts and painted by Michelangelo. Meanwhile, people with a firm biblical faith find it difficult to accept the idea that human ancestry has anything in common with apes, which are regarded as degrading, subhuman caricatures totally incompatible with the dignity of a human race made in the image of God.[1]

Both sides concentrate enormous effort in attempting to argue what they see as the key flaws in the arguments of the opposition. For example, rationalists ask how the Ark could possibly have held two each of all the millions of creatures we now know have existed throughout all time since the Creation, and what the carnivores (especially the large ones that capture the public imagination, like dinosaurs) could have eaten on the Ark whilst still allowing the survival of two each of all the herbivores. Creationists of many persuasions are united in their rejection of the social and theological implications of a theory that sees apes as the ancestors of humans. The details of these arguments are often wrong and always distracting, and lead only to what has been called The Tyranny of Small Decisions: quick fixes of peripheral problems (such as where do the fossils of the dinosaurs fit into the story of the Ark? Could there have been several successive Creations?) lead to ignorance of

---

1.   M Midgley, *Evolution as a Religion* (London: Methuen, 1985).

the central problem, which concerns the intellectual basis of faith and reason—the deeper question, how do we know anything at all?

Models and metaphors
The central problem of belief, both in science and religion, is the failure to recognise that human knowledge is not concrete and eternally solid and reliable, valid in all times and places and passed down from one generation to the next in a cultural vacuum. Far from it: all forms of knowledge are expressed in terms of culturally defined metaphors and models,[2] as interpreted through personal experience. Metaphors that carry the ring of truth in one culture, such as many in the New Testament, fall flat in a different one. (How many sheep in modern Australia are known by their names, as were those in the small, non-commercial flocks of first-century Palestine? And, how do the flock management policies and motivations of our shepherds compare with those of the Good Shepherd of the gospels?)

In this paper I am using the definition of a model provided by Peacocke:[3] Models are imaginative human constructs selectively representing certain aspects of reality for particular purposes. They allow a limited picture of what is not observable, but because they are neither exactly real nor merely useful fictions, they must be taken seriously but not literally. The same definition is appropriate for models in both science and theology.

Knowledge itself is inseparable from these necessary intellectual frameworks, especially when we are describing things that are real but invisible. Invisible realities in science include anything outside the rather small range of sizes of things that we can see directly, that is, tiny structures from cells down to subatomic particles, and large ones from geological formations up to the movements of the planets and stars. In theology, spiritual realities such as intense guilt or overwhelming grief are invisible themselves but can have some very visible consequences.

---

2. S McFague, *Models of God: Theology for an Ecological, Nuclear Age* (Philadelphia: Fortress Press, 1987).
3. A Peacocke, *Theology for a Scientific Age* (London: SCM Press, 1993).

Because intellectual frameworks are only as good as the observations they are built on, metaphors and models describing these things in both science and theology are *in principle* subject to modification in the light of accumulating new knowledge. Living, life-giving knowledge is *intrinsically dynamic*. Knowledge of a particular time elevated to the status of eternal, unchangeable truth becomes fossilised, which does not mean it is useless, but it may be difficult to interpret and have rather few future prospects.

Quine's web of beliefs
Of course, prior knowledge does to some extent determine perception, and conversely, the capacity to add to existing knowledge in the future is strongly influenced by present knowledge. One theory that explains these relationships very well is that of Quine, who proposed in 1951 that a person can be seen as an entity quite separate from his or her experience.[4] Each person develops their internal own truth values, which make contact with real experience only at the boundaries of the person, the conflict zone between personal experience and reality.

Experience is interpreted through a complex web of beliefs, which make the links between the outside and the inside. On the edge are peripheral beliefs—simple things like the results of taking actual measurements, which can easily be adjusted and corrected without any wider implications. At the centre are the core beliefs which are given maximum truth value and which will be defended with the greatest possible vigour—these are the more complex things such as the fundamental belief that God is real, rational, good and supremely loving. In between are the intermediate beliefs, which make sense of the interaction between the core beliefs and the experience of any given person.

For me as a scientist, this means that, because Christian theology assures me that the world is rational, the measurements I take will be constant, the same from one day to the next. Because God has given

---

4. N Murphy, 'Postmodern Apologetics, or Why Theologians Must Pay Attention to Science', in *Religion and Science: History, Method, Dialogue*, edited by WM Richardson and W Wildman (1996), 105–120.

Creation freedom within set laws, the world is contingent, that is it could be other than the way it is, it is necessary to take measurements rather than deduce the form of things by speculation or logic. The rationality, goodness and necessity of Western science are based in Judaeo-Christian theology.[5] Conversely, for people with no scientific background but profound fundamentalist convictions, the interaction between experience and core beliefs makes more sense in terms of a theory of direct creation. Either scheme can be totally convincing—it all depends how an individual's core beliefs interpret experience. However, not all belief systems are equally valid, as we shall see.

Simple and complex models
The models that we use to understand the world start with simple, culturally determined mental interpretations of direct observations. Those that are compatible with our core beliefs tend to be accepted quickly and usually uncritically—we label them as 'obviously true'. That is the power of deep-seated cultural stories like the Eden myth, because at some level we all want to believe that a world made by a good, all-powerful and loving Creator should not contain the weeds, thorns, sweat and hard labour. And even though we know it is the earth that moves, not the sun, it is still not difficult to imagine Joshua holding back the sun in its course until the Israelites had defeated their enemies (Joshua 10:11–14). (On many a long day at the office one might wonder who is up to the same trick again!)

On the other hand, observations incompatible with expectations may not even be visible. If new information cannot be put into context, or its potential significance estimated, it means nothing at all. The story goes that the first Aboriginals to see a European sailing ship on the horizon ignored it, because they had no means of telling what it was or of predicting what it would mean for them —meanwhile, they still needed to concentrate on the daily necessity to search for food.[6] In other words, our core beliefs determine our perceptions—and that conclusion goes a long way towards

---

5.   CB Kaiser, 'The Creationist Tradition in the History of Science', *Perspectives on Science and Christian Faith*, 45 (1993): 80–89.
6.   K Willey, *When the Sky Fell Down: The Destruction of the Tribes of the Sydney Region, 1788–1850s* (Sydney: Collins, 1979).

explaining the futility of many political and religious debates. People with a background in science see much traditional theology as completely irrational—and yet, those traditional beliefs are internally consistent and 'obviously true' to people soaked in them, and for them, no other explanation of the world is possible or necessary.

More complex models emphasise the logic of the invisible processes behind the direct observations—they are interested more in the game than in the cards. The development of this attitude is the indispensable prerequisite for understanding how to manipulate those processes. So, for example, a description of the chemical structure of DNA counts as a simple model, even though it is a very complex molecule, because merely knowing the structure of it says nothing about how it is made. Only when the natural process of DNA replication was worked out could it be controlled and manipulated, which opened the way to genetic engineering and all its many consequences.

Therefore, what we see in front of our eyes depends substantially on what is behind them. Different people can look at the same view and see completely different things. Imagine a group of four standing on a hill overlooking a new hydroelectric dam and discussing their reactions. The first might grieve over the insult to the spiritual values of the river and the destruction of many important cultural sites and productive farms; the second might remember with anger the political horse-trading behind the decision to build and the extensive disturbance to wildlife habitat in the river valley and surrounding area; the third might see a triumph of technology against huge human and geological odds; and the fourth might appreciate most of the others' arguments but, given a *fait accompli*, try to make the best of it.[7]

Inconsistencies between core and peripheral beliefs can be ignored up to a point, depending on what other forms of knowledge and

---

7.   CM King, 'Changing Values and Conflicting Cultural Attitudes Towards Plants and Animals in New Zealand', in *Biodiversity: Papers from a Seminar Series on Biodiversity,* hosted by Science and Research Division, Department of Conservation, Wellington, 14 June–26 July 1994, edited by B McFadgen and P Simpson (Wellington, New Zealand: New Zealand Department of Conservation, 1996), 69–88

experience need to be integrated within the same web of beliefs. The difficulties arise when these inconsistencies become too great, and eventually force a traumatic change in one or more of the core beliefs, which in turn may drive dramatic and sometimes quite sudden changes in perception of the world. This process is usually described as a paradigm shift, or, in religious terms, a 'conversion'. According to Hans Kung, every major discontinuity in church history has been marked by a paradigm shift.[8] It may replace the old core beliefs with a new series of models, often more searching than the previous ones. Before he took the road to Damascus, Saul could see only the damage that the early church was doing to the settled traditions of strictly monotheistic Judaism: afterwards, all he could say was, 'Who are you, Lord?'

In the modern world, a useful tool available to all of us during such an experience is the concept of *critical realism*, which assumes that there is a pre-existing reality that sets limits to our speculations.[9] During some periods of the history of Christian theology, critical realism has been in acutely short supply, which explains some doctrines that make rather little sense to the ears of a biologist. Conversely, it was the paradigm shift forced by the resurrection which drove the early church to ask new questions about the role of the Messiah, and to reach new conclusions about the nature of God. Critical realist accounts of complex issues in theology and in science cannot be neatly mapped one onto the other, because each has dimensions of experience unknown to the other. Nevertheless, they can be productive working partners, because they can set boundaries for each other's speculations, and point out deeper meanings in each other's data.

Scientific models
There are many examples of how gradual changes in intellectual models have affected our understandings of key concepts, in both

---

8.　H Küng, 'Paradigm Change in Theology: A Proposal for Discussion', in *Paradigm Change in Theology*, edited by H Küng and D Tracey (Edinburgh: T&T Clark, 1989), 3–33.
9.　IG Barbour, *Religion and Science: Historical and Contemporary Issues* (New York: HarperCollins, 1997), 118.

science and religion. In science, the shifts from geocentric to heliocentric models of the universe, and the shift from one model of evolution to another, took centuries to complete. The shift from the assumption of fixed continents to the acceptance of continental drift took only a few decades. All three transitions have given birth to new sciences (modern astronomy, genetics and plate tectonics) based on fruitful paradigms that constantly stimulate and support new questions.

Astronomy

The geocentric model was not invented by Dante, but he gave the clearest description of it and its implications for the theology of his time, in his three-volume masterpiece The Divine Comedy.[10] It assumes, for theological rather than scientific reasons, that the earth must be the centre of the universe, and that Jerusalem must be at the centre of the northern hemisphere. Satan is eternally punished in the deepest pit of hell, and Purgatory is a mountainous island in the southern hemisphere. This elaborate geography was deduced by pure speculation, untroubled by reference to any pre-existing realities, and was regarded in Dante's time as self-evidently true. It is a good example of how a simple model can turn into a fantastic myth (poetically beautiful but literally unrealistic) when it is free to develop for centuries free of the restrictions imposed by critical realism.

Above the earth the orbits of the seven planets (which included the sun and the moon) were described as necessarily perfect circles wheeling across the sky against the background of the fixed stars. This model depended, again, on theological rather than observational arguments—it was regarded as inconceivable that the planetary orbits could be otherwise than circular, since they had to demonstrate the perfection and creative activity of God. God was 'up there' in the perfection of heaven (we still look up to find inspiration!) and the earth was at best imperfect and at worst corrupt.

The challenge of Copernicus to this established system was resisted as much for theological as for scientific reasons. However,

---

10. DL Sayers, *The Comedy of Dante Aligheri, the Florentine* (Harmondsworth: Penguin, 1949).

the inconsistencies accumulated—Kepler could not make the mathematics work—and finally, came the paradigm shift to the heliocentric model, which envisages a quite different system: four small rocky inner planets, and four giant gaseous outer planets, not including the sun or the moon and none with perfectly circular orbits, and no fixed stars. The curious thing is, a person standing on the ground at night, gazing up in awe at the starry heavens, cannot see any reason why this model should be regarded as more true than the other. It all depends on what else that person knows, what their core beliefs are, and what other models of invisible realities have to be reconciled with what can be seen with the naked eye and integrated into a single, coherent model of the universe.

Evolution

A similar history of replacement of one model by another has happened in biology. The first biologist to construct a serious theory on how species might change over time was not Darwin, but Lamarck. He envisaged all living things being driven by an inborn desire to achieve greater complexity, while new, simple ones were added at the bottom by spontaneous generation. He postulated that *individual* animals are able to figure out what physical characters they 'need' in order to meet their 'goal', that use of those characters causes changes in bodily form during their lifetime, and that these changes can be passed on to their offspring. The mechanism Lamarck envisaged, the inheritance of acquired characters, was equivalent to saying that the children of a champion athlete can inherit the physical results of their parent's training; or that the offspring of urban hedgehogs that need to run from oncoming traffic will inherit that habit rather than curling up; or that the flightless birds of countless remote islands can be expected to develop wings because they need to escape from alien predators brought by European colonisers.

The contrasting model proposed by Darwin works by natural selection (he never called it 'evolution', because he disagreed with the implications of progress attached to that word). Darwin did not know about genes, but his crucial insights were that every individual animal is slightly different, and that many of these differences are somehow heritable. If there is competition for limited resources, and if some individuals happen to have an advantage in the local circumstances (it doesn't have to be a large advantage), then those individuals have a slightly better chance of producing surviving offspring than others. In the next generation there will be slightly more individuals carrying those genes, and again in the next and so on—over a long time, the best genes accumulate in the collective genome of the population.

In contrast to Lamarck's idea, Darwinian evolution can be perceived only in populations, not in individuals, and it is not directed or progressive. Neo-Darwinism is the twentieth-century integration of natural selection and genetics, the two cornerstones of evolutionary theory, independently discovered during the nineteenth century. (If Darwin had known of Mendel's proof of the particulate nature of inheritance as he developed his insights into the action of natural selection, the history of biology might have been very different). The ultimate origin of variation is random, and has nothing to do with an individual's needs, but the accumulation of useful characters in the population is not random at all.

The two key differences between the two theories are that (1) Lamarck thought that changes in physical characters could be induced in individuals during their own lifetimes, whereas Darwin saw them as changes in the population averages observable only over many generations, and (2) Lamarck's theory suited those who thought of evolution as purposeful, whereas the change in gene frequencies from one generation to the next described by neo-Darwinism is the *consequence* of natural selection, so to the biologist it is quite wrong to think of natural selection as a purposeful process, and it cannot work for the good of the species. A process that can be understood only backwards cannot logically be driven or used by anyone, not even God.

Theological models

Historical changes
The history of theology, like that of science, also offers many examples of models of invisible realities which have changed with time. For example, the Hebrew understanding of God as a tribal warlord dedicated to fighting on behalf of his chosen people, *against* all other people, was over the centuries replaced by the Christian

understanding of God as Love, the Lord of *all* people. The Old Testament idea that God's blessing is conditional on obedience, which was already being questioned by Job, was decisively abolished by Jesus' ministry—although the national expectation of a heroic, military messiah continued, at least until the destruction of Jerusalem by the Romans. In more recent times, the traditional image of the passive role of the woman in reproduction (as merely a seedbed for her husband's sperm) has been discounted by medicine and biology. In many countries the Roman Catholic teaching against artificial contraception, based on ancient philosophical ideas very different from those of today, is seen as contrary to both the dignity of women and to healthy marital relationships and is widely ignored. So paradigm change in theology is possible, but is much more difficult than in science, and takes much longer.

Two among many possible reasons for this difference are that, first, competing scientific models are (usually) recognised as intellectual exercises, and second, it is possible to design experiments that can conclusively discriminate between them. In theology, the arguments supporting alternative models are treated as matters of life and death, and knock-down proofs to distinguish them are hard to come by. Dissenting theological positions can remain entirely reasonable and tenable for years, or even centuries, as church history amply demonstrates. In the early church, arguments between competing interpretations of the definition of the nature of Christ raged for hundreds of years, and in the modern world, the debate on conflicting views of creationism shows no sign of fizzing out. Quine's concept of how we all construct our own webs of belief is helpful here: perception depends on how one's own internal truth values condition what else can be integrated into one's central core of belief. For example, knowledge of palaeontology made acceptance of the official Roman Catholic interpretation of the Eden story impossible for Teilhard de Chardin, but that was no problem for his Jesuit superiors.

Then and now, the choice between competing models often comes down to reconciling our personal experience of God and with our knowledge about the outside world, with the help both of spiritual wisdom and of critical realism. Two competing models will often agree on many of the basic observations, but disagree fundamentally on how to interpret them—and more important, how to integrate ancient principles with the stream of new knowledge constantly being introduced by science. Is there any valid way to judge between them? I think there is.

In science the most widely acceptable and useful models are the ones that are (1) credible, because they are internally consistent and explain the most independent observations, and (2) fruitful in leading to new insights, generating new hypotheses, and opening the way to positive advances in understanding in the field. The heliocentric model of the universe, neo-Darwinism and plate tectonics are all examples of fruitful scientific models that have galvanised their respective subjects and made possible many advances that were formerly inconceivable. Surely we can also use the criteria of credible, consistent explanation and of fruitfulness to evaluate alternative models in theology (one immediately thinks of the comment, 'By their fruits shall ye know them.'). But although theological models capable of speaking to an educated world must be consistent with current science, we do not need to reject the insights of older, less useful models. The trick is to distinguish the message from the model and then find new models to convey the same message. Here are some examples.

Intelligent design
In the secular world, the replacement of discredited theories is often total—for example, among professional biologists, neo-Darwinism has completely replaced Lamarckism, and debates on the details of natural selection do not at all weaken the solid basis of evolutionary biology as a whole. Religious people who do not accept the materialistic implications of evolutionary biology, and have not yet discovered theistic science, need a scientifically credible alternative that can stand up in court. They have found, after decades of legal battles in the southern US, that various forms of creationism are difficult to defend. However, what is basically the same philosophical position is now reappearing in a new form, Intelligent Design Theory (IDT).

Supporters of IDT assert that random and mostly damaging mutations could not have lead to the interlocking beneficial adaptations we observe in nature.[11] If chance mutations are indeed the only source of novelty, as biology claims, then surely they must be initiated by God, therefore, the complexity of nature demonstrates divine guidance of, or even intrusion into, evolutionary processes. It is certainly true that the theory of evolution by natural selection is counter-intuitive and hard to grasp, which may be why it was discovered only so recently. But their claim that IDT is a far more probable alternative model, both mathematically and theologically, does not constitute a credible model to a biologically informed theist. First, it is based on an improper comparison, and second, it leaves the most vital question unanswered, concerning *what* has been created.

Most versions of IDT go back to Paley's argument from design, which proceeds from observation of the complex and obviously purposeful construction of a pocket watch to the conclusion that the complexity of the universe itself must also be the product of deliberate construction by a purposeful intelligence. But the concept of IDT is not served well by this example, because the processes of natural selection that control the construction of the natural world are not the same as the processes of cultural selection which control the construction of a watch. The one involves the consequences of differential reproductive success of animals and plants over many generations, and the other involves the deliberate generation of ideas within human minds. One moves slowly, the other fast; culture accelerates the pace of information transfer by orders of magnitude, much as jet planes have accelerated the pace of modern travel compared with the age of horses and carts. Humans inherit information by both pathways, and both are necessary to human life. To compare these two processes as if they were the same is a category error, and leads to false conclusions, just as horses and jet planes both carry people and goods but cannot be yoked together.[12] Paley cannot be blamed for making a comparison that was convincing at the time

---

11. MJ Behe, *Darwin's Black Box: the Biochemical Challenge to Evolution* (New York: Simon & Schuster, 1996); WA Demski, *Intelligent Design: The Bridge between Science and Theology* (Downers Grove: InterVarsity Press, 1999).

12. H Rolston III, *Genes, Genesis and God* (Cambridge: Cambridge University Press, 1999).

but which modern knowledge has made invalid. Contemporary Christians do not have the same excuse, so must find other examples than Paley's pocketwatch.

Among the favourite cases of IDT writers are aerobic metabolism and the clotting of blood, both complex functions of modern cells—and in the case of blood, specifically functions of multicellular animals. Their relevance to the arguments about the origins and development of complexity in the world over the last three and a half billion years is not clear. All the earliest forms of life, for at least the first half billion years, were necessarily anaerobic, since the atmosphere then was like that of the lifeless planets, about 98 per cent carbon dioxide,[13] and aerobic metabolism would hardly have counted as a useful adaptation in such an environment. Free oxygen has constituted about a fifth of the atmosphere only since around two and a half billion years ago, and multicellular animals have had a use for a blood-clotting mechanism only since around one and a half billion years ago.

The greatest difficulty presented by the IDT model to a biologist concerns the question of why the products of evolution do not seem, on close inspection, worthy of a divine designer. The usual example given is the vertebrate eye, which seems to be perfectly designed for its function. It has all the physical requirements—a dark internal chamber, an iris to control the amount of light entering it, a lens to focus light rays on a photosensitive surface, and all the associated mental equipment needed to form and interpret a sharp image—plus even, in hunting animals, a means of integrating images from two forward-looking eyes and using the parallax effect to judge distances. To a person whose core beliefs, in Quine's terms, are untouched by medical training, such an engineering marvel could only have been deliberately designed by God. But to an ophthalmic surgeon, the human eye is not well designed at all.

The retina is placed within the eye-ball inside out, with the photo-receptive cells facing away from the incoming light, their nerves trailing behind them. That means that the light has first to travel through a mat of nerves before it reaches the photo-receptive surface itself, which blurs the information received, or in places (over the

---

13.   J Lovelock, *Gaia* (Oxford: Oxford University Press, 1979).

optic nerve) creates a completely blind spot. Moreover, the retina is not actually attached to the inside of the eyeball, but merely held there by fluid pressure. In certain circumstances the retina can become torn, or even totally detached, confusing or destroying the perception of visual images. Surely any competent designer god with eternal foresight would not have left humans, the alleged crown of all creation, dependent on such an inefficient visual system. To me the alternative explanation is more realistic: eyes of all sorts evolved from simple, superficial light-sensitive spots on the skin, and the full sequence of capabilities, from merely distinguishing day from night to the formation of a sharp image, can be reconstructed in five completely independent lineages of animals.

Similar arguments can be applied to various other aspects of the human anatomy. A wise and loving director of evolution would surely have avoided producing humans with disadvantages that would later comprise serious embarrassments for theology ('*Inter urinam et faeces nascimur*,' groaned Tertullian[14]) but which can be explained quite simply in terms of the evolutionary history of the vertebrate urinogenital system. The facts are poor advertising for any designer, but easily understood as the result of sequential tinkering and adjustment to an ancient, basic four-legged vertebrate body plan.

It is a truism in human life as well as in biology, that every advantage has a cost, balanced against its disadvantages across time. In human evolution, the price of speech was an extensive modification of the larynx, which also introduced a new danger unfamiliar to primates, that of choking. The price of walking upright was a rigid, box-shaped pelvis with balancing muscles, plus slipped discs and fallen arches. The price of producing more and more intelligent babies was (and is) the pain of squeezing their heads through a birth canal that leads, for historical reasons, through that same rigid pelvis.

The two competing models, IDT and evolution by natural selection, both have to explain the facts of nature, including all the difficult ones. But IDT has a problem which evolution does not have, to answer and additional question: If a wise and benevolent God

---

14.   M Midgley, *Beast and Man: The Roots of Human Nature* (London: Methuen University Paperback, 1978), 290.

designed the primate lineage with the intention of producing talkative, upright, and intelligent humans out of it, why did the divine foresight not see these problems coming? A model has to be credible in explaining not only *how* things have been created, but also, even more difficult, exactly *what* has been created, and in the process be fruitful, in generating new ideas about life and about God.

At first sight, IDT might suggest that the long rearguard action by the nineteenth-century church against the theory of evolution and all its implications was a

> bizarre tactical aberration . . . the church exhausted, distorted and discredited itself in order to combat a quite imaginary danger. Most Christians today readily accept that the earth does not have to be in the centre of the universe, and that God, if he could create life at all, could do it just as well through evolution as by instant fiat.[15]

This is a common compromise view much favoured by IDT theorists and others keen to find an easy middle ground between science and theology, but it contains an unexpected hurdle. The same people who are so ready to assert that God works through evolution also believe, with equal fervour, that creation is good. Yet the concept of God using evolutionary processes *directly* to create parasitic worms and hyenas introduces contradictions with other things that clearly have to be believed by Christians, such as that *God* is good. The compromise formula also demonstrates a worrying misunderstanding of two key biological aspects of evolutionary biology.

First, the mechanism of natural selection cannot be personalised or utilised, even by God. Evolution is defined as successive changes in gene frequencies across generations, which is a *consequence* of differential reproductive success of the bodies they inhabit, not a driving force to be harnessed. Natural selection is not in itself a creative process; it is a sieve, not a sculptor[16]—ie it cannot create fit organisms, only eliminate the unfit. In a world of free creatures, it is

---

15.   M Midgley, *Beast and Man: The Roots of Human Nature, op cit*, xix.
16.   SJ Gould, editor, *Eight Little Piggies* (London: Penguin, 1993), 317.

entirely possible that not even can God predict the outcome over the long term. This is no insult to the dignity and divine power of the Creator: no-one is diminished by their inability to perform a logical impossibility, least of all the supreme source of all rationality.

Second, natural selection is not the only source of evolutionary change, and to argue that is to underestimate the key role of contingency in the history of life on earth. Many drastic events that changed the course of evolution were non-selective, and their effects could not be anticipated or explained in terms of any theory—for example the cosmic impact that saw off the last of the dinosaurs and opened up the stage for the early mammals, or the unknown catastrophe that buried the Burgess fauna.[17] Even at the level of individual lineages, historical choices favouring some adaptive changes preclude others in the future, because they reduce the options available to descendant forms. The modern giant panda needs an opposable thumb for handling bamboo, but it is descended from ancestors that walked on bear-like feet with all five toes in line. The genes needed to construct an opposable thumb were not available, but slight changes in the structure of the wrist proved a useful substitute, and over time have developed into what serves the giant panda almost as well.[18]

As Augustine pointed out, Christians who refuse the help of critical realism and continue to defend interpretations of scripture that any scientifically knowledgeable non-Christian would recognise as nonsense are not doing their faith any good.[19] So the proposition that God used evolution fails on the criterion of credibility and consistency with other information. More significantly for theology, it also fails on the criterion of fruitfulness. If all questions about the complexity of nature can be answered only as 'God's creative

---

17. DM Raup, *Extinction: Bad Genes or Bad Luck?* (New York: WW Norton, 1991).

18. SJ Gould, *The Panda's Thumb: More Reflections in Natural History* (New York: WW Norton, 1982).

19. HJ van Till, *Basil*, 'Augustin, and the Doctrine of Creation's Functional Integrity', *Science and Christian Belief*, 8 (1996): 21–38.

activities cannot be explained in terms of natural laws,'[20] then all enquiry is stifled. But it *is* possible to develop new models of God's action in the universe that are both credible and fruitful, and old ideas must be discarded. IDT retrieves purpose for theology, but only by making God responsible for all natural evil. As Haught[21] points out, its obsession with orderliness is too narrow for—and in great measure irrelevant to—the genuine engagement of theology and science. Love, not knowledge, is the substance of faith.

Original sin
One of the most significant contests between rival models, whose outcome has had incalculable effects on the Western church and thereby on Western civilisation, was the one between Eastern and Western concepts of original sin.[22] If the influence of Gregory of Nyssa, Julian and other Eastern theologians had prevailed, rather than that of Augustine, the West might have been spared centuries of tragic misunderstandings of the nature of evil and of human sexuality.[23]

The early church celebrated a doctrine of universal acceptance of humanity by God and an ideology of moral freedom, especially of women.[24] Clement of Alexandria (c 180 CE) regarded sexuality in marriage as a conscious co-operation with God in the work of creation[25]—which is, along with the idea of sex as crucial to pair-bonding, a surprisingly modern concept. Clement also extended the statement in Genesis that God had created all humanity in his own image as evidence of the equality and infinite value of every individual human life, each one entrusted with free will and moral responsibility. For over 300 years, Christians regarded various forms

---

20. W Gitt, *Did God Use Evolution?* (Bielefeld, Germany: Christliche Lieteratur-Verbreitung e V, 1993).
21. JF Haught, *God after Darwin* (Boulder, Colorado: Westview Press, 2000).
22. E Pagels, *Adam, Eve and the Serpent* (London: Penguin, 1988).
23. J Hick, *Evil and the God of Love* (San Francisco: HarperCollins, 1977).
24. E Pagels, *Adam, Eve and the Serpent, op cit.*
25. Clement, *Paidagogos* 2,83, quoted by Pagels, *ibid*, 27.

of freedom as the primary message of Genesis 1–3—freedom of will, freedom from demonic powers, from social and sexual obligations and from tyrannical secular government. The threat of persecution proved insufficient to counter the attraction of the message of freedom for thousands of converts.

Yet over a short period in the fourth century this intoxicating freedom was suddenly replaced by a totally different model, one that emphasised universal *bondage*. The work of Augustine, conducted in a totally new post-Constantinian environment that regarded freedom with suspicion (in case it might prove to be an enemy of the emperor) was based on a different interpretation of Genesis, that Adam's sin corrupted all hope of moral freedom, and indeed made us all incapable of genuine freedom or moral responsibility of any sort. He extended the JE creation story, which to the Hebrews was only a just-so explanation of why life is hard in a world created by a good God, to become the explanation of why all humans are helpless without the redemption which only the church could offer. Augustine effectively eliminated all belief in freedom from the early church, and ensured that it was replaced by the more politically expedient idea that humans *need* external government. He also added some bizarre interpretations of sexuality, and the blank denial of mortality and sexual desire as natural at all.

In patriarchal times, when the church was more authoritative and rival theories were suppressed as heresies, the whole intellectual history of Christendom was influenced by this important example of the struggle between rival interpretations of similar ideas. Augustine was vigorously opposed by Irenaeus, Justin, Tertullian and Clement, but he eventually succeeded in reducing the early variety of Christian ideas about freedom to the single and very different idea of universal corruption—especially of women.[26] At least with respect to this key central doctrine, there has been no cumulative increase in complexity as scholars learned more, but rather a 'collapse into simplicity'.[27]

Augustine persuaded many bishops and several Christian emperors to drive out of the churches as heretics those who held on

---

26.   E Pagels, *Adam, Eve and the Serpent, op cit*, 73, 97.

27.   J McManners, editor, *The Oxford Illustrated History of Christianity* (Oxford: Oxford University Press, 1992), 84.

to the earlier traditions of Christian freedom. From the fifth century on, his pessimistic views of sex, politics and human nature became the dominant influence on Western culture, replacing all early variety as surely as the vertebrates replaced the Burgess fauna. Neither development could have been predicted in advance—both illustrate the general rule that the processes of adaptation are contingent and chancy, not a grand march to Omega.

Picking up on Gould's conclusion about the Burgess fauna, that if the tape of creation were run again there would be no guarantee that humans would reappear,[28] could we be sure that if the tape of Christian history were run again, the same doctrines would have emerged as successful? It seems unlikely, since so much depends on the individual protagonists, the circumstances of the conflict, and chance events that influenced the judgments of the participants and the listeners. Convergence of religious doctrines under cultural selection is not at all the same process as convergence of body forms under natural selection given the physical constraints of the material world, so my guess is that Gould is right, the particular run of Christian history we have experienced was unique.

That conclusion raises the question of why Augustine's elaboration of the Eden story in pursuit of the doctrine of original sin became one of the foundational paradigms of Western culture, given that it involved some very strange reasoning. His insistence that Adam's sin introduced death to a humanity previously free of it was preposterous:

> To claim that a single human will ever possessed such power reflects a presumption of supernatural human importance. When Augustine claims that a single act of Adam's will changed the structure of the universe itself, he denies that we confront in our mortality a natural order beyond human power.[29]

---

28. SJ Gould, *Wonderful Life: The Burgess Shale and the Nature of History* (New York: WW Norton, 1989).

29. E Pagels, *Adam, Eve and the Serpent, op cit*, 144–145.

Actually, Augustine did not claim that the whole universe was corrupted, only the human capacity for moral judgement.[30] According to Santmire,[31] Augustine denied that the Fall affected wild nature, which he regarded as full of radiant beauty, portraying the transcendent and fecund glory of God. If the humanised parts of creation made life difficult for humans, that was only because it was obeying God's command to punish Adam's descendants. The idea of transmitted guilt affecting nature was totally absent from the Patristic tradition;[32] the extension of it to the whole cosmos was a consequence of the adoption of Aristotelian cosmology into theology by Aquinas in the thirteenth century.

But to the people of Augustine's time, the human and natural worlds were practically the same. The distinction between them is not relevant to Pagels' question: Why did Catholic Christianity adopt such a paradoxical doctrine, in the teeth of opposition from other theologians and in the face of all ordinary reason? Her answer illustrates the power of self-interest at the corporate level, which, then as now, is capable of subverting the motives of even the most idealistic organisations:

> Such beliefs validate the church's authority, for if the human condition is a disease, Catholic Christianity, acting as the Good Physician, offers the spiritual medication and the discipline that alone can cure it.[33]

On the other hand, if Augustinian theology served only as a device for social manipulation, why would reasonable people accept such sophistry? According to Pagels, one of several reasons why

30. CB Kaiser, 'The Integrity of Creation and the Social Nature of God', *Scottish Journal of Theology*, 49 (1996): 261–290.
31. P Santmire, *The Travail of Nature: The Ambiguous Ecological Promise of Christian Theology* (Minneapolis: Fortress Press, 1985), 66.
32. AE McGrath, *Christian Theology: An Introduction* (Oxford: Blackwell, 1994), 371.
33. E Pagels, *Adam, Eve and the Serpent, op cit*, 145.

Augustine's theory of the Fall eventually triumphed was that it made palatable the uneasy alliance between the Catholic church and Roman imperial power,[34] and it gave the church a monopoly on forgiveness of sin.[35] The latter argument was especially useful in serving the corporate survival (ie the self-interest) of the church.

The reason, Pagels points out, might have been that from ancient times until now, and independently of any religious belief, the most common immediate reaction of anyone suffering some sort of disaster is to ask what they had done to deserve it. There seems to be a strong and almost irrational human tendency to seek blame for natural misfortune, which is certainly not confined to the early Christian church, nor to the unpleasant personal consequences of individual bad moral decisions. The Jews of Jesus' time were ready to believe that the eighteen unfortunate people killed by the fall of a tower in Siloam must have been worse sinners than those who escaped (Luke 13:1–5). Pagels suggests that people need to find a *reason* for their sufferings, so,

> Had Augustine's theory not met such a need—were
> it not that people often *would rather feel guilty than*
> *helpless*—I suspect that the idea of original sin would
> not have survived the fifth century.[36]

Augustine taught that natural events are not random, but lie within the moral sphere, and so potentially within human control. The rival theory of Julian and his many supporters offered less prospect of human control over nature. The illusion of control came at the price of personal and corporate guilt, but, as history shows, the desire for power and its associated privileges is among the most powerful default settings of human nature. In terms of our two criteria for choosing between competing models, Augustine's was less credible and less fruitful than that of Irenaeus even at the time, but more politically expedient. Now that we live in very different circumstances, that advantage has evaporated. It is a different matter

---

34.   *Ibid*, 126.
35.   *Ibid*, 145.
36.   *Ibid*, 147 (author's emphasis).

to ask why his view is still so dominant in the more conservative branches of the church, but the answer is probably the same.

Evolutionary theology

These examples illustrate some of the reasons why, on the criteria of credibility and fruitfulness, the models summarised above cannot facilitate real dialogue between science and theology. We need a completely new paradigm which can capture the deeper meaning that a robust theological vision might discover in an evolving universe—in short, we need an evolutionary theology. Haught[37] offers a suitable definition:

> Instead of trying to prove God's existence from nature, evolutionary theology seeks to show how our new awareness of cosmic and biological evolution can enhance and enrich traditional teachings about God and God's way of acting in the world.

The field is huge and the literature vast. For example, Ruth Page's definition of the action of God in the world as 'a continuous giving room to explore what is possible', and Arthur Peacocke's definition of evolution as 'theology's friend in disguise' have in common a profound respect for the real freedom that God has granted to all life. Science may explain the consequences of this freedom in different ways, but they are not incompatible with theology, and must not be, because theology needs to understand the same world as described by the sciences.[38] Researchers working to understand the invisible realities in both disciplines need to take the same attitude:

> The model of natural science proposed by Galileo is an experimental, inductive one which seeks knowledge of the world *a posteriori* from its own concrete particulars rather than *a priori* from abstract generalities. It is in fact a model wholly consonant

---

37. JF Haught, *God after Darwin, op cit*, 36.
38. A Peacocke, *Theology for a Scientific Age, op cit.*

with proper theological method, and true of
theology's own subject, God, as well. The methodological axiom that the world is to be investigated
etsi deus non daretur (as if God were not part of the
picture) is also fundamental to proper scientific
investigation, and an essential part of the doctrine of
creation. It reflects the contingency of creation, the
fact that God has created something which is other
than Godself, and therefore to be investigated out of
itself. Galileo was entirely correct about this—as
indeed he was about the exegesis of scripture;
indeed it might be argued that he was a better
theologian than scientist![39]

Page, Peacocke and Haught and many others have presented
theological models of creation that are not only completely
compatible with evolutionary biology, but also fruitful in generating
new theological insights.[40]

Evolutionary theology offers an alternative model of the origin of
evil, which does not depend on a literal interpretation of the Eden
myth, and is consistent with theistic science. In nature, as in human
life, it is merely a logical consequence of creaturely freedom that,
when a lot of independent and non-sociable animals pursue their
own self-interest at the same time and place, many forms of evil are
the direct result. Evolutionary theology sees the universe as
unfinished and creatures as necessarily imperfect—a key point in
Irenaeus's ancient perception of nature, suppressed by Augustine but

---

39. S May, 'The Galileo Affair, or, How NOT To Engage in the Theology
     /Science Debate', in *Science and Christianity: Festschrift in Honour of
     Harold Turner and John Morton*, edited by LRB Mann (Auckland:
     University of Auckland Centre for Continuing Education, 2001),
     29–48.
40. K Ward, *God, Chance and Necessity* (Oxford: Oneworld, 1996); D
     Edwards, *The God of Evolution* (New York: Paulist Press, 1999); JF
     Haught, *God after Darwin, op cit.*

now being recovered by modern scholarship.[41] It therefore also sees evil as the unavoidable consequence of freedom: God could not have prevented it.[42] This is the simple and obvious answer to Gould's concerns about the cruelty of ichneumon wasps.[43] The problem of evil, for the biologically informed theist, is not the existence of evil, such as the apparently useless suffering of the ichneumon's caterpillar victims or of the last-hatched 'back-up chicks' of the pelican,[44] but the *extent* of it.

But it is in human affairs that evolutionary theology is both most needed and most exciting, especially in the long-vexed questions of moral responsibility. Traditional theology has always made a distinction between original sin as an inescapable predisposition which 'contaminates our lives from birth',[45] and personal sin as an individual, deliberate act. If original sin is equated with the conflict between natural selection for individual advantage and cultural selection for group advantage,[46] which is inherent in human nature, then it certainly is an inescapable predisposition. We may know very well that there are good reasons why we should be honest, chaste, sober, hardworking, faithful and public-spirited in this life, if only in the hope of being happy in the next, yet somehow it is never as easy as that. St Paul hit the nail right on the head:

> . . . when I want to do the right, only the wrong is in my reach. In my inmost self I delight in the law of God, but . . . there is in my bodily members a different law, fighting against the law that my reason approves . . . miserable creature that I am,

41. RF Brown, 'On the Necessary Imperfection of Creation: Irenaeus' Adversus Haereses, iv, 38', *Scottish Journal of Theology*, 28 (1975): 17–25.
42. J Hick, *Evil and the God of Love, op cit.*
43. SJ Gould, 'Nonmoral Nature', *in Hen's Teeth and Horse's Toes*, edited by SJ Gould (New York: WW Norton, 1983), 32–45.
44. JB McDaniel, *Of God and Pelicans: A Theology of Reverence for Life* (Louisville, Kentucky: Westminster/John Knox Press, 1989).
45. AE McGrath, *Christian Theology: An Introduction, op cit*, 374.s
46. DT Campbell, 'The Conflict between Social and Biological Evolution and the Concept of Original Sin', *Zygon*, 10 (1975): 234–249.

who is there to rescue me out of this body doomed
to death? (Romans 7:21–24)

Paul could hardly have written a better description of the inner
conflicts generated by the meeting of our animal and cultural
heritages if he had been schooled in evolutionary biology.

The ancient distinction between the concepts of original sin, a
general predisposition, and immorality, individual acts of
wrongdoing[47] holds no challenges for biology. The first refers to
what we *are* (any species that has survived the winnowing processes
of natural selection must necessarily have equipped its members to
be self-centred in some sense), the second to what we *do*—how we
make those choices between self-interest and group interest. Sociable
animals are not so much 'survival machines' built by selfish genes[48]
as 'adaptive decision makers' descended from primates who had got
the processes of social negotiation down to a fine art even before the
evolution of human language.[49] The assumption that human nature
is malleable by culture and circumstances, to produce altruistic or
individualistic behaviour (usually equated with good or evil,
respectively) according to the odds on whatever strategy might pay
best in the social environment of the moment, helps to explain the
multiple dilemmas of social life.

The differences between the traditional and evolutionary models
of evil go right back to the primary assumption of how God acts in
creation, which governs all the other consequences that follow (Table
1).

---

47.   AE McGrath, *Christian Theology: An Introduction, op cit*, 374.
48.   RDawkins, *The Selfish Gene* (Oxford: Oxford University Press, 1989).
49.   F de Waal, *Good Natured: The Origins of Right and Wrong in Humans
      and Other Animals* (Cambridge, Mass: Harvard University Press,
      1996).

Table 1. Two models of the origin of evil

	Traditional model	Evolutionary model
Primary assumption	God is both good and omnipotent	God is good but not omnipotent
Means of creation	Direct, hands-on	Indirect, via cosmic law
Consequences	God could not be responsible for imperfections of nature, moral evil So creation is not as God designed it Only humans have freedom Evil must be due to human sin	Imperfections and evil expected, necessary All life is free Natural and moral evil both caused by conflicts of interest among free agents, unavoidable
Historical reconstruction	OT Eden myth adapted to explain origin of moral evil Adam's fall explains necessity of redemption Emphasis on original sin, conditional acceptance mediated by church Hell is for those who cannot be forgiven	Morality gradually developed from animal roots Eden is a powerful symbol only God's acceptance unconditional, unaffected by frequent failure Hell is for those who cannot accept they are already forgiven
Problems	Vested interests; fear of loss of biblical authority; fear of immorality	Traditional creation theology needs fundamental rethinking
Representative authors	Gitt[50]	McFague,[51] Page,[52] Ward,[53] McGrath,[54] Edwards[55]

---

50.   W Gitt, *Did God Use Evolution?*, *op cit.*

Evolutionary theology is not only credible to modern ears, but also can generate some fruitful new theological insights. For example, why does the ritual of adult baptism often have such marvellous restorative consequences? The power of this simple action depends on the fact that all terrestrial animals fear drowning, and most humans have a panic reaction to having their heads forcibly shoved under water. The traditional practice of baptism by total immersion imitates the experience of rising from death to a new life, so is therefore a powerful symbol of the theological doctrine of Christian faith as death to our natural life and the beginning of a new life in Christ.

Critics of the practice of infant baptism point out that infants do not need redemption before they have had the opportunity to commit sin. But just by being human and sharing in the human genetic and cultural heritage, infants share the same predispositions as all the rest of us, so to the extent that baptism cancels original sin, we all need it, infants included. This interpretation assumes that the sacraments generally are causative rather than declarative.[56] If baptism is understood as causative (it effects forgiveness of original sin) it is perfectly appropriate to apply to infants; if it is understood as declarative (it demonstrates forgiveness), it is not. The difference between the two has been argued at length by theologians; in general, the Anglo-Catholic tradition seems to opt for the first, and various other Protestant communities for the second.

The role of women in history and the virgin birth is another subject on which the incorporation of modern genetics into an evolutionary model of theology can produce wonderful new insights. Age, sex and death constitute an alliance, all derived from errors in copying the genes—the process that causes individual bodies to

51. S McFague, *Models of God: Theology for an Ecological, Nuclear Age,* op cit.
52. R Page, *God and the Web of Creation* (London: SCM Press, 1996).
53. K Ward, *God, Chance and Necessity, op cit.*
54. AE McGrath, *The Foundations of Dialogue in Science and Religion* (Malden, Massachusetts: Blackwell Publishers Inc, 1998).
55. D Edwards, *The God of Evolution, op cit.*
56. AE McGrath, *Christian Theology: An Introduction, op cit,* 446.

decay but the genetic message to be preserved. Senility is caused by cumulative copying errors in the mitochondria of the body cells, which reduce energy production, also, many inherited diseases appear in later life as bad side-effects linked to reproductive advantages to the young. But the cells that later become sperm and eggs are set aside, separate from the rest of the body, from well before birth. During the processes of sexual reproduction, which compare and re-match the two separate copies of each gene drawn by the two partners from the species gene pool, many errors are found and deleted. Indeed, one of the main tasks of sex is to undo the damage done by mutation to the body of every prospective parent during its own growth years—in other words, sex functions for mutual proofreading of genes. Jones[57] therefore draws a parallel between mutation in the 'corruptible body', and the life-giving effects of sex and resurrection.

> The story of mutation unites, as nothing else, scientific and spiritual views of the human condition. It gives the idea of resurrection 'a corruptible body raised in incorruption'—a new and precise meaning.[58]

A woman makes her full complement of around a million egg cells before she is born, and releases them at intervals throughout her reproductive life. A man makes millions upon millions of sperm cells every day. Since the sperm are made at a vastly greater rate, the mutation rate is higher in them, whereas in ova the self-checking processes operated by armies of repair enzymes are slower and can be more comprehensive. Hence, says Jones, the conventional [Augustinian] idea of women as the source of corruption is wrong; by this definition, women are the essence of resurrection.[59]

Evolutionary theology also generates some fruitful new ideas about the virgin birth, and not for the obvious reason that only a girl could be produced by a parthenogenesis. If Jesus was truly fully

---

57. S Jones, *In the Blood* (London: HarperCollins, 1996).
58. *Ibid*, 247.
59. *Ibid*, 277.

human, as the patristic Church insisted, he must have been not only bone of our bone but also (in modern terms) DNA of our DNA. He must have had a Y chromosome complete with all the genes that define masculinity and which connected him to our earliest human ancestors via the immense span of historical linkages that determine the male part of the evolved human condition. As Gregory of Nazianus (329–389 CE) put it, 'What he has not assumed he has not healed'—so it is *theologically necessary* that the birth narratives be seen as legend—as conveying truth, without being factual. For both biological and theological reasons, the doctrines of the virginal conception and of the incarnation are different, and must be separated.[60] Gregory himself would have approved this development, since he recognised the evolutionary nature of theology:

> By gradual advances and . . . partial ascents, we should move forward and increase in clarity, so that the light of the Trinity should shine.[61]

The real stumbling block to reconciling evolution with faith, says Haught[62] is not evolution itself but the scandalous image of God's humility that comes right from the heart of religious experience, rather than from the logic of design arguments. Evolutionary theology allied with critical realism can reject Dennett's claim that Darwin's idea was dangerous for the theological enterprise, and replaces it with an even more dangerous idea of its own, that of an incarnate God who suffers along with creation. Both ideas are offensive to those whose models of the invisible realities of science and faith insist on obsolete notions of materialism, on the one hand, and divine omnipotence, on the other. But a more realistic understanding of the metaphorical nature of all knowledge could help understand where that offence comes from, and perhaps how it can be disarmed.

---

60. A Peacocke, 'The Challenge of Science to the Thinking Church', *Modern Believing*, 36 (1995): 15–26.

61. Quoted in AE McGrath, *Christian Theology: An Introduction, op cit*, 244.

62. JF Haught, *God after Darwin, op cit*, 52.

Conclusion

Science and theology are alike in several important things, including that both are systems of human knowledge, necessarily based on models and metaphors, which cannot be regarded as immutable over the long term. I suggest that this basic similarity between science and theology, starting with their agreement founded in the Christian assertion that the world is good, rational and contingent, offers new hope for resolution of their traditional differences.

They have other features in common too. For example, proper understanding of any model depends on getting the ideas in the correct order. In both the English language and in the genetic code, the sense conveyed is contained in the *sequence* of symbols, not, as in Chinese, in the symbols themselves. In words, the sequence GOD means something different from the sequence DOG, even though the symbols are the same; in the genetic code, the sequence AGC codes for a different product than CGA. Both science and theology are vulnerable to what might be called the 'cart-before-the-horse' syndrome, by which the meaning of a model can be completely reversed. The most common cause of misunderstanding of neo-Darwinism is that people tend to think of adaptive evolution as a horse, and talk of it as 'driving' changes, and even of God 'harnessing' it. Actually, evolution is the cart, and the horse it follows is the differential breeding success of animals in a variable population. For Christians, love and grace are the horses that pull the cart called 'good works' along a road called 'justification'. Much of Luther's work was about getting the horse back in front.

For both science and theology, there are penalties attached to hanging on to inappropriate models. Individual scientists who refuse to allow modification of their favourite models delay progress towards better understanding of their field, and may even damage the credibility of their institutions, as Lysenko destroyed Soviet agricultural research over the period from the 1930s to 1964. In theology, there is widespread reluctance among ordinary believers to consider any radically updated theology of creation, which hampers the efforts of theologians to counter the materialist propaganda of atheistic science that destroys the credibility of faith for countless young people.

On the other hand, there are signs of progress. According to Moltmann,[63] the temporary estrangement between the sciences and theology is now over. It began when the sciences emancipated themselves from cosmology, while theology detached its doctrine of creation from cosmology and reduced it to a personal belief in God as Creator rather than in the things that have been created. The two disciplines established, after many struggles, their own identities on either side of accepted demarcation lines, and achieved a peaceful coexistence based on mutual irrelevance. Now they are becoming companions in tribulation, under the pressure of the ecological crisis and the search for new directions in both which must be found if humanity is to survive at all. In this newly cooperative atmosphere, the mutual demarcation lines are no longer necessary. In a global situation where it is one world or none, says Moltmann, theistic science and theology cannot afford to divide up the one, single reality.

I wonder, in what ways might the science-religion debate be different, perhaps even more productive, if we celebrated what we have in common more often than what divides us?

63.　J Moltmann, *God in Creation* (London: SCM Press, 1985).

Part Two

Evolutionary Biology

Interpretations of Complexity in Nature: Teilhard to Maynard Smith

Carolyn M King

Introduction

One of the most important and frequently recurring challenges in the history of theology is the question: How can we make sense of the world around us? Particularly, in the context of this conference, does the wonderful complexity of the natural world mean anything, and if so can we draw any valid conclusions about the nature of God from observations of nature?

People have asked this question in every generation since time out of mind. The Book of Job records an untypically honest response of the pre-scientific age: God's ways are inscrutable, but trustworthy. Then, as now, humans are constantly being challenged to seek a new understanding of God appropriate to their times, which means that every generation has to ask again how to fit their knowledge of God with their knowledge of the secular world.

This paper is based on the belief that, although contemporary theology need not be beholden to science, it must be consistent with it in order to remain credible to contemporary listeners. That does not mean simplistically judging the one by the standards of the other, but that both sides need to engage in a sincere and meaningful dialogue. Theologians must neither dismiss nor imitate science, and scientists must disengage themselves from materialistic propaganda[1] and

---

1. The writings of several high-profile anti-theists claim that science and materialism are inseparable, but I agree with Haught (JF Haught, *God after Darwin* (Boulder, Colorado: Westview Press, 2000), 47) that 'it is quite possible to distinguish evolutionary science from the obsolete materialism that cripples . . . public presentations of it'. On the contrary, theistic science is not only possible, but intellectually rigorous: see N Murphy, *Theology in the Age of Scientific Reasoning* (Ithaca, New York: Cornell University Press, 1990) and A Peacocke, *Theology for a Scientific Age* (London: SCM Press, 1993).

neither dismiss nor patronise theology. We need more people on either side willing to enter serious debate on the contemporary issues with those on the other side, and earnestly try to understand what the other is saying.

This might sound like a new idea, but it is not:

> St Augustine insisted that 'The literal meaning . . . may never stand in contradiction to one's competently derived knowledge about the earth, the heavens and the other elements of this world . . . [that are] certain from reason and experience . . . Augustine soundly reprimands those Christians who defend interpretations of scripture that any scientifically knowledgeable non-Christian would recognise as nonsense.'[2]

The advances of science over the last 300 years have made it even more important than ever that modern Christians heed Augustine's advice, but even though it is not easy, we have plenty of historical precedent for the task, and no real excuses for avoiding it. In my view the credibility of our faith depends on it.

Definitions of complexity

Complexity in biology
The complexity of nature is difficult to define, but two obvious criteria are the variety and sheer improbability of living things, and the apparent increase in these over time. The paleontological record is certainly incomplete, but even so it catalogues a staggering list of fossil species which have arisen, flourished and passed on since life first appeared as blue-green algae about 3.5 billion years ago. The history of life has generally proceeded from the simple to the complex, from the first few basic molecules in the primordial soup to the staggering variety and diversity of life crowding every

---

2.   HJ van Till, 'Basil, Augustine, and the Doctrine of Creation's Functional Integrity', *Science and Christian Belief*, 8 (1996): 30

conceivable habitat on earth today.[3] After the blue-green algae, there was a long pause. Then, the earliest multicellular animals appeared about 1.8 billion years ago, the earliest mammals and dinosaurs about 235 million years ago, and the earliest true humans *H. sapiens* from about 150 thousand years ago.

The fossil record has been improving for centuries, and more than ninety per cent of all species that have ever lived are known only from fossils. However, the real extent of the huge complexity of life on earth has become known only since the development of molecular biology, because the vast majority of global genetic diversity is microbial. Of the three main branches of the tree of life, two (the Archaea and the Bacteria) are entirely microscopic. All visible animals and plants are classed only as two rather remote twigs of the third branch, the Eucarya.

Another possible definition of complexity in biology might be the upper-level order which arises from interactions at the lower levels of the biological hierarchy. At each new level of complexity in organisation, living organisms acquire new and often unpredictable emergent properties. Within each level, differentiation among the components and intercom-munication between them also increase with time. For example, at the level of the cell, eukaryotes are more complex than earliest archaea and prokaryotes, among organs, the human brain is the most complex ever, with a multi-level internal messaging system and emergent consciousness, animal and human societies range from simple family groups to larger associations including unrelated members to permanent tribes with division of labour and emergent social structures, the most complex ecosystems are usually the most stable and resistant to invasion.

Complexity in theology

Traditionally, the historical *increase in the complexity of nature* has been seen as progress towards God. The medieval idea of the 'Great Chain of Being' visualised all creation as ranged in order from the inert physical substrate through the lowliest of invertebrates up to humans, and, above them, the angels and archangels. To start with,

---

3.   EO Wilson, *The Diversity of Life* (Cambridge, Mass: Belknap Press, Harvard, 1992).

rank order was thought of as fixed, but an element of progress had been introduced at least by the eighteenth century. For example, Lamarck (1774–1829) envisaged organisms being driven up an escalator by innate 'desire' towards greater complexity, while new organisms were continually created at the bottom by spontaneous generation.

It was common to interpret this general pattern as an inevitable upward march towards the crown of creation, *Homo sapiens*. Indeed, that is still a required assumption for Christians who want to substitute evolution for special creation as God's route to the incarnation—including, most notably, Pierre Tielhard de Chardin. Others, eg Burhoe[4] go further and substitute evolution for God, seeing the whole process as a passport for escape from the degrading animal company that contaminates the human past, a guarantee of a glorious, rational future. Critical responses to this idea, known as 'the escalator fallacy' are decisive.[5] Teilhard de Chardin was even more explicit in identifying his 'Omega Point' with the culmination of a progress towards God led by humans, the 'leading shoot' of creation.

Conversely, the more recent idea of '*irreducible* complexity' is being promoted as evidence for divine action in creation, and incidentally as a means for theology to resist the domination of atheistic science, widely seen as incompatible with faith. The fundamental proposition is that the interlocking components of very complex systems, such as the chemical machinery of aerobic respiration or the anatomy of the vertebrate eye, could not have evolved gradually by natural selection.[6] A whole new branch of natural theology has been constructed on this basis, known as Intelligent Design Theory (IDT). For biological reasons discussed in more detail in my companion paper, and theological reasons given by Haught,[7] this theory contributes nothing to advancing the debate.

---

4. RW Burhoe, 'Natural Selection and God', *Zygon*, 7 (1970): 30–63.
5. M Midgley, *Beast and Man: The Roots of Human Nature* (London: Methuen University Paperback, 1978), 197, and *Evolution as a Religion* (London: Methuen, 1985), 67.
6. MJ Behe, Darwin's *Black Box: The Biochemical Challenge to Evolution* (New York: Simon & Schuster, 1996).
7. JF Haught, *God after Darwi, op cit.*

The extent and variety of biological adaptations possible over evolutionary time is much more difficult for theologians to accept than for biologists. That may well be because modern biology is itself a very complex subject, and there are too few biologists who, like Ursula Goodenough, are willing to take theologians seriously and to discuss with them the contemporary theory in sufficient detail.[8] This is unfortunate, because it obstructs understanding on both sides of the religion-science debate. On the religious side, people's difficulty about seeing themselves as members of the one creation remains stuck in a crude, narrow, highly abstract notion of what the other members were like.[9] On the scientific side, most mainstream biologists see it as safer for their career prospects to follow Richard Dawkins in assuming that, because biology can now prove Paley mistaken,[10] all other forms of theology can also be dismissed.

Interpretations of complexity
The general observation of historical order in creation, whereby the simplest creatures appeared first and the more complex ones only later, has long been recognised. At least one strand of Hebrew tradition, represented by the first (P) creation story in Genesis 1, has plants and animals appearing before humans. That is not evidence of the compatibility of scripture and science, since any such argument misses the point of P's story, and invites questions about why the second (JE) Eden story has the same God creating humans first. However, many ordinary people uninterested in the academic details are happy to think of Genesis 1 as a metaphorical or prophetic version of what is now the standard geological story, and are thereby open to the science-religion debate in ways that hard-line literalists are not.

The historical increase in biodiversity is well documented in the fossil record, despite its imperfections. There is a recurring pattern of periodic mass extinctions, each followed by a period of recovery to

---

8. U Goodenough, *The Sacred Depths of Nature* (New York: Oxford University Press, 1998).
9. M Midgley, *Beast and Man: The Roots of Human Nature*, op cit, 95.
10. R Dawkins, *The Blind Watchmaker* (Harlow, Essex: Longman Scientific and Technical, 1986).

the same or even higher levels of diversity as before—as in the stock market, growth eventually resumes after even catastrophic slumps. Over the past 600 million years there have been three main casts in the drama, three recognisably different sets of animals now preserved as hard fossils. The first set was the ancient Cambrian fauna (represented by only a very few modern survivors), then the Palaeozoic fauna (now relatively rare), and then the Modern fauna, (still rapidly expanding). In addition to these there are the soft bodied organisms, which are much better represented in recent sediments than in older ones, so our concept of their numbers and lifestyles is very patchy. One particularly well-preserved and studied set of them, the Burgess fauna of the Canadian Rocky Mountains, gives us a glimpse into a hugely diverse lost world of ancient and very strange creatures.[11]

There is no evidence of steady improvements of types in the fossil record. If there were, we should be able to detect a smooth, or at least unidirectional, development of forms from a simple beginning to a complex later state; the present should be predictable from the past. The earliest known fossil assemblages should contain fewer types than later assemblages. But, as the Burgess fossils show, that is simply not the case. Most scientists therefore deny that evolution is progressive in any ordinary sense.

For theologians, there are two conflicting interpretations of the complexity of life. For the anthropocentric determinists such as Tielhard de Chardin[12] and Michael Behe,[13] geological history is evidence that *God directs evolution,* and that humans capable of entering into a conscious and loving relationship with God have always been the purpose of it. Natural selection could not possibly have done the job alone. Conversely, for atheistic evolutionists such

---

11. SJ Gould, *Wonderful Life: The Burgess Shale and the Nature of History* (New York: WW Norton, 1989) and S Conway Morris, *The Crucible of Creation: The Burgess Shale and the Rise of Animals* (Oxford: Oxford University Press, 1998).
12. T de Chardin, *The Phenomenon of Man* (London: Fontana, 1965).
13. MJ Behe, *Darwin's Black Box: The Biochemical Challenge to Evolution, op cit.*

as Richard Dawkins,[14] Stephen Jay Gould[15] and Daniel Dennett,[16] the same data provide conclusive evidence that *there is no God*, or at least not one bearing any resemblance to the God of love claimed by Christianity. They are adamant that natural selection does not need any divine help—what Dennett calls 'skyhooks'—to produce the riotous complexity of the natural world.

For anyone not totally committed to one side or the other, both of these interpretations are deeply unsatisfactory. Theological determinism ignores much contrary evidence from evolutionary history, showing that most lineages lead to dead ends, and that most adaptations are the result of jury-rigging of whatever designs happen to be available. The hypothesis of divine direction is therefore universally rejected by those most familiar with biology, but that tends to leave them without spiritual foundations. The alternative interpretation, especially the more aggressively materialistic versions of gene-centred evolution, allows no room for God, so that alternative leaves believers without any rational tools with which to explore the possible relationship between the divine life and the complexity of nature. The only other possibilities are either radical atheism or, if that raises the fear of a world governed by random purposelessness, 'creation science'.

Is there a middle course? Yes, I believe there is. IDT theorists are correct to reject the idea that natural selection alone could be the source of order in nature, but then, so do evolutionary biologists. Living beings are neither inert nor the product of solely random processes. Rather, it is the *interaction of chance and law over time* which provides the crucial conditions for natural selection to operate. Peacocke[17] describes chance as 'the search radar of God', sweeping through all potential fields of statistical possibility. Without chance

---

14. R Dawkins, 'Replicators and Vehicles', in *Current Problems in Sociobiology*, edited by anon (Cambridge: Cambridge University Press, 1982), 45–64

15. SJ Gould, 'Nonmoral Nature', in *Hen's Teeth and Horse's Toes*, edited by SJ Gould, (New York: WW Norton, 1983), 32–45

16. DC Dennett, *Darwin's Dangerous Idea* (New York: Simon and Schuster, 1995).

17. A Peacocke, *Creation and the World of Science* (Oxford: Clarendon Press, 1979), 95.

there could be no new variations; without order, all new variations would be immediately lost. Favourable variations are accumulated over many generations, and evolution—ie changes in gene frequencies from one generation to the next—is the result. It is the *consequences* of natural selection that produce new life forms, and the process is always subject to modification, certainly by historical contingency,[18] and perhaps also by the more controversial potential self-organisation of matter.[19] Moreover, the emergent properties of higher levels of organisation are unpredictable and not due only to natural selection, for example it cannot explain the properties of populations or ecosystems, or the emergence of human consciousness from the structure of the brain. Dennett's idea, that evolution works as an algorithm[20] is quite wrong: law plus initial conditions is no good at explaining how more evolves out of less.[21]

In this paper I will consider the significance of complexity in creation from a biologist's point of view, and specifically at two levels: first, how the complex machinery of life operates in the present, and second, how the diversity of life developed from simple to complex over time. To me it is clear that contemporary biology and theology have *mutual* implications—advances in the one may well affect our images of, and therefore our understanding of, the other. Mutual criticisms based on outdated concepts are invalid and serve neither cause.

Therefore, the debate must be based on *current* knowledge, which is constantly advancing in both fields. In biology this is called the Red Queen effect, because Lewis Carroll's image of the Red Queen constantly running in order to stay in the same place is a potent metaphor for the struggle of all species to remain well adapted in a natural world constantly being changed by adaptations in other

18. SJ Gould, *Wonderful Life: The Burgess Shale and the Nature of History, op cit.*
19. S Kauffman, *At Home in the Universe: The Search for Laws of Self-Organisation and Complexity* (London: Viking, 1995).
20. DC Dennett, *Darwin's Dangerous Idea, op cit.*
21. H Rolston III, *Genes, Genesis and God* (Cambridge: Cambridge University Press, 1999), 151.

species.[22] So if we want to make real progress in the science-theology debate, and avoid pointless arguments, science and theology must take each other seriously enough to keep up with each other's advances. But so far, the vast majority of materialistic scientists ignore theology, and to a great extent, theologians still think and write almost as though Darwin had never lived.[23]

Complexity in the present

Complexity is hard to measure or evaluate in any objective terms: for example, although the 'higher' animals don't always need more genes to construct their complex bodies, nevertheless there is some obvious sense in which sentient mammals are more complex than worms, and bacteria more than the first replicating molecules. The recurring question is: How did this complexity arise?

The basic principle we need to understand before going into any details is an unfamiliar one, developed only recently and most clearly explained by Williams:[24] It is that there are *two different forms of reality.* One is the material domain, which comprises the familiar, tangible stuff of ordinary observable life, from molecules to cells and bodies, from trees to paper. The other is the codical domain, which comprises non-material coded information such as is carried in the form of genes, or in the words of human language. The interactions between them are unimaginably complicated, but essential to life in the every day. Over time, they are the source of all natural, historical and cultural diversity.

It can be argued that the most stable basic unit of life is not the individual or the cell, but the gene. The genes governing vital body functions such as the feedback controls governing breathing, heart rate and digestion remain unchanged over the long term, and exist in millions of identical copies. Every individual animal must have a co-ordinated set of these genes, and every one holds and uses this information inherited from its ancestors, and then passes it on to its

---

22. M Ridley, *The Red Queen: Sex and the Evolution of Human Nature* (London: Penguin, 1993).

23. JF Haught, *God after Darwin, op cit,* 2.

24. GC Williams, *Natural Selection: Domains, Levels and Challenges* (New York: Oxford University Press, 1992).

offspring. But the gene is not the DNA molecule, which is a material entity destroyed by death along with the rest of the body: the gene is the *transcribable information coded by* the molecule, in three-letter codons ('words') that mean the same in all organisms. Genes are absolutely real, but only in the *codical* (non-material) domain. They do not eat, run, sweat, watch for predators or produce young, but they make bodies that do all these things.[25]

By contrast, the bodies constructed by genes are only temporary, but every one is unique. Except for twins or asexual clones, each body is a single, once-only individual expressing the information contained in a particular aggregation of coded information, modified by its own interactions with the environment. Each combination of genes works together for this generation only, and is split into new combinations in the next generation. So bodies show extensive variation between generations of the same lineage, and no son is ever quite like his father. Copies of the genes carried by successful bodies live on in new bodies, for long after the old bodies were destroyed at death.

Both codical and material domains are involved in reproduction, but genes can replicate themselves exactly from one generation to the next, whereas bodies cannot. Both are real, but they are not the same kind of reality. Genes are equivalent to sheet music, but bodies are like a concert performance. Genes are like musical notation—a real code, comprising any number of written or printed copies all identical, carrying information that remains stable over centuries, but they are only *potential* experience. So long as they remain only coded information on paper, no-one will hear the music. It takes an entity belonging to the material domain—a musician (or more often a group of individual musicians working together), to lift the musical code off the page and express it as a temporary, variable performance. Like bodies, concerts may be imperfect and are always influenced by circumstances, but they are *experienced reality* in a sense that the score, though also real, can never be.

Units of information (genes) recycle down the generations indefinitely through a succession of material bodies. Parents draw

---

25. R Dawkins, 'Replicators and Vehicles', *op cit*, and *The Selfish Gene* (Oxford: Oxford University Press, 1989).

copies from the gene pool, and those that succeed in breeding return copies to the pool in their offspring.[26] Meanwhile, all bodies die and are destroyed, with their material DNA, however successful they were. Generations of repetition of this process slowly changes the representation of genes in the pool. Copies of the most useful genes are returned to the pool somewhat more often than copies of less useful genes. This differential rate of return causes changes in gene frequency (ie the mixture of genes in the pool), which accumulate in the relatively stable, collective genome of the species.

These changes not directed, progressive or predictable, since the basic variation on which they depend is random, but the cumulative change in the genome is *not* random—it leads either to increased (or at least maintained) adaptation, or to extinction. Evolution is the *consequence* of these differential processes: inevitably, genes having effects that favour their own survival are best represented in the pool. They are not 'selfish', as in Dawkins' provocative and widely misunderstood analogy, but it stands to reason that, for example, since white fur is a better camouflage against ice than black fur, the gene for white fur is more often passed on by white polar bears successfully producing cubs than would any freak reappearance of their ancestral gene for dark fur. The key point to grasp is that evolution is a follower, not a leader—it does not drive natural selection, or anything else. Evolution is what we see when natural selection has done its work.

In turn, natural selection can choose only between available alternatives, so it works only when there are (1) bodies carrying heritable variants (genes), eg body shape or colour, size or running speed, and (2) competition for insufficient resources or danger from predators. Darwin's name for this process was 'descent with modification', because he wanted to avoid any implication of progress as implied (then and now) in the word 'evolution'.

The very recent recognition of the significance of the difference between the domains of reality underlies important advances in our understanding of animal behaviour and evolution. For example, the

---

26. GC Williams, *Natural Selection: Domains, Levels and Challenges, op cit.*

problem of altruism in animals, called by Wilson[27] the 'central problem of sociobiology', is thereby explained in genetic terms, and in the natural world this insight has proved extraordinarily fruitful. Any act of what might appear to be unselfish generosity, such as sharing food or feeding a relative's cubs, may lead to evolutionary advantage in terms of enhanced reproductive success if it improves the propagation of copies of the family genes. Similar cultural processes create group cohesion around systems of shared ideas in human societies, ever since the evolution of language. And the full significance of sexual reproduction becomes clear only in when it is understood in terms of what is happening in the codical domain. The separate copies of the same genes drawn from the same pool by the two parents are not only shuffled to produce unique combinations in every new individual, but also checked for copying errors when the chromosomes are matched at fertilisation.[28]

Regrettably, the difference between the characters of the material and codical domains has also been used to support ultra-materialism and scientism—the philosophies criticised by Appleyard[29] as starting from the reasonable proposition that science can investigate only certain kinds of questions, and ending with the completely invalid conclusion that only those questions that can be investigated by science are worth considering, or even real. Hence Dawkins' assertion that, because genes are virtually immortal compared with bodies, they must be more important. He visualises bodies as merely 'robots' built as 'survival machines' for genes: and since genes are blind, the universe is necessarily purposeless.[30] Philosophers point out that this is nonsense.[31] but for everyone else this concept makes all previous interpretations of the meaning and significance of human life untenable.

---

27. EO Wilson, *Sociobiology: The New Synthesis* (Cambridge, Mass: Harvard University Press, 1975).
28. S Jones, *In the Blood* (London: HarperCollins, 1996).
29. B Appleyard, *Understanding the Present: Science and the Soul of Modern Man* (London: Picador, 1992).
30. R Dawkins, *The Selfish Gene, op cit.*
31. M Midgley, 'Gene-juggling', *Philosophy*, 54 (1979): 439–458.

Theological interpretations

The concept that the material domain is less important because it is only temporary is an old one, and at first sight might offer an unexpected link between science and theology. It is true that Christian history is full of comparable affirmations, but this attitude is less appealing now than it was a few hundred years ago. For a start, too rigid a division between the material and spiritual worlds has led in the past to some spectacular excesses of world-denying spirituality. Even now, by drawing such a sharp line between the world of nature and the world of the soul, Christianity still contributes to attitudes that have encouraged irresponsible environmental exploitation.[32] To this day there remains a correlation between a high level of fundamentalist and/or apocalyptic expectations in a local congregation and a general disinterest in conservation.[33] But, as Barbour points out,[34] when God is confined to the realm of the self, the natural order is deprived of any religious significance except as a background for the drama of human existence. Rather, we should insist that the natural world is not simply 'the stage on which the larger drama of history is played, but has a key role in that drama itself'.[35]

Theologians interested in the science-religion debate can and should assert that codical realities such as genes are indeed real, but are neither more nor less significant because they last longer than bodies. It is the interaction between the codical and material realities that produces life, because although natural selection ultimately measures the fitness of genes, it cannot 'see' genes until they are expressed in a body. The score is *not* more important than the performance, or recipes than cakes—neither makes any sense alone.

---

32. IG Barbour, *Religion and Science: Historical and Contemporary Issues* (New York: HarperCollins, 1997), 268.
33. DL Eckberg and TJ Blocker, 'Christianity, Environmentalism, and the Theoretical Problem of Fundamentalism', *Journal for the Scientific Study of Religion*, 35 (1996): 343–355.
34. IG Barbour, *Religion and Science: Historical and Contemporary Issues, op cit*, 89.
35. W Granberg-Michaelson, 'Creation in Ecumenical Theology', in *Ecotheology: Voices from North and South*, edited by DG Hallman (Geneva: WCC Publications, 1994), 96–106.

In nature, 'adaptation' is an ecological word, not a genetic one: a coyote in a zoo still has genes, but no fitness.[36] In the human world, our material lives are brief, puzzling and contradictory, but they are experienced reality, and our interactions in the real, material world are our meeting place with God. In different words, Haught[37] makes the same point: 'Information is quietly resident in nature . . . it abides patiently in the realm of possibility, waiting to be actualised in time . . . it is not an abstraction that vanishes when we stop thinking about it but is, rather . . . the foundation of anything being actual at all.' Haught describes this 'information' as 'scientifically unspecifiable', so he was not equating it directly with Williams 'codical domain', but there could be grounds for discussion on that.

A second theological interpretation of the two-domains theory is relevant to speculations about the nature of the soul. We are familiar with the ideas that personal individuality resides more in information (genome/personality) than material characters (anatomy), and may be more permanent. On the one hand, DNA fingerprinting works to identify criminals from genetic information alone, and the files containing this information can remain real and useful even after the bodies they represent have died. On the other hand, all human bodies are basically similar in anatomy, and I can be confident that the surgeon to whom I entrust my life will have trained on a large number of basically similar bodies and will know exactly what to look for when searching for my appendix.

The higher degree of individuality in the codical domain has an interesting implication relevant to theology. Stories about or memories of a person are information, which is, like a file of DNA codes, independent of their physical bodies and can last longer. Even we as fallible humans can keep alive personal memories of our loved ones while we live, even if those memories are selective and fade with time. How much clearer and longer might God remember us? As Page[38] puts it, certain moments and things so please God that they concur with, and so become part of, the divine experience. Whatever natural or human event God has concurred in is thereby

---

36. H Rolston III, *Genes, Genesis and God, op cit*, 66.
37. JF Haught, *God after Darwin, op cit*, 70–71, 76.
38. R Page, *God and the Web of Creation* (London: SCM Press, 1996).

taken, with the creatures involved, into eternity, while what does not concur is relegated into non-being.

Concurrence with God, then, holds the key, for what God has concurred in cannot be lost. Those whom God remembers therefore become immortal. Think of the dying thief's request, 'Lord, remember me when you come to your kingdom,' and Jesus' response, 'Today you will be with me in Paradise.' Dawkins himself asserts the authority of science in claiming that the codical domain is more important and longer lasting than, and independent of, the material domain. Suppose God uses some comparable process to carry the redeemed into Paradise, there to provide them with a new, non-material body?

Complexity in the past

The Principle of Uniformity is one of the basic assumptions of geology, dating back to Charles Lyell (1797–1875). It requires that all interpretations of past events should be assumed to be the product of processes comparable to those we can see today, eg the observable effects of water, wind and ice on the contemporary landscape. The same applies in biology, so, armed with a new understanding of how life operates in the present, we can now return to the question: How did all the successive levels of complexity in creation arise, and what are the implications for theology?

Many interpretations could be considered, but here we will discuss only two. They span the range of possibilities, from the first serious attempt to integrate the fossil record with theological assumptions, by Pierre Teilhard de Chardin,[39] to the latest biologically authentic account given by Maynard Smith & Szathmáry.[40]

Teilhard de Chardin

Teilhard de Chardin (1881–1955) was a French scientist and philosopher with impeccable scientific qualifications. He was ordained as a Jesuit in 1911, took a PhD in palaeontology at the Sorbonne in 1922, and lectured in geology at the Institut Catholique

---

39.   T de Chardin, *The Phenomenon of Man, op cit.*

40.   J Maynard Smith and E Zachary, *The Major Transitions in Evolution* (Oxford: WH Freeman, 1995).

in Paris (1920–23 and 1924–26). After a visit to China in 1923–24, he returned to teaching, and developed a theory which concluded that the traditional view of original sin can be reconciled with cosmic evolution, so does not entail a rejection of Christianity. His superiors did not agree, and in 1926 he was required to give up his teaching and return to China under a lifetime ban on producing any non-scientific publications. He worked in China for the next twenty years (1926–46), and made important contributions to palaeontology. He respected the silencing order, which continued to the end of his life, but in private he completed the manuscript of his major work, *The Phenomenon of Man* (published posthumously in 1955 and translated into English in 1959). His ideas are still widely discussed, and promoted on various websites such as www.teilhard.asso.fr and www.mnhn.fr/teilhard/FondAss1.htm.

Teilhard's theory started from the generally accepted observation that, at least on the broadest scale, the cosmos is becoming successively more complex over time. Secular scientists part company from him, however, as soon as he adds his two crucial assertions: (1) that the process is linear and unidirectional, and (2) that the process is guided by God actively assisting the cosmos in striving to reach its ultimate purpose, the 'Omega Point', variously interpreted as the integration of all personal consciousness or as the second coming of Christ.

Because Teilhard's ideas still have wide appeal for Christians, and are very relevant to the theme of this conference, it seems worth taking some time to spell out the three main reasons why they are inconsistent with secular biology. They are: (1) the processes of natural selection are incapable of acting as Teilhard assumed, (2) global development of biodiversity has not been linear and (3) the assumption that humans are the central figures in the story was (and still is) orthodox Catholic theology but unacceptable biology. Teilhard was a very competent scientist, so these disagreements are due, not to ignorance, but to his isolated working environment and to later developments that have overtaken his understanding of how evolution works.

The rules of natural selection

Like most scientists of his time (and most people today), Teilhard assumed that genetic evolution works for the good of the species. It seems natural to interpret almost everything we see animals doing in nature as unconscious expressions of loyalty to their kind. Until the 1960s this was commonly assumed even among scientists. So birds feed their chicks, bears defend their cubs, monkeys and meerkats post lookouts while the others feed, and groups of lionesses feed each other's cubs indiscriminately, all because such behaviour is good for the survival of the species. Christians of the Teilhardian school still like this interpretation, because it readily fits with the idea of the workings of God pushing the collective development of creation in the direction of the foreordained emergence of humans capable of making moral decisions.[41] The problem is that this view cannot account for many contrary observations in the real world, which are inescapably real but very *bad* for the species.

For example, when a group of male lions take over a pride of females, they can expect to stay in charge for only about two years before they are defeated by new, challenging males. It also takes about that long for the lionesses to rear a litter of cubs to independence. So the timing is critical, and therefore each group of incoming males will kill all the existing cubs, in order to reduce the time before the females will come into heat and produce cubs for their new mates.[42] It seems cruel and wasteful for the species as a whole, but that is irrelevant to the outcome—what matters in terms of evolution is that the next generation of cubs will be fathered by the incoming males. The genes of more merciful males cannot survive such ruthless competition—they will simply be eliminated.

These observations simply could not be reconciled with the traditional good-of-the-species argument, and the solution was not found until more complex questions had been tackled, such as, what controls breeding rates and population numbers from year to year. These issues were the subject of fierce debates through the 1960s and

---

41. L Galleni, 'Relationships between Scientific Analysis and the World View of Pierre Teilhard de Chardin', *Zygon*, 27 (1992): 153–166.
42. AE Pusey and C Packer, 'The Evolution of Sex-biased Dispersal in Lions, *Behaviour*, 101 (1987): 275–310.

1970s. On the one hand, there were those who believed, with Teilhard and Wynne-Edwards,[43] that natural selection could act on a group of animals to ensure social survival, say by encouraging breeding restraint in times of food shortage. On the other side, there were those who followed Lack and Williams in insisting that natural selection on individuals at the genetic level is much stronger than group selection, so the genes of individuals that 'cheat' by producing a few more young than the average would over time be better represented in the following generations.[44]

The general conclusion, amply confirmed by decades of field studies on a huge variety of animals, is that the presence or absence of group-oriented behaviour in nature is understandable only in terms of genetic strings. (Cultural selection in humans is different, because it can work for the good of the group, by a comparable process acting on ideas instead of genes—see below). The underlying processes are understandable only in terms of the key distinction between the codical and material domains.

Progress in evolution
The second problem biologists have with Teilhard's theory is that it is simply not correct to equate the increasing complexity of nature with progress. There are many examples of creatures that have changed little, progressively or otherwise, from one generation to the next over hundreds of millions of years—such as the horse-shoe crabs, the coelacanth and the crocodiles. There are even more types of animals that have vanished without leaving any descendants at all. The famous Burgess fauna records a community of marine animals of Cambrian age (530 million years ago), which came in an astonishing range of different body designs, suggesting that, against all expectations, the sweep of anatomical variety reached its maximum soon after the first diversification of multicellular animals.[45] They

---

43. V Wynne–Edwards, *Animal Dispersion in Relation to Social Behaviour* (Edinburgh: Oliver & Boyd, 1962).
44. GC Williams, *Natural Selection: Domains, Levels and Challenges, op cit.*
45. SJ Gould, *Wonderful Life: The Burgess Shale and the Nature of History, op cit.*

suggest that the explosive diversification of multicellular life that was made possible by, among other things, the evolution of sexual reproduction. Most of them bore no relationship to any living forms, and cannot be fitted into any existing system of classification, because they have no modern representatives. Modern seas certainly do contain many more *species* than those of Burgess times, but most are variations upon a few basic *designs*. Indeed, *all* the familiar 'higher animals' of the modern world, the fish, amphibia, reptiles, birds and mammals, are the product of endless variations on only *one* single design, that of the vertebrates.

On the other hand, we have to remember that evolution is a cumulative process, which adds complexity only if that is advantageous. In some lineages it has been, but not in all, and the process was not inevitable in any—it depends on habitat and on the contingencies of mutation. Moreover, the cumulative changes can comprise *losses* of old characters as well as development of new ones: over thousands of generations, ancestral whales lost their hind legs, snakes lost all their legs, and apes lost their tails.[46] Some very advanced life forms, such as parasites, have extremely complex life cycles but are anatomically very simple. So Teilhard's idea of any species comprising a 'leading shoot' of creation cannot be confirmed from the fossil record. In all the best-known lineages such as the horses, whales, and primates, the relationships between earlier and later species are more like those of the branches of a bush than the rungs of a ladder.

Anthropocentrism

Teilhard's understanding of evolution as a steady march to braininess is conditioned by his concept of the 'noosphere' as the ultimate purpose of the cosmos. His concept of 'hominisation', all nature reaching to God and led by the accelerating intelligence of humans, certainly requires some such proposition. But for all those who see no evidence of or need for such a concept, it looks like human hubris in its most breathtaking, anthropocentric form. It exposes religious convictions to ridicule by devaluing the rest of

---

46. EH Colbert, *Evolution of the Vertebrates* (New York: Wiley International, 1969).

nature ('What is an ocean? It is a body of water occupying about two-thirds of a world made for a species that has no gills.') and grossly overvaluing the supposed product ('If the purpose of the universe was to produce human intelligence, why did it take so long to produce so little?'). It cannot explain the problem of the extinction of the other species of *Homo*, whose independent marches to braininess were cut off at the roots after the global expansion of *H. sapiens sapiens*. Teilhard knew that other human species existed—he was closely involved in the early excavations of *H. erectus* in China—but his theory does not help us understand what happened to them, or why.

'Hominisation' and the Internet
On the other hand, there is one aspect of Teilhard's thought which has been attracting particular attention recently, because it has interesting implications and could possibly be reinterpreted in terms of modern theory. There is a profound distinction between two sorts of selective processes. *Natural selection* can work only by propagation of copies of genetic information from one generation to the next, and it benefits only the genes carried or shared by individual animals that successfully reproduce. But *cultural selection* works by propagation of copies of cultural information (ideas, or 'memes'), and it *can* benefit a whole group, especially in humans using conscious, moral choice to over-rule natural selection.

Moral systems have developed as part of our nature, and they work to smooth the constant conflict of interests between members of the community.[47] The seeds of conflict are always there when we do things that favour our own genetic self-interests over the cultural interests of the group, and an intuitive recognition of that conflict clearly lies behind the Augustinian idea of original sin.[48] But in close-knit social groups all individual behaviour is a continual series of compromises that usually benefit the cohesion of the immediate group. Campbell points out that 'for every commandment we may

---

47. RD Alexander, *The Biology of Moral Systems* (New York: Aldine de Gruyter, 1987).
48. DT Campbell, 'The Conflict between Social and Biological Evolution and the Concept of Original Sin', *Zygon*, 10 (1975): 234–249.

reasonably hypothesize a biological tendency running counter to some social-systematic optimum'.[49] Could Teilhard's notion of 'noosphere' be a precursor or a parallel concept to cultural and moral development?

The recognition of cultural selection acting on memes as a constructive process working for the good of group requires clear distinction between genes and memes (ideas). This distinction was unknown to Teilhard, but he might well have been delighted with modern theories using it to explain the key selective value and social functions of early religions, which was that they reinforced and fostered group-centred altruism[50] Of course there is also competition for cultural and biological success *within* the group,[51] but that is temporarily set aside when the group is faced with a threat from outside. Within the group, the basis of community responsibility or 'public spirit' is the development of a widespread congruence between personal and group interest. When a religious cultural story is widely accepted and regularly reinforced through rituals such as worship services, the group is seen to be more important than the individual. Could this process lead eventually to the 'hominisation' of all creation, envisaged by Teilhard? Is it possible that the concept of noosphere was a prophetic anticipation of the Internet?

Well, maybe, but there is a problem. Teilhard's theory makes hardly any provision for moral evil, and does not consider the costs of freedom in either the human or the animal worlds. Part of the reason why community responsibility seems to be waning in the contemporary Northern world is that the traditional stories underlying Christian society so familiar to Teilhard have lost their influence on individual ideals and behaviour, and the more basic

---

49. *Ibid*, 243.
50. EO Wilson, *On Human Nature* (Cambridge, Massachusetts: Harvard University Press, 1977), RW Burhoe, 'Religion's Role in Human Evolution: The Missing Link between Ape-man's Selfish Genes and Civilized Altruism', *Zygon*, 14 (1979): 135–162, and IG Barbour, *Religion and Science: Historical and Contemporary Issues, op cit*, 263.
51. W Irons, 'Cultural and Biological Success', in *Human Nature: A Critical Reader*, edited by L Beitzig (Oxford: Oxford University Press, 1997), 36–49.

forces of human nature are freer than they were. The Internet is one of the best possible places to see that. The idea that a religious concept such as the noosphere could now be realised through the Internet is attractive at first sight, but when one considers the way in which the Internet facilitates the propagation of all kinds of frightful pornography on a equal footing with genuinely useful material, I am not sure that Teilhard would agree.

For all these reasons and more, Teilhard's ideas are no longer useful to explain the complexity of creation in terms acceptable both to science and to theology. We need to consult what contemporary biologists are saying about the origins of biodiversity, and then re-open the debate with theologians on the basis of current understanding on both sides.

Maynard Smith and Szathmáry
John Maynard Smith is one of the most widely respected living theorists in evolutionary biology, and Eörs Szathmáry is a biochemist. Their book, *The Major Transitions in Evolution,*[52] describes eight key stages in the evolution of complexity over time.

The first transitions preceded the beginning of the fossil record, so their existence was unknown until the development of molecular biology. They were:

1. From isolated replicating molecules to populations of molecules aggregated within compartments.
2. From independent replicators to chromosomes.
3. From RNA operating as both gene and enzyme to DNA (gene) coding for enzymes and proteins.
4. From prokaryotes (simple cells) to eukaryotes (cells with nuclei).
5. From asexual clones to sexual populations.

The last three transitions have been documented both by fossils since the Cambrian explosion, 535 million years ago, and by comparisons between modern species:

6. From simple to multicellular animals/plants/fungi.

---

52.   J Maynard Smith and E Zachary, *The Major Transitions in Evolution,* *op cit.*

7. From solitary individuals to colonies (including non-reproductive castes).
8. From primate societies to human societies (with language).

Some transitions were unique, such as the origin of the genetic code, which apparently happened once only. That is why the same system by which instructions for making proteins are translated from the genes coded on the DNA to the machinery of the cell is now common to all life, from beetles to bananas, from bacteria to bonobos. Other transitions were repeated, for example multicellular organisms evolved three times in independent lineages (animals, plants and fungi). Either way, each of these major transitions released huge bursts of new diversity, because they facilitated rapid increases in the variety of new forms and complexity of life. A graph of the most impressive of these, the Cambrian explosion, shows an almost exponential rise in the number of recognisable taxonomic orders over a very short period.

The most important reason for these sudden explosions in biodiversity is that each of these profound transitions was associated with a significant change in the *codical* domain, specifically in the means by which information is transmitted from one generation to the next. After every transition from one level of organisation to the next, entities that were capable of independent replication before the transition could replicate only as part of a larger whole after it. This observation raises a problem common to each transition in turn: Why did the formerly independent entities allow themselves to be taken over? Why did not natural selection between entities at each lower level disrupt integration at the next higher one?

The current explanation is that organisms are composed of subunits, including genes, and are themselves subunits of larger entities such as social groups. Natural selection is a multilevel process that operates on a nested hierarchy of units.[53] When all the members of a group have the same fitness and a shared fate (like all the organs of one body, or the eight members of a rowing crew), they lose their individuality and are treated as subunits of a larger whole. Because selection chooses only between organisms—that is, units

---

53. D Wilson, 'Introduction: Multi-level Selection Theory Comes of Age', *American Naturalist*, 150, supplement (1997): S1–S4.

differing in fitness—it can only treat each organ or rower as similar subunits of a larger unit. It has to shift up a level until it can choose between separate bodies, or boats, that have different fitness and are in direct competition.

The normal definition of an organism is the individual animal, but the concept can be frame-shifted up or down from the individual level. When genes differ in fitness, they become competing organisms and the individual body is their environment. 'Outlaw' or 'rogue' genes occasionally appear, which have effects favouring their own propagation at the expense of the integration of the whole body.[54] They are normally counteracted by 'the parliament of genes', which suppresses the outlaws and enforces the coadaptation of all the units of the genome. The same applies to somatic cells: cancer develops when normal cells escape the control over growth and differentiation exerted by their genes, and begin to multiply at the expense of the rest of the body.

At the other end of the scale, in a colony of ants, each individual ant is an organ, a subunit, of a genetically defined organism, a colony, which is in competition with other such organisms. This arrangement means therefore, the eusocial insects are among the very few examples in nature of genetic selection at the group level. In humans, altruism at the group level is very important, but controlled largely by cultural, not genetic, mechanisms

The immediate selective advantage to individual replicating units at each level explains the historical sequence and the stability of evolutionary transitions. For example, the cells of all multicellular organisms are descended from free-living, single-celled protists, once capable of surviving on their own, but today they can exist only as parts of a larger organism. If members of stable partnerships tended to survive better than solo operators, then those partnerships would eventually become essential to survival. A cancer cell may run rampant within one body, but it has no hope of returning to the free-living independence of its remote ancestors.

---

54.   LA Dugatkin, DS Wilson, L Farrand III and RT Wilkens, 'Altruism, Tit for Tat and "Outlaw" Genes', *Evolutionary Ecology*, 8 (1994): 431–437.

When stable partnerships became necessary to life, all members of the partnership came to share the same fate, and to compete together against other partnerships but not against each other. For example, all multicellular organisms develop from a single fertilised egg, so all their cells are genetically identical, and the genes carried by each cell can survive only if they all cooperate to build a functional multicellular body. Natural selection could then shift to choose between these unbreakable partnerships at the next level. Hence the progression, from single replicators to chromosomes to multicellular bodies to colonies. It is only where the interests of all parties are identical[55] that there is no competition. Human communities, by contrast, require the collaboration of genetically different individuals which definitely do not have identical interests. This insight from cell biology is enormously significant in understanding failures in human cooperation, from biblical wars to the Body of Christ.

One might ask why other apparently important transitions in the history of life that certainly had a profound effect on the development of complex new faunas—such as the emergence of land animals and of internal fertilisation, or the origins of flight and of warm blood—are not included in the list. The answer is that all of these, though dramatic, were simple material adaptations achieved by sexual populations of multicellular animals (level 6) through the machinery of interaction using the genetic code already available to them. These transitions required no radically new forms of interaction between the codical and material domains, and none appeared until the origin of true societies with permanent division of labour.

Theological significance of complexity in nature
Models of natural selection based on population genetics concentrate on the codical domain, and regard the material domain as a by-product. Theology has always recognised the existence of non-material realities but is also deeply concerned with the material domain, the scene of all our lives, experiences and morally significant decisions. In my view, theology need have no qualms about

---

55. Later in life. accumulating mutations in the somatic cells introduce relentlessly increasing genetic differences within the body, which inevitably leads to ageing, and death (S Jones, *In the Blood, op cit*).

accepting the concept of cumulative change by natural selection. It is not, as Williams[56] asserts, an 'evil . . . unreasoning enemy',[57] but a statistical, often very small, difference in the probability of reproductive success between slightly different individuals. The real freedom that God has given to all creatures places no limits on the actions of natural selection in the natural world, and their use of it determines what will be available for God to take up into the new creation at the end of time.[58]

On the contrary, creaturely freedom is limited most often by opportunity, moderated by the consequences of past choices. Obviously, the complex interactions of free agents cause friction, which in turn causes all forms of natural evil including earthquakes, parasites, predators and war. Death is the simple consequence of accumulated copying errors in the codical domain controlling the workings of the body cells, much as a sheet of white paper becomes black after a few dozen passes through a photocopier. Birds sing for their own reasons, usually in language aggressive to other birds but which sounds to us like one of the definitions of innocent beauty. Our enjoyment of birdsong is a matter of grace rather than translation. None of these questions need any special explanation in an evolutionary world, and theology is thereby relieved of the responsibility of finding answers to them.

In the human world, the same arguments apply. God has not limited the multilevel processes which eventually led to the emergence of cultural selection in the human world, and eventually to the abandonment of selection in the spiritual world.[59] With Haught,[60] I would assert that God accepts the consequences of creaturely freedom, and loves the resulting riotous variety of amoral

---

56. GC Williams, *Plan and Purpose in Nature* (London: Weidenfeld & Nicolson, 1996), 156.

57. Darwin himself called natural selection 'clumsy, wasteful, blundering, low and horribly cruel'. (Quoted by H Rolston III, 'Does Nature Need To Be Redeemed?' *Zygon*, 29 (1994): 219–229.)

58. R Page, *God and the Web of Creation, op cit*, 173, and JF Haught, *God after Darwin, op cit*, 160.

59. G Theissen, *Biblical Faith: An Evolutionary Approach* (London: SCM Press, 1984).

60. JF Haught, *God after Darwin, op cit*.

natural life presumably as much as God loves the variety of moral and immoral human life that evolved from it. Haught advocates an evolutionary theology which envisages God as creating, not individual organisms, but the *possibility* through which, first the universe itself, and then living organisms within it, could create themselves.

This is not such a modern idea as it sounds: it was already foreshadowed in the historic creationist tradition, which in turn is the foundation of modern science. The scientific view of the rational, ordered universe is entirely compatible with the theistic, Christian affirmation that we can make sense of the world because God's faithfulness stands behind it. The three main themes of the historic creationist tradition, asserting that the universe reflects the goodness, rationality and freedom of God and therefore creation itself must be good, rational and contingent, were in due course incorporated within Christian faith.

In our time we are faced with the challenge of constructing an updated creation theology that is also true to current science. One of the fundamental aims of such an enterprise must be to find intellectually respectable ways to integrate the unlimited freedom of nature with the unlimited love of God, in terms acceptable to both sides. Haught has gone further than most in laying the foundations for such a theology. He argues that it can and must be done at the most fundamental level, without selective burrowing by one side in the complex fields of knowledge of the other. Take, for example, the unexpected insight from Maynard Smith and Zachary,[61] that every major transition in evolution has involved closer collaboration of formerly independent units. A Teilhardian interpretation of life's history could be constructed from this, since it implies progress in cooperation, a distinctly Christian idea. But that interpretation would be to ignore the same authors' point that biology cannot support any interpretation of progress, because progress cannot be defined in biological terms. Maynard Smith and Zachary were analysing transitions from one codical-material interaction to the next, not within a settled form of that interaction, such as governs all

---

61.   J Maynard Smith and E Zachary, *The Major Transitions in Evolution*, *op cit*, 6.

multicellular animals. We cannot pick and choose scientific ideas, any more than we can do the same with biblical texts.

On the other hand, it is true that there is a large body of evidence supporting the view that, *within* the realm of human life, co-operation *can* beat raw rivalry, given certain well-defined circumstances. Until very recently most human interactions have almost always been repeated interactions with family, friends and colleagues within long-term, stable communities. And repeated interactions allow every encounter to be treated *as a deal rather than as a match*. The difference is that between a zero-sum game such as football or tennis, in which only one side can win, and a non-zero-sum game such as social life generally, in which the more people cooperate together the more they all benefit.

Real life is usually a non-zero-sum game, so the implications of this insight from game theory for social evolution are profound. At long last, it seems, science has discovered an empirical confirmation for what philosophers and moralists have always known, that the world is a better place when everyone restrains their personal self-interests. In terms of evolutionary psychology, the ethical systems of the world's major religions are (among many other things) comprehensive schemes of conscious instruction for maximising non-zero-sum social interactions. As with Linux, an open-code operating system developed by free collaboration between independent computer scientists, everyone benefits when everyone else takes a positive and helpful attitude. The contrast with Microsoft Windows is thought-provoking. Likewise, Christians believe that God creates and saves through love, allowing us freedom to choose to co-operate with each other or not.

> The God of evolution does not fix things in advance, nor hoard selfishly the joy of creating. Instead, God shares with all creatures their own openness to an indeterminate future. Such an interpretation does not destroy the cosmic hierarchy but by its openness to new being brings special significance to every

epoch of nature's unfolding, including humanity's
unique history in a still unfinished universe.[62]

Conclusion

Understanding the origin and maintenance of complexity in creation inevitably invites inspection of the Christian theology of creation. In turn, all credible theologies must take into account the view of reality current in their own day.[63] Over the long history of Christianity, that has meant periodic reformulations of doctrine: so Augustine integrated Christian concepts with the world view of neo-Platonism, Aquinas with that of Aristotle, and Paley with that of Newton.[64] In any age, when the secular picture of reality undergoes a significant paradigm shift, theology must attend to it, despite its general suspicion of innovations.[65]

The contemporary science-religion debate is enormously exciting for a Christian biologist, because we are at last seeing a serious attempt to introduce Darwinian perspectives into traditional creation theology. Some authors call for a restructuring of the entire framework of Christian thought about the relationships between God and the world.[66] Others maintain that the only change required is a more faithful understanding and preaching of established doctrine.[67] McGrath[68] opts for 'starting all over again', because

---

62. JF Haught, *God after Darwin, op cit*, 191.

63. A Peacocke, *Theology for a Scientific Age, op cit*, 7, and S McFague, *The Body of God: An Ecological Theology* (London: SCM Press, 1993), 73–74

64. C Kaiser, *Creation and the History of Science* (Grand Rapids: Eerdmans, 1991).

65. H Küng, 'Paradigm Change in Theology: A Proposal for Discussion' in *Paradigm Change in Theology*, edited by H Küng and D Tracey (Edinburgh: T&T Clark, 1989), 3–33.

66. D Gosling, *A New Earth: Covenanting for Justice, Peace and the Integrity of Creation* (London: Council of Churches for Britain and Ireland (CCBI), 1992), 49.

67. RJ Berry, 'Creation and the Environment', *Science and Christian Belief*, 7 (1995): 21–43.

68. AE McGrath, *The Foundations of Dialogue in Science and Religion* (Malden, Massachusetts: Blackwell Publishers, 1998).

what once seemed as if it might be a wonderfully creative and interesting discussion appears to have degenerated into little more than a slanging match between a group of natural scientists bent on eliminating religion from cultural and academic life, and a group of religious people who seem to know (and care) nothing for the natural sciences. What the Renaissance envisaged as a dialogue has degenerated into what is depressingly often a mutual display of ignorance, hostility and spite.[69]

We can recover the Renaissance vision, provided both sides are willing to take each other seriously. For theology, the challenge is to recognise nature's ability to create itself, and the consequences of accepting that for all traditional understandings of the relationship between God and the world. 'What is needed now,' says Ruth Page, in *God and the Web of Creation*, 'is not another skirmish on the green fringes of belief but a rethinking of fundamental doctrine.'[70] Conversely, for science the challenge is to accept the limitations of its own models. Far too few scientists aware of the Fallacy of Misplaced Concreteness[71]—the tendency to organise knowledge in terms of abstractions, and then to reach conclusions and apply them to the real world as if abstractions and reality were the same thing (the best-known example of this is the selfish gene metaphor).

Naturally, both sides see such an adjustment of their usual positions as threatening their authority, and the process may well be resisted in some quarters, more so at parish level than in theological colleges. And it is important that both sides listen to what the other can contribute to the debate, because otherwise science and religion will continue to talk past each other, leading to the impasse described by Appleyard:[72]

---

69. *Ibid*, 7.
70. R Page, *God and the Web of Creation, op cit.*
71. AN Whitehead, *Science and the Modern World* (Cambridge: Cambridge University Press, 1927), 64.
72. B Appleyard, *Understanding the Present: Science and the Soul of Modern Man, op cit.*

> Science [has become] the lethally dispassionate
> search for truth in the world whatever its meaning
> might be; religion [has become] the passionate
> search for meaning whatever the truth might be.

If we are to understand the scientific and theological meanings of complexity in creation, there is a lot to be done.

A World Made to Flourish: Divine Design and the Idea of Natural Self-organisation

Niels Henrik Gregersen

Divine creation through natural self-organisation

In the present essay I am going to discuss two ideas that are often set in contrast to one another: The one is the theological doctrine that the world of creation (everything that does or can exist within the framework of time, space and matter) is created by God out of divine love, and for the purpose that it shall thrive and flourish. The other idea is the notion of nature's character as self-developing over time, triggered by trial and error processes and yet undergirded by nature's seemingly built-in capacity for self-organisation.

The discussion that follows can thus be seen as a variant of the classic dialogue between creation theology and evolutionary biology. And yet the present essay is guided by presuppositions that are not shared by all biologists. I am thus going to discuss with proponents of an extended Darwinism, who believe that chance and natural selection need to be supplemented by self-organising principles in order to account for the actual trajectory of evolution. For, as argued by Stuart Kauffman and other theoretical biologists, there is an overall trend towards complexification of the universe that leads from matter to life, and from simpler life-forms to more complex life-forms. This is not accidental, but happens due to the formative principles of physical chemistry. We are the expected children of the universe, as it were.[1]

Neither will my theological aims be shared by all theologians, so let me also begin by stating them briefly.

Some theologians want to escape the notion of a personal God altogether (for example, Gordon Kaufman.[2]) Others want to argue

---

1. Stuart Kauffman, *At Home in the Universe: The Search for the Laws of Complexity* (New York: Oxford University Press, 1995).
2. Gordon Kaufman, *In Face of Mystery: A Constructive Theology* (Cambridge, Mass: Harvard University Press, 1993), 75–82.

that God's purpose for the world must at every instant be construed as a divine design that has a specific purpose in mind and then makes it real in the history of nature (the Intelligent Design Movement). I am here going to take a middle position. I believe that personal language is indeed applicable to God, since God cannot be thought to be less than personal. God *is* eternally Word or utterance, and assumes personal traits when communicating with human beings. The personal agency of God, however, should not be identified with an all too humanised concept of God as a spatio-temporal planner. I therefore believe that we should be careful to avoid an over-attribution of the idea of 'design' to God, as if God were a finite subject placed in a temporal nexus and located at a certain place. For all, the difference between 'getting an idea' in the intellect and then 'making it real' through will and agency (which is so well known from human experience) should not applied to God. There are indeed also limits to anthropomorphic language: under-standing thinking and willing as two discrete stages in the mind of God means finitising God and may trivialise our understanding of God's self-communicative character.

Let me also briefly say how I see the positive relation between the belief in creation and the idea of self-organisation in complexity theory. I am going to argue that on the basis of a prior assumption of God's benevolence and generosity, we should naturally be inclined to think of self-organisation as the apex of divine purpose. Making room for otherness is already logically implied by the idea of creation; making the creatures make themselves can be seen as a further emphasis on the urge for exploration and autonomy generously bestowed by God on creatures. From this perspective God's creatures can be said to be designed for self-organisation. God's design of the *world as whole* favours the emergence of autonomous processes in the *particular course* of evolution, a course at once constrained by and propagated by a built-in propensity towards complexification.[3] Rather than seeing self-organisation as a threat to

---

3. Niels Henrik Gregersen, 'Beyond the Balance: Theology in a World of Autopoietic Systems', in *Design and Disorder in Science and Theology*, edited by Niels Henrik Gregersen, Willem B Drees and Ulf Görman (Edinburgh: T&T Clark, 2002), 53–92.

religion, I believe we should see God as continuously creating the world by constituting and supporting self-organising processes. This is a thesis that I have developed elsewhere concerning the theological significance of the theory of autopoietic or self-productive processes.[4] What I am now going to add is that the idea of autopoietic systems does not necessarily break with all notions of pre-established structures or 'designs'. True it is that autopoiesis often takes place by breaking down previously established structures, however it is also a fact that self-developing processes thrive in environments that are particularly hospitable to the emergence and stabilisation of these processes. General physical laws and chemical propensities may well support autopoietic processes and make them flourish.

This brings us to ask a further question. Where do the laws of nature come from? For sure, the believer will see God the creator as the eternal source of the laws of nature. But as we shall see in discussing the so-called anthropic principle, the theological answer is not without alternatives. Nonetheless I shall argue that there may be a natural connection between the theological idea of an 'anthropic design' of the laws and initial conditions of our universe to the trend towards self-organisation and complexity in cosmic evolution. While granting the possibility of a non-theistic interpretations of this general direction from big bang to the world that flourishes all around us, it is my thesis that the world of nature, as discovered for us by the sciences, possesses many of the qualities that we would expect the world to exhibit, if our physical universe is eventually created out of a divine zest for novelty, variation and plenitude, as zest rooted in God's creative love.

Self-organisation does not mean self-creation
It should be noted that this general argument presupposes that self-organisation does mean self-creation. Self-organisation never starts from scratch, from point zero. Rather the ideas of divine design and

---

4. Niels Henrik Gregersen, 'The Idea of Creation and the Theory of Autopoietic Processes', *Zygon*, 33:3 (1998): 333–367, and Niels Henrik Gregersen, 'Autopoiesis: Less than Self–Constitution, More than Self-Organization: Reply to Gilkey, McClelland and Deltete, and Brun', *Zygon*, 34:1 (1999): 117–138.

self-organised complexity are only compatible on two conditions which specify the respective domains of their applicability:[5]

First, the notion of divine design relates to the constitution of the world of creation *as a whole* and to the coordination of the basic laws of nature, but not to the *details* emerging within the framework of the world. Accordingly, even if the basic laws of nature were to unified in a Theory of Everything, they would not give us a sufficient scientific explanation for *particular features* within cosmic evolution, such as the informational structure of the DNA, the upright gait of human beings, the AIDS epidemic, or the election of President George W Bush. This is, as shown by theoretical physicist John Barrow,[6] a result of a necessary distinction between laws and outcomes, equations and solutions. Even though the laws of physics may be simple, their outcomes are nonetheless complicated, for the outcomes depend on the initial conditions and the special contexts that are not part of the equations. The same insight is taken by Stuart Kauffman, who argues that if the world is tuned for the emergence of autonomous agents, the theory of evolution cannot explain evolution. We cannot prestate the 'configuration space' of the biosphere.[7]

Second and conversely, the concept of self-organisation should not be elevated into a metaphysical principle that is able to explain all-that-exists. There is no observational basis for claiming that either selection processes or principles of self-organisation are responsible for laws of physics such as gravity, quantum mechanics, cosmological constants etc. In fact, standard science offers good evidence for believing that some laws of physics are basic, and it is these laws that make our planet (and perhaps other planets) habitable. Neither selection nor self-organisation start from scratch,

---

5. What follows is adapted from my article, 'From Anthropic Design to self-Organised Complexity' (Gregersen 2003).
6. John B Barrow, *Theories of Everything: The Quest for Ultimate Explanation* (New York: Ballantine Books, 1991), 156–157.
7. Stuart Kauffman, 'The Emergence of Autonomous Agents', in *From Complexity to Life: On the Emergence of Life and Meaning*, edited by Niels Henrik Gregersen (New York: Oxford University Press, 2003), 64–71

rather, they presupposes a sufficient flow of energy and are channelled within an already existing order.

I thus believe that there are good reasons for steering a middle course between two parties in today's discussion: those who believe that self-organisation simply replaces the idea of a divine designer, and those who believe that unless the belief in God is cashed out in some supernatural explanation of particular affairs of nature (in contrast to naturalistic explanations), God is pushed out from the world of nature. Thus, the two positions I want to argue against are on the hand the proponents of a replacement hypothesis, on the other the proponents of the anti-Darwinian hypothesis of 'intelligent design'. Both parties seem to me to make a common fallacy of misplaced concreteness: If God is not to be traced in the details of scientific exploration of nature, God cannot be present in the tissues and texture of the world.

According to the replacement thesis, Nature Herself does the job that God was once assigned to do. This metaphysical position has recently been uncompromisingly stated by the cosmologist Lee Smolin:

> What ties together general relativity, quantum theory, natural selection, and the new sciences of complex and self-organised systems is that in different ways they describe a world that is whole unto itself, without any need of an external intelligence to serve as its inventor, organiser, or external observer.[8]

This is clearly a highly metaphysical interpretation of science, since one could hardly say that any such conclusion is implied by any of the above-mentioned sciences. It is true that the physical sciences are silent about God, but this silence is a methodological requirement

---

8.   Lee Smolin, Lee, *The Life of the Cosmos* (New York: Oxford University Press, 1997), 194, cf Lee Smolin, 'Our Relationship with the Universe', in *Many Worlds: The New Universe, Extraterrestrial Life, and the Theological Implications*, edited by Steven J Dick (Philadelphia: Templeton Foundations Press, 2000), 84 ff.

that offers no evidence for or against the reality of the divine. Smolin's judgment rests on his particular hypothesis that not only are systems self-organising but so are also the physical laws of nature. According to Smolin, all laws of nature have been pruned in a grand cosmological selection process beyond our reach. Consequently basic laws of nature do not exist. Interesting as this philosophical hypothesis is, it is definitely not implied by either quantum theory, relativity, evolutionary biology, nor by complexity studies. Even strong critics of religion such as Steven Weinberg admit that

> if we were to see the hand of the designer anywhere, it would be in the fundamental principles, the final laws of nature, the book of rules that govern all natural phenomena.[9]

Smolin's argument against design rests on the metaphysical assumption that there exists no basic framework of laws to be explained. Because the *explanandum* has disappeared, we should also take leave of the *explanans*. Unless one is prepared to follow this speculative proposal to its very end, there is no inherent conflict between the traditional doctrine of creation and the principles of self-organising systems.

Naturalistic vs anti-naturalistic design theories
As is evident from the last thirty years of theistic interpretation of the Anthropic Principle, the classic idea of God as designer of the universal laws is far from outmoded, even though the idea of design (as we shall see in a while) is not without alternatives. More dubious is a more recent version of design arguments propelled by the so-called Intelligent Design Movement. According to this group of scholars, a divine design can be inferred from particular features of nature in so far as these resist a full explanation in naturalistic terms. The intelligent design theorists remind us that there exist important gaps in the scientific knowledge of nature, especially about the origins of life. As a matter of fact, no-one has yet come up with a

---

9.   Steven Weinberg, 'A Designer Universe?', *The New York Review*, 21 October (1999).

satisfactory theory about how the interaction between DNA and RNA came about in the first place.[10] They also rightly point out that the sequential order of the DNA-molecules (the 'specified information') cannot be derived from the chemical affinities of the constituent building blocks themselves. If this were the case, evolution would take place in a chemical straightjacket that would not allow for much variation.[11] I believe, however, that the importance of the many existing subexplanations, eg on proto-metabolism (see de Duve[12]), is either ignored or belittled. Intelligent design theorists seem to be playing an all-or-nothing game. Since we have in our hand *no full* explanation of biogenesis in terms of biochemistry, we have *no* explanations *at all*. But, as it has been rightly pointed by critics of the intelligent design theories, 'complexity' is a redundant phenomenon of ordinary chemistry, and the 'specificity' of information is what one would expect of a DNA profile which has been carved out through a long history of variation and selection.[13] Unsatisfied by the partial explanations of current science, the intelligent design theorists offer a wholly other type of explanation: intelligent design. Just as we are used to detecting intelligent agency in every day life as well as in the social sciences, so we can infer a divine mind from the subtlety of 'specified

---

10. This is underlined in the recent collection of essays by André Brack [*The Molecular Origins of Life: Assembling Pieces of the Puzzle*, edited by André Brack (Cambridge: Cambridge University Press, 1998)]. The editor points to the fact that most of the earth's early geological history is erased by later events, and that current theories in the field, many of which are untested, have a puzzle-like character.

11. Stephen C Meyer, 'The Explanatory Power of Design: DNA and the Origin of Information', in *Mere Creation: Science, Faith and Intelligent Design*, edited by William A Dembski (Downers Grove: InterVarsity Press, 1998), 132 ff.

12. Christian de Duve, 'Clues form Present-day Biology: The Thioester World', in *The Molecular Origins of Life: Assempling Pieces of the Puzzle*, edited by André Back (Cambridge: Cambridge University Press, 1998).

13. Niall Shanks and Karl H Joplin, 'Redundant Complexity: A Critical Analysis of Intelligent Design in Biochemistry', *Philisophy of Science*, 66 (1999): 268–282.

information' in the DNA world. What could not be explained naturalistically, is economically explained by design. So the argument goes.

To me this is an example of an impatient science which changes the level of explanation from natural causes to philosophy of mind, when (wherever?) there are gaps in the explanatory of current science. My main objection, however, is of a theological nature. If one wants to speak of divine design, God's purposes may well be compatible with both and chance. In fact, God's constituting of the basic laws of nature makes up a core tenet in the inherited notion of design. But as often argued by Arthur Peacocke,[14] it is the intricate interplay between laws (which guarantee the overall order) and chance (which introduces novelty into the world) that drives evolution forward. In fact, the open-endedness of evolutionary processes (within a given phase space) is highly congruent with the idea of a benevolent God. Who, by analogy, are the more loving parents—those who specifically instruct their children to become, say, lawyers, or those who let their children explore their individual possibilities within a well-proportioned balance of safe background conditions and an influx of time and circumstance?

Perhaps the most distinctive move of the Intelligent Design movement lies in the presupposition that divine design can be best (or only) detected in the absence of naturalistic explanations. William Dembski's 'explanatory filter' of design via the exclusion of first law and then chance, seems to rely on a competitive view of God and Nature (see Dembski[15]).

Below I intend to show that this presupposition is not in accord with the general thrust of a religious way of perceiving nature. The logic of both the Jewish Bible on creation and the New Testament texts of the Kingdom of God presuppose that the more creative nature is, the more benevolent and the more beautiful is the grandeur

---

14. Arthur Peacocke, *Paths From Science Towards God: The End of All Exploring* (Oxford: Oneworld, 2001), 75–78
15. William A Dembski, *Intelligent Design: The Bridge Between Science and Theology* (Downers Grove: InterVarsity Press, 1999), cf William A Dembski, *The Design Inference Eliminating Chance Through Small Probabilities* (Cambridge: Cambridge University Press, 1998), 55–66.

of God's creativity. Similar views can be found in other traditions as well. This internal religious perspective can, I believe, be reformulated in the context of a philosophical theology. Bringing the Anthropic Principle in communication with the theory of self-organised complexity thus may give theology rich resources for re-describing, in religious terms, a cosmos that has already been described and (at least partially) explained by the sciences. There is no need to turn to the oppositional thought pattern of God versus Nature. By contrast, my hypothesis is that God's splendour is enhanced by the capacities unveiled by the evolutionary history of our cosmos.

The internal religious perspective
Let us take a closer look at the logic that persuaded some to think that the principles of self-organisation have devastating implications for religion. Simply put, the argument was as follows: 'If nature makes itself, God does not make nature.'

God's transcendence and immanence in an inventive universe
In 1975 physicist K G Denbigh, in his widely read book *An Inventive Universe*, made the claim that the denial of nature's self-generative powers is a logical consequence of the idea of divine transcendence. According to Denbigh, God's transcendence means that God has created, and still rules, the world *'as if from the outside'*; this religious view is then said to lead on to the idea that the world's material constituents have no creative powers of their own; nothing essentially new could ever be produced by matter.[16]

It should be conceded that, on a theistic view, nothing happens in separation from God, but Denbigh's alternative—God or nature—misses the religious point of view. In fact, according to standard theism, God is believed to be at once transcendent as well as immanent. Here is but one example from the New Testament:

> The God who made the world and everything in it,
> he who is Lord of heaven and earth, does not live in

---

16. KG Denbigh, *An Inventive Universe* (London: Hutchinson, 1975), 11, cf 149.

> shrines made by human hands, nor is he served by
> human hands, as though he needed anything
> [transcendence!] . . . indeed he is not far from each
> one of us [immanence]. For 'In him we live and
> move and have our being,' as even some of your
> poets have said, 'For we too are his offspring' (Acts
> 17:24–28).

Thus God is perceived to be infinitely beyond any empirical event, yet God is also qualitatively present in the world without losing God's self-identity. Conversely, also the world may be said to exist in God (a view often termed pan-en-theism).

Both in the scientific and philosophical literature on self-organisation we nonetheless often find views like Denbigh's. Lee Smolin has been mentioned already; another example is the philosopher-engineer Paul Cilliers, who in passing claims that self-organisation implies that 'nothing 'extra', no external telos or designer is required to 'cause' the complex behaviour of a system'.[17] This statement holds true within an empirical context, but the sentence wrongly suggests that God is denied by way of logical implication: 'If self-organisation, then no design.'

However, the alternative 'divine design vs natural self-organisation' only appears if one fails to distinguish between the theory level of science and the worldview assumptions that may (or may not) be associated with a given domain of science. The search for scientific explanations is always pursued under the condition of a *methodological naturalism*. Therefore, God cannot and should not be found in the epistemic gaps left over by the limits of current scientific explanation. Such methodological naturalism may also include the stronger ontological stance that David Ray Griffin has dubbed a *minimal naturalism*, namely the assumption that 'the world's most fundamental causal principles are never interrupted'.[18] But this by no means rules out the view that the observed processes of self-

---

17. Paul Cilliers, *Complexity and Postmodernism: Understanding Complex Systems* (London: Routledge, 1998), 143.
18. David Ray Griffin, *Religion and Scientific Naturalism: Overcoming the Conflicts* (Albany: SUNY Press, 2000), 44.

organisation are placed in the framework of cosmic conditions that could well be in need of a metaphysical or religious explanation.

God: the source of self-organisation
Indeed, the idea of self-organisation is far from foreign to the great world religions. In Hindu scriptures, such as the *Rig-Veda* (X, 129), we find the notion that in the beginning a golden germ of fire sprang up within the water. This could well be interpreted as an expression of creation as rooted in emergent processes. Later in the Upanishads, we find the idea of 'the egg of Brahman', which implies that the world starts off as an undivided whole which is then subsequently divided and complexified.[19]

But also in the Jewish and Christian tradition, the notion of spontaneous generation is present. As pointed out by Rabbi Louis Jacobs, the Hebrew word for creating, *bara*, literally means 'cutting out' of existing material.[20] In the book of Genesis, God is portrayed as the one who grants the creatures a power to emerge and reproduce. God creates by letting the earth bring forth vegetation with self-sustaining capacities:

> Then God said, 'Let the earth put forth vegetation: plants yielding seed, and fruit trees of every kind on earth that bear fruit with the seed in it' (Genesis 1:11).

Biblical scholars believe that we here find traces of a Mother Earth mythology which has been inscribed into the theology of creation. Be that as it may, it is evident that God is depicted as the one who elicits the created powers in order to let them grow, increase and be fruitful. God's generosity is highlighted, accordingly the motif of God's blessing of the creaturely powers is emphasised.

---

19. *Aitareia Brahmana* II, 17.8, and RF Gombridge, 'Ancient Indian Cosmology', in *Ancient Cosmologies,* edited by Carmen Blacker and Michael Loewe (London: George Allen & Unwin, 1975), 114-18.
20. Louis Jacobs, 'Jewish Cosmologies', in *Ancient Cosmologies,* edited by Carmen Blacker and Michael Loewe (London: George Allen & Unwin), 71.

If we turn to the New Testament, we also find that the Kingdom of God (ie God's active and qualitative presence in the world) is likened to the self-productive capacities of nature. In the teaching of Jesus, we find the following parable:

> The Kingdom of God is as if someone would scatter seed on the ground, and would sleep and rise night and day, and the seed would sprout and grow, he does not know how. The earth *produces of itself* [Greek: *automatike*], first the stalk, then the head, then the full grain in the head (Mark 4:26–28).

As is evident, neither the Jewish nor the Christian scriptures conceive of God as being in competition to nature's capacities. Rather, God is the facilitator of self-generative processes manifest in nature. Against widespread opinion, there is not a hint of contradiction between God's creativity and the creature's self-productivity. Rather, we seem to be facing a two-phase relation between God and world: First, God unilaterally creates the world and its capacities, second, creatures partake in a bilateral flow between divine and natural powers.[21]

Combining anthropic principle and self-organised complexity

In the following, I wish to propose a differentiated notion of God's relationships to an evolving world. By 'differentiated' I mean that theology should be able to employ different thought models in relation to different problems. The idea of design, as we have seen, may be illuminating with respect to the fundamental structure of reality, but the inherited notion of design seems to be misplaced in relation to self-organisational processes. My proposal is therefore that theology should move beyond a stereotypical use of its models and metaphors. In some contexts, the notion of design may be appropriate, in other contexts it may be unpersuasive.

---

21. Michael Welker, 'What Is Creation? Re-Reading Genesis 1 and 2', *Theology Today* 48 (1991): 56–71.

Limiting the metaphor of design in theology
The idea of a divine master plan is one standard model of design, derived from the field of human prudence. As phrased by Thomas Aquinas, 'It is necessary that the rational order of things (*ratio ordinis*) towards their end pre-exists in the divine mind.' The preconceived divine plan is then presumed to be carried out (*executio*) in the course of history, though in such a manner that God normally uses natural means (*executrices*) to accomplish the divine purpose (*Summa Theologica* I q. 22.3). This teleological-instrumental model of divine activity may have its uses, but since it is framed within a deterministic thought model, it is often generalised and used without acknowledging its internal limitations. Accordingly, the design idea tends to have a very low informational value.[22]

Of course, one can hold the position that the basic physical laws are divine instruments, and *so* are the mathematical orders of complexity, and *so* are the Darwinian principles selection and chance, and *so* are the workings of the human brain. This strategy, however, seems feeble from a theological perspective. Moreover, it is incapable of differentiating between questions pertaining to cosmology (concerning the basic laws of physics), and questions pertaining to self-organising systems (concerning the regularities of complexity).

---

22. A recent attempt to pursue the Thomistic thought model (moderated through Bernard Lonergan) is found in Happel [Stephen Happel, 'Divine Providence and Instrumentality. Metaphors for Time in Self-Organizing Systems and Divine Action', in *Chaos and Complexity: Scientific Perspectives on Divine Action*, edited by Robert J Russell *et al* (Vatican City/Berkeley: Vatican Observatory Publications, CTNS, 1995), 177–203)]. Happel points out some important implications of the distinction between first and secondary causalities: God never acts 'directly', but always 'mediated' in the world of nature, and that 'there is no other causal nexus than the self-organisation of the entity itself', (197). Thus, this teleological-instrumental model is friendly to a general naturalist perspective: 'Rocks cooperate [with God] as rocks, plants as plants, and dogs as dogs', (198). However, it is exactly this sweeping character of the teleological thought scheme which limits its explanatory power. Explaining everything does not, after all, explain the distinctive features of our natural world.

Explaining the framework of the world as such does not always explain the particular features emerging *within* that framework.

In what follows, I will therefore argue for a more limited use of the concept of design in theology. More precisely, I want to bring a theistic interpretation of the Anthropic Principle into conversation with the paradigm of self-organised complexity. The fact of anthropic coincidences fits well with religious expectations of how a generous God would set up a world. However, the robustness of self-organising systems seems not to call for any design hypothesis. I am nonetheless going to argue that the hypothesis of a divine design of all-that-exists is corroborated by the fecundity and beauty that result from the working of self-organisational principles. From a theological perspective, the effectiveness and variety of self-organisation may be seen as exemplifying a principle of grace written into the structure of nature. Self-organisational processes are always risky and fragile, but cooperation and the building up of higher-level structures do pay off in the long run. Without claiming to 'explain' the causal routes of self-organisation in religious terms, the fertility of self-organisational processes can be seen as the blessing of nature by a generous God. Later on more is to be said on the interaction between religion and scientific inquiry; but it is wise to start out acknowledging the working divisions between science and religion: Whereas science is concerned with the laws and mechanisms of nature, religion deals with the interpretation or rereading of the processes resulting of these laws and mechanisms. Only from this starting point we can approach appropriately the many zones of contact between a theology of creation and a scientific view of the world as depending on laws of nature and principles of self-organisation. I begin by discussing varieties of the so-called anthropic principle.

The strong version of the anthropic principle
According to the anthropic principle, the nature of the physical universe is highly constrained by the fact that we are here to observe it. There is a link between the basic laws and constants of our physical cosmos and our being as human observers (therefore the term 'anthropic' cosmological principle). The fact of intelligent life tells a story about the kind of universe we are inhabiting. The question, then, is how strong or weak the connection is, and whether

one can legitimately infer any theological conclusions from the many anthropic coincidences. According to the *Strong Anthropic Principle* (SAP),

> The universe must have those properties which allow [intelligent] life to develop within it at some stage of its history.[23]

On this view the constants and laws of nature are *necessarily* as life-supporting as they are, because we are here to observe the universe. To paraphrase Descartes, 'I think therefore the world is as it is.' On this view, the interrelation between the cosmos and intelligent life (such as ourselves) does not only impose restrictions on our location in the universe (we could, for example, not have arrived 5 billion years earlier), but also on the fundamental parameters of the universe. This point was already made by the cosmologist Brandon Carter when he first, in 1974, introduced the idea of the anthropic principle.[24]

The large number cosmic coincidences are open for a theistic interpretation: our particular universe may be fine-tuned by God for the purpose of generating intelligent beings. Obviously, this is not a physical but a metaphysical explanation, but it is one which explains the particular features of the anthropic-cosmological coincidences that cannot easily be explained within a physical framework—after all, it is the very framework of physics that calls for an explanation.

This immediate theistic interpretation, however, is not without alternatives. The most widespread is the so-called Many World Interpretation (MWI) which holds the following position,

---

23. I am here following the definition by Barrow and Tipler [John D Barrow and Frank J Tipler, *The Antropic Cosmological Principles* (Oxford: Oxford University Press, 1986, 1996), 21].
24. Brandon Carter, 'Large Number Coincidences and the Anthropic Principle in Cosmology', in *Modern Cosmology and Philosophy*, edited by J Leslie (Amherst: Prometheus Books, 1998), 134 ff.

An ensemble of other possible universes is
necessary to the explain fact that our particular
universe is as life-supporting as it is.

On this interpretation, we are simply the lucky inhabitants in the
universe (or in one of many universes) that seem *as if* geared to the
emergence of life. The existence of many universes can then be
imagined either as standing in a temporal sequence (oscillating
universes replacing one another) or as simultaneous universes placed
in different regions of a larger Universe of universes. So far MWI
appears as a purely metaphysical hypothesis which, compared with
the design hypothesis, has the disadvantage of being construed
purely *ad hoc*, for the purpose of explaining the 'problem' of large
number cosmic coincidences, without explaining anything else. On
this score, the traditional designer hypothesis may be judged not only
as more economic but also as capable of explaining far more features
than MWI (eg the comprehensibility of the world, the beauty of the
universe, the overall progress of evolution, the urge to love another,
independent attestation of religious experience etc etc).

However, quantum versions of MWI have been proposed that
have a stronger linkage to scientific theory building. Already in the
1950s Hugh Everett argued that quantum mechanics supplies a
mechanism for generating separate worlds. His proposal was that
wave-functions never truly collapse (as it is presupposed in the
Copenhagen interpretation). Rather, at each quantum time the world
splits into branches which thereafter hardly interact. With one
notable exception, though. According to Everett, the existence of
other universes explains the otherwise unexplained effects of
quantum wave interference in the famous double split experiment.[25]
More recently, David Deutsch has revived Everett's ontological
interpretation of quantum theory. Deutsch explains the observations
of quantum wave interference as an interference between the single
photon (that has been detected by the measuring apparatus as
passing through one of the two slits) with other undetectable photons
in an infinity of adjacent universes. These universes are claimed to be

---

25. John D Barrow and Frank J Tipler, *The Antropic Cosmological
    Principles, op cit*, 458–509.

real, since only real things can have real effects: the wave interference. In this manner, Deutsch infers a whole world view on the basis of the double split experiment. Our so-called universe is in reality a 'multiverse', that is, a multilayered structure of quantum time instants. Each time (each snapshot of observation) constitutes a whole universe of its own, without any overarching framework of time or observational perspective. What is a shadowy universe to one quantum event is the real universe to another, but all possible states of quantum processes are fully real:

> We exist in multiple versions, in universes called 'moments'. Each version of us is not directly aware of the others, but has evidence of their existence because physical laws link the contents of the different universes. It is tempting to suppose that the moment of which we are aware is the only real one, or is at least a little more real than the others. But that is just solipsism. All moments are physically real. The whole of the multiverse is physically real. Nothing else is.[26]

It is of course highly adventurous to draw so far-reaching ontological messages on the basis of the features of wave inter-ference. But this is not our issue here. The question is what the theological options are for dealing with the many world assumption (if it were plausible). One option is to understand the idea of God as an explanatory rival to the MWI. This strategy, however, would only be legitimate if God's vision for the world were confined to letting into being just one single universe, for which God has a very definite 'plan'. But is this the only theological option? Certainly, this was the notion of design that has been presupposed in the influential strands of religious determinism (for example, in Islam and in some forms of Christian tradition). But also a deterministic design theory can be coupled with MWI, as we see it in the Stoicism which taught the

---

26. David Deutsch [David Deutsch, *The Fabric of Reality* (London: Penguin, 1997, 1998), 287, cf 32–53 (on the double split-experiment) and 275–285 (on the multiverse)].

doctrine of oscillating universes in the context of a deterministic cosmology. But also indeterminism is a theological truth candidate, and indeed a more flexible one. If we understand God as the creator of creativity,[27] God´s intention is to let the world flourish according to its own, God-given possibilities. In Jewish tradition, we thus find the idea that God blesses the world already created by God. In Neo-Platonic tradition we find the idea of the 'principle of plenitude' which has influenced also Christian philosophers from Augustine to Leibniz.[28] This understanding of a divine design as a creative and self-giving design is highly compatible with MWI. Indeed, the theological notion of God's superabundance would be open to many forms of divine creativity, in this universe as well as in other universes. Even though this remains a thought experiment (since we cannot know about other universes), we find in the Narnia books of CS Lewis a modern awareness of the possibility of multiple parallel universes, in the context of an orthodox Christian thinker. As we will see below, the idea of design can be placed at higher logical levels than the notion of one particular design for one particular world.

Michael Denton's naturalistic version of the strong anthropic principle (SAP)

Let us nonetheless stay within the boundaries of the observable universe and here focus on the degree of coordination between the laws of physical chemistry and biological life. In *Nature's Destiny. How the Laws of Biology Reveal Purpose in the Universe*, biochemist Michael J Denton has pointed to the long chain of anthropic coincidences from the basic laws of physics to the life-supporting contribution of sunlight and the hydrosphere, and to the aptness of water and especially carbon as bearers of intelligent life. None of these properties are created by Darwinian evolution, since they precede biological life. Denton's observations are by no means new, taken individually, but he should be credited for having added

---

27. Niels Henrik Gregersen, 'The Creation of Creativity and the Flourishing of Creation', *Currents in Theology and Mission*, 28:3–4 (2001): 400–410.
28. Arthur O Lovejoy, *The Great Chain of Being: A Study of the History of an Idea* (Cambridge, Mass: Harvard University Press, 1936).

further weight to the hypothesis that life is the property of a uniquely concerted universe. He points to the fact, for instance, that silicon would not work as a replacement for carbon, since 'it falls far short of carbon in the diversity and complexity of its compounds'. In particular, he underlines that carbon's aptness for life 'is maximal in the same temperature range that water is fluid ', which is not the case for silicon.[29]

Against this background, Denton argues that the cosmos is a 'uniquely prefabricated whole with life as it is on earth as its end and purpose'.[30] This is SAP, for Denton's thesis is (a) that intelligent human-like life will *necessarily* arise given the way the world is construed, and (b) that the physical-chemical structure of the universe has been *uniquely designed* for that unique purpose.

Denton is aware that his position cannot be proven, after all, a necessity does not follow from even a very long chain of contingent coincidences. But he underlines that his hypothesis could be falsified, eg by the evidence of extraterrestrial life on non-carbon templates. Furthermore, Denton makes clear that his teleological argument (unlike the Intelligent Design theory) is developed on fully naturalistic foundations, namely that our cosmos is

> a seamless unity which can be comprehended ultimately in its entirety by human reason and in which all phenomena, including life and evolution, are ultimately explicable in terms of natural processes.[31]

Denton thus escapes both the Scylla of a principled anti-teleology and the Charybdis of a design theory which erases naturalistic

---

29. Micheal J Denton, *Nature's Destiny: How the Laws of Biology Reveal Purpose in the Universe* (New York: Free Press, 1998), 101, cf 109–116. Some (but not all) of these unique capacities are also pointed out by Barrow and Tipler [John D Barrow and Frank J Tipler, *The Antropic Cosmological Principles, op cit*, 524–548].

30. Micheal J Denton, *Nature's Destiny: How the Laws of Biology Reveal Purpose in the Universe, op cit*, 367.

31. *Ibid*, xviii.

explanations. Denton carefully distinguishes the causal explanations of science from the semantic explanation of a natural theology.[32] Therefore, one could subscribe to Denton's long list of cosmic coincidences without necessarily explaining them in terms of divine purpose. The fact that intelligent life *must* happen, given the physics we have, does not prove that we *must* have the physics we have by virtue of God's benevolent design. The category of design certainly has an illuminating power, but there is no cogent inference to be made from the existence of a vast number of lucky coincidences to the existence of a designing God.

Another strength of Denton's position is that he avoids the view which Barrow and Tipler named the *Final Anthropic Principle* (FAP):

> Intelligent information-processing must come into existence in the Universe, and, once it comes into existence, it will never die out.[33]

The latter part of the sentence simply overstates what we know about the cosmic conditions. An eternal future of life processes cannot be deduced from the many happy coincidences of past cosmic history.

George Ellis' theological interpretation of the Weak Anthropic Principle (WAP)

The *Weak Anthropic Principle* (WAP) has more followers. According to this version, the universe can only be understood as *actually* providing the right physical conditions for intelligent life. Barrow and Tipler state the principle as follows:

---

32. In fact, the substance of Denton's argument of carbon's unique properties for life also questions the hope that carbon-based information in a far future could be transferred into a silicon medium, and thus make life everlasting. Cf Frank Tipler's argument that the persistence of intelligent life is only possible if 'an exact replica of ourselves is being simulated in the computer's minds of the far future' [Frank Tipler, *The Physics of Immortality: Modern Cosmology: God and the Resurrection of the Dead* (New York: Doubleday, 1994), 227].

33. John D Barrow and Frank J Tipler, *The Antropic Cosmological Principles, op cit*, 23.

The observed values of all physical and cosmological quantities are not equally probable but they take on values restricted by the requirements that there exist sites where carbon-based life can evolve and by the requirement that the Universe be old enough for it to have already done so.[34]

This weak version has sometimes been called a truism. Barrow and Tipler thus described WAP as a mere restatement of a well-established principle of science, namely to take into account the limitations of one's measuring apparatus when interpreting one's observations. As pointed out by the South African cosmologist George Ellis, however, the weak version can be seen as a meaningful research program for understanding the road from physics to life by asking:

How much variation in laws and initial conditions can there be, and still allow intelligent life to exist, including the unique features of the mind such as consciousness and self-consciousness.[35]

As a matter of fact, most of the basic observations of the cosmological coincidences that favour life are not questioned in the scientific literature—it is the interpretation of the facts (especially the SAP and FAP versions of the Anthropic Principle) that have been under attack. The existence of consciousness does indeed impose extremely narrow conditions on the basic laws of the universe (such as gravity, weak and strong nuclear force) and on its initial conditions (such as size), *if* life and intelligence is to evolve. These coincidences include the following features:[36]

---

34. *Ibid*, 16 (italics in original).
35. George FR Ellis, 'The Theology of the Antropic Principle', in *Quantum Cosmology and the Laws of Nature: Scientific Perspektives on Divine Action*, edited by Robert J Russell, Nancey Murphy and CJ Isham (Vatican City/Berkley: Vatican Observatory Publications, CTNS, 1993), 377.
36. See the concise overview in Leslie [John Leslie, *Universes* (London: Routledge, 1996), 25–56], probably the best book on the anthropic principle.

* To avoid a nearly immediate re-collapse of the cosmos, the *expansion rate* at early instants needed to have been extremely fine-tuned (perhaps to one part in 10^{55}).

* Had the *nuclear weak force* been a little stronger, the Big Bang would have burned all hydrogen to helium; no stable stars could then have evolved. Had the force been weaker, the neutrons formed at early times would not have decayed into protons.

* For carbon to be formed within stars, the *nuclear strong force* could vary only up to one to two per cent in each direction.

* Had *electromagnetism* been appreciably stronger, stellar luminescence would fall, and all stars would be red stars, probably too cold to support the emergence of life, and unable to explode as supernovae. Had electromagnetism been slightly weaker, the main sequence stars would be too hot and too short-lived to sustain life.

* Gravity also needs to be fine-tuned and correlated with electromagnetic forces in order to create long-lived stars that do not burn up too early.

In a second step, these extremely delicate balances of the life-giving physical condition may then be taken as a warrant of the widespread religious belief that a divine designer is responsible for creating and maintaining the extraordinary contrivances of laws and initial conditions in our universe. These contrivances are *a priori* more probable under the presupposition of a theistic world view than under the assumption of a pointless universe. As we saw, however, the *design idea* is only one interpretation among others (interpretation 1). One could mention the ancient Greek notion of the *eternal necessity* of the world (interpretation 2), the chaotic cosmological idea of the *high probability* of cosmos (interpretation 3), and the above mentioned *many world interpretation* (interpretation 4).[37]

Note again, however, that these interpretations are not necessarily rivals. In particular, the theistic notion of design is flexible enough to accommodate elements of all three other interpretations. The design idea is compatible with the doctrine of the world's necessity (interpretation 2), provided that God is not the creator of this world but only a formative principle who shapes an already self-existing world. Thus understood the notion of divine design would be akin to Plato's concept of God as Demiurge (in the *Timaeus*), but would be different from the Jewish, Christian and Muslim conceptions of God.

With respect to interpretation 3 and 4, God may be invoked as a higher-order explanation for the mathematics of probability, or even for the mathematical structures that may allow for different physical laws and different initial conditions in multiple other universes. Thus, one could imagine different types of 'meta-Anthropic' design in order to account for the contingencies of the orders of the universe.[38]

My aim here is not to review the *pros* and *cons* of the anthropic design argument in itself, but to clarify its philosophical nature. First, the design argument refers here to strictly *universal* features of the world. Divine design is invoked to explain the framework of reality (with its bearings on life and consciousness), without claiming to explain particular features such as the development of elephants, dolphins, and humans. (The term 'anthropic' is here misleading since the argument does not concern humanity in particular, but life and consciousness in general).

---

37. George FR Ellis, 'The Theology of the Anthropic Principle', *op cit*, 372–376.

38. See the original proposal by Russell [Robert John Russell, 'Cosmology, Creation, and Contingency, in *Cosmos as Creation: Theology and Science in Consonance*, edited by Ted Peters (Nashville: Abingdon Press, 1989), 177–210], 196–204.

Second, the meaning of the term 'divine designer' is highly ambiguous. The design argument suggest that God is utterly transcendent in relation to the designed world, since a designer is imposing an order on a given material or object. *Who* or *what* the divine is remains unspecified. Usually, the divine designer is tacitly assumed to be the Creator of all-that-is (and not only a forming principle), but historically as well as logically the idea of creation is *not* entailed in the notion of design. God could well be a designer without being the world's creator. In fact, this is the Platonic position revived in the twentieth century by the mathematician-philosopher AN Whitehead. Nor is the Biblical notion of God as Creator always combined with the idea of a 'grand divine masterplan'. As a matter of fact, the teleological idea of a divine design cannot be inferred from the Old and New Testament texts themselves, but is the result of a later Christian appropriation of Platonic and Aristotelian philosophy.[39] The semantic fuzziness of the very notion of design

---

39. In English Old Testament translations, the reference to what God has 'purposed' (eg Jeremiah 4:28) or 'planned' (eg Isaiah 14:24, 27, 19:12) are usually derived from the Hebrew verbs *zamas* (meaning 'thinking and doing something deliberately') and *azah* (meaning 'forming something', like a pot, and 'counseling, willing, and making real what one wills'), see Jenni and Westermann (Ernst Jenni and Claus Westermann, *Theological Lexicon of the Old Testament*, volumes I–II (Peabody: Hendrickson, 1997)), 566–568. When reading English translations of the Bible, one should always bear in mind that Indo-European translations of *zimmah* as 'purpose' and *ezah* as 'plan/counsel' always refer to substantivised Hebrew verbs that connote a circumstantial, yet very intensive divine intention-and-action (eg Isaiah 46:9). God pursues this or that purpose, but it is nowhere assumed that God has a fixed plan for the history of creation in general. In the New Testament, by contrast, we do find some references to God's one purpose for all-that-is (God's will, *boulé*, God's predetermination, *prothesis*, or God's plan, *oikonomia*) but the purpose referred to here is always the purpose of salvation, not a general cosmic plot (eg Ephesians 1:4–11). Thus, in the Old Testament, we have a highly context-bound concept of design: a theology of God's will in relation to historical situation (a local teleology, if one so wishes); in the New Testament we have a concept of global design, but a design about eternal salvation (a transcendent

demonstrates that 'design' is not an indigenous religious concept. Rather, it is a second-order theoretical construct used by philosopher-theologians to defend the rationality of religious belief. Helpful as the concept of design may be in the context of a philosophical theology, it is not of primary concern in religious life.

Third, the theistic interpretation of the Anthropic Principle gains its strongest plausibility from the need to explain the *extremely narrow fine-tuning* of the laws and boundary conditions necessary for the development of intelligent life. It is this explanatory need which is satisfied by the reference to a divine designer who deliberately selects the laws and boundary conditions with respect to their intrinsic fruitfulness. A balanced theological position will have to notice both the strengths and weaknesses of the concept of design. Earlier we have seen some of its strengths. One of its weaknesses, however, is that a theology which has so fallen in love with fine-tuning will tend to see an enemy in the *robustness* which is so characteristic of self-organising systems. But how can theology spell out the significance of self-organisational principles which are not in need of fine-tuning?

Why design arguments are misplaced in relation to self-organising systems
For several reasons, the *'laws of complexity'* (or rather, the general tendencies towards complexification) underlying the emergence and further propagation of complex orders, differ from the laws of physics as we usually think of them. These 'laws' deal with the cooperative behaviour of huge systems which cannot be understood

---

global teleology), never about a mundane harmony (an immanent global teleology), cf Gregersen (Niels Henrik Gregersen, 'Providence', in *The Oxford Companion to Christan Thought*, edited by Adrian Hastings (Oxford: Oxford University Press, 2000)). Historically speaking, the idea of a global this-worldly design is derived from late Jewish Apocalyptic (texts which did not find entrance into the canonical writings) in combination with the great Platonic idea of an artistic God (*deus artifex*). This teleological idea was appropriated in the Early Middle Ages by Platonising Christians and became later, in Early Modernity, a standard concept of natural theology. Against this background, it is somewhat paradoxical that evangelicals today often appeal to this Enlightenment concept of the designer God as an identity mark of 'orthodox' Christianity.

synchronous holistic influence without which one cannot account for the structures that emerge only at the level of the system-as-a-whole.[40] But there is also a *diachronous* aspect to the laws of complexity. Since the systems produce themselves in the course of time, and since the rules for self-formation are built into the systems themselves (they don't have the status of Platonic formative principles), the *probability rates are changing during history*. As pointed out by Karl R Popper, if we want to take probabilities seriously from an ontological point of view, they are 'as real as forces' and not a set of mere abstract possibilities. By changing the situation, the probabilities are changing also.[41]

To me this suggests that we should take leave of the older thought model of nature as 'the one great chain of being' pouring down as an emanation from a Supreme Being, or (in the naturalist translation) as the immediate expression of the basic physical entities. Rather, nature is a continuous 'story of becoming' whose outcome can only be predicted in general terms; the important details are open for a historical determination.[42] What matters is not only, 'What is out there in nature?' (on the constitutive level of physics), but also, 'How does nature work?' (within complex higher-level orders). We have moved away from a materialistic clockwork picture of the universe to an image of the world as consisting of local, very peculiar networks floating in a wider cosmic network governed by physical laws.

Now, which are the theological options in the light of this change from being to becoming? How can theology creatively respond to this new inquiry into the nature of self-organised systems? Let us face how different the features of self-organisation are from those features addressed by the Anthropic Principle.

---

40. On different versions of whole-part causation, see Peacocke [Arthur Peacocke, 'The Sound of Sheer Silence: How Does God Communicate with Humanity', in *Neuroscience and the Human Person*, edited by Robert J Russell *et al* (Vatican City/Berkeley: Vatican Oberservatory, CTNS, 1999), 215–248].

41. Karl R Popper, *A World of Propensities* (Bristol: Thoemmes, 1990), 12–15.

42. Cf DJ Bartholomew, *God of Chance* (London: SCM Press, 1984).

(1) Even if the drive towards pattern-formation can be found at many places in cosmos, the phenomenon of information-based self-organisation is not as ubiquitous as gravity. Self-organisation is only realised here and there, at once propelled and sheltered by the specific environmental conditions. Similarly in theology, there is a difference between speaking of a *meta-design* that explains the world as a whole (in relation to the Anthropic Principle), and a *design process* which is related to God's involvement in particular processes within the world.

(2) Whereas the notion of God as the external designer is related to God's activity as creator, the idea of God's interaction with a developing world suggests some intimacy (perhaps even a two-way relationship) between God and the mundane existence. In the context of the Anthropic principle, God is seen as the *context-constitutive* creator of all-that-is (the meta-design). However, if we introduce the concept of design in relation to a self-organising and self-developing world, we assume that God may guide the particular pathways within the evolutionary phase space. This notion of a design process presupposes God's activity as a *context-sensitive* interaction with the world of nature.[43]

(3) The theory of self-organised complexity needs no divine designer to solve the problem of fine-tuning. This problem is already solved by the flexible, internal dynamics of self-organising systems. Complexity 'can and will emerge "for free" without any watchmaker tuning the world,' according to Per Bak[44] and Stuart Kauffman.[45]

Provided that this analysis is essentially correct, theology seems to face a stark dilemma. After all, religious life is more interested in the active presence of a providential God in the midst of the world, rather than in a designer God at the edge of the universe. Yet the design argument is viable in the context of the Anthropic Principle

---

43. On this difference, see Gregersen [Niels Henrik Gregersen, 'Three Types of Indeterminacy. On the Difference between God's Action as Creator and as Providence', *Studies in Science and Theology*, volume 3 (Geneva: Labor et Fides, 1997), 165–184], 177ff.

44. Per Bak, *How Nature Works: The Theory of Self-Organized Criticality* (New York: Oxford University Press, 1997), 48.

45. Stuart Kauffman, *At Home in the Universe: The Search for the Laws of Complexity, op cit*, chapter 4.

(where its religious significance is rather faint), whereas the design argument seems to be without value in the context of self-organised complexity (where its application would be religiously significant).

Are there ways out of this dilemma? I believe there are at least two options for theology, a *causal* approach in the tradition of philosophical theology, and a more qualitative and *descriptive* approach, which aims to redescribe the world rather than explaining it. I believe that this latter qualitative approach (which is relatively unconcerned about design) is the more congenial to the spirit of the sciences of complexity, and at the same time more appealing from a religious point of view. I intend to show, however, that the two theological options—the first concerned with divine causality and the other concerned with meaning—are indeed supplementary.

The causal approach: re-connecting design and self-organisation

The first option consists of an attempt to reconnect the two lines of argumentation that we have so far, for the sake of the analysis, differentiated from one another. Ontologically, the evolving laws of self-organisation cannot be disconnected from the basic laws of physics, since the former always follow trajectories conditioned by the latter.[46] Any fitness landscape—even if it is open-ended—is always finite, rooted as it is in the specific mathematical properties of chemical systems.[47] All biological adaptations move in the phase space of possibilities constrained by the Anthropic Principle.

Against this background, we might reconcile the *apparent lack of design* at some levels of reality (eg the level of evolutionary selection, or of self-organised complexity) with the idea of a divine 'meta-design' that affords and even favours complexification in the long run. A solution along this line has been developed both by proponents of a Christian reading of the anthropic principle such as

---

46. See, in this volume, the contributions from Davies, Stewart, Loewenstein and Morowitz.

47. Ian Stewart, *Life's Other Secret: The New Mathematics of the Living World* (London: Penguin, 1998). The importance of the finitude of phase space was made clear to me by George Ellis (personal communication in Cape Town, 8–9 August 1999).

George Ellis[48] as well as by proponents of a more general theism such as Paul Davies. Recently, Davies has thus proposed a modified uniformitarianism: God may be compared with a chess legislator who, on the one hand, selects certain rules from the set of all possible rules in order to facilitate a rich and interesting play, and yet leaves open the particular moves to the players.[49] After all, some laws are inherently fruitful for the development of life. Life, however, is not a step-by-step guided process.

I believe that one can add to this view the possibility of an objectively real divine agency within the world in terms of a 'design process'.[50] In the science-theology dialogue several options have been proposed in order to conceptualise God's special actions within the world without assuming a view of God as breaking physical laws.

(1) God may continuously influence the world in a bottom-up manner through the quantum processes.[51] Since quantum processes can generate mutations at the genetic level, and God, in inscrutable ways, may select between otherwise indeterminate quantum processes (as long as the overall probabilities are not violated), there are potential channels everywhere for God's exercise of a continuous influence on the course of evolution.

(2) God may act in a top-down manner by constraining the possibilities on the world as a whole, and thereby effectively influence the course of evolution.[52]

---

48. George FR Ellis, 'The Theology of the Antropic Principle', *op cit*, 375.
49. Paul Davies, 'Teleology without Teleology: Purpose through Emergent Complexity', in *Evolutionary and Molecular Biology: Scientific Perspectives on Divine Action*, edited by Robert J Russsel *et al* (Vatican City/Berkeley: Vatican Observatory Publications, CTNS, 1998), 155.
50. Here, as elsewhere in this article, 'process' is not alluding to the specifics of Whiteheadian 'process theology'.
51. Cf many voices in the Vatican/CTNS project on 'Scientific Perspectives on Divine Action', including Robert J Russell, Nancey Murphy and George Ellis.
52. Arthur Peacocke, *Theology for a Scientific Age. Enlarged Edition* (London: SCM Press, 1993), 191–212.

(3) Elsewhere I have proposed a third possibility, which focuses on the changeability of the probability patterns throughout evolution.[53] The point here is that the dice of probabilities are not loaded once for all, but are constantly reloaded in the course of evolution. Given any phase space, the probabilities for future development are constantly changing. With every step, some new steps are facilitated, whereas the probability of other possibilities is greatly diminished. Such changeability is always taken for granted by the practising scientist. In fact, one could argue, with philosopher Nancy Cartwright, that the measurement of such capacities or propensities is what the empirical sciences are really about, whereas the search for mathematically universal laws is more philosophically than scientifically motivated.[54] I would not follow her that far, though. But Cartwright makes the important point that even if there are higher-order laws of nature, lower-level probabilities are constantly re-created in the process of procedure. This applies especially to *autopoietic systems*, ie systems that are not only self-organising but also produce (or at least change) the elements of which the systems are made up. Examples of such autopoietic creativity is the production of lymphocytes in the immune system, the formation of neural pathways in the brain, or the invention of words in human language.

Now the question is: How can we account for the preferred pathways of evolution (and their changing probability rates) if these are *not* fully explainable from the underlying laws of basic physics? How can we explain how nature *works*, if the workings of nature cannot be predicted from the constituent level of the parts, nor from basic laws of physics? The fact is that we cannot, and I suggest that this is given by the role of autonomous agents.[55]

Again we have an array of metaphysical possibilities. For what is the *preferential principle* (respectively the principle of exclusion) which

53. Niels Henrik Gregersen, 'The Idea of Creation and the Theory of Autopoietic Processes', *op cit.*

54. Nancy Cartwright, *Nature's Capacities and their Measurement* (Oxford: Clarendon Press, 1989).

55. Stuart Kauffman, 'The Emergence of Autonomous Agents', *op cit*, 49–80.

explains why nature follows *this* particular route rather than all other energetically possible routes: (1) a dynamical theism, (2) necessity, or a determinism invoking hidden variables, or (3) chance, or ultimate tychism.[56] Again I believe that we have both a competition between these views, and the possibility of combining them. Evidently, a dynamical and process-oriented theism is opposed to determinism and tychism as long as these latter interpretations are taken as ultimate explanations of reality. However, the notion of divine agency is indeed compatible both with natural causation and with a certain range of chance. In fact, only a dynamical theism (including a design process) is able to embrace the other options. The other way around is not possible. An ultimate determinism would exclude not only an ultimate tychism, but also a dynamical theism, and also an ultimate tychism would exclude both theism and determinism. By comparing the three explanatory candidates, theism seems to be the more flexible and open cosmological explanation.

Thus, God may act as a preferential principle guiding the pathways of evolution without determining the individual steps of evolution. God would then not act as a *triggering cause* (like my finger tip on the computer keyboard), but rather as a *structuring cause* which constantly wires and rewires the probability rates of self-organising processes (like the computer programmer who makes the machine do what I want it to do). In general, what would support a dynamical (non-uniform) theism is a situation where one could say that the overall fruitfulness of self-organisational processes is *more* than one would a priori expect knowing the general laws of physics. There must be more than pure regularity, and more than pure chance, if the notion of God's continuous, yet non-uniform activity is to be plausible. A delicately coordinated balance between law and chance seems to be congenial to the hypothesis of a steadfast yet dynamical God who is interacting with a developing world.[57]

---

56. Note that the option of 'infinite possibilities' (comparable to the many world hypothesis) is not viable here, since the phase space is finite.

57. Note here similarities and dissimilarities to the Intelligent Design movement. The penultimate sentence may seem to resonate with William Dembski's 'explanatory filter': Intelligent Design can be inferred where features *cannot* be explained by law, nor by chance

The non-causal qualitative approach

We are here already on our way to the qualitative approach which is also about discerning God in nature without appealing to specific divine influences on the evolving world. The lead question here is not, 'What effective difference does God make during evolution?', but rather, 'How does the nature of the world *express* the nature that God eternally *is*'? Whereas the causal approach usually attempts to *infer* God from the structures and processes of the world, or at least understand God as an explanatory principle, the reality of God is here *assumed* (on the basis of religious experience) and subsequently *re-cognised* in the external world. In terminology familiar to theologians, we are here moving from a 'natural theology' to a 'theology of nature'. Self-organising systems are here seen as prime expressions of God's continuous creativity. Thus the focus is here on how we may theologically *re-describe* the results of the self-organising processes which may or may not need special divine guidance.[58]

Above we noticed how the robustness of self-organising systems implies a high degree of autonomy, that is, independence from external conditions. We also saw that the theory of self-organisation, in this respect, constitutes a new challenge to theology since self-organisation is not in need of any specific fine-tuning. However, complexity theory also offers new options for theology if theology can learn to redescribe, in the language of religion itself, those important features of self-organising systems that are open for a religious interpretation. What is awe-inspiring about self-organisation is not the delicacy of the coordination of the many

---

(William A Dembski, *Intelligent Design: The Bridge Between Science and Theology*, op cit, 127–239). The last sentence, however, makes the difference: it is exactly the delicate (natural!) interplay between law and contingency that is open to a religious interpretation.

58. On the difference between (causal) explanation and (semantic) re-description, see Gregersen [Niels Henrik Gregersen, 'Theology in a Neo–Darwinian World', *Studia Theologica*, 48 (1994): 125–149], 125–129, further elaborated in Gregersen (Niels Henrik Gregersen, 'The Creation of Creativity and the Flourishing of Creation', *op cit*, 400–410). See also van Huyssteen [J Wentzel van Huyssteen, *Duet and Duel? Theology and Science in a Postmodern World* (London: SCM Press, 1998), 125–128].

parameters (as in the Anthropic Principle), but the sheer fact that the most variegated processes of diversification and creativity are driven by relatively simple laws. These laws, given time and circumstance, *guarantee* that the world of creation attains increasingly complex levels of orders—'for free'.

I therefore suggest that the engagement of theology with complexity studies is not best served by rehabilitating or revising ideas of intelligent design. What is of more interest to theology is the possibility that a *Principle of Grace* seems to reign in the creative orderliness of nature. Redescribed in a Judeo-Christian perspective, the theory of self-organisation suggests that God is not a remote, a-cosmic designer of a world but God is the *blessing God* who creates by bestowing on nature a capacity for fruitful albeit risky self-development. The transcendence of God—revealed in the richness of possible pattern formations—is at work *within* the world. As such God is not identical with specific evolutionary patterns, but God is viewed as the wellspring of the always unprecedented and always changing configurations of order. *God creates the world by giving free freedom—gratuitously. God creates by creating creativity.*

Accordingly, we might need to redescribe our traditional expectations concerning the orderliness of the world. The lesson to be learnt both from evolutionary theory and from Self-Organised Criticality is that the laws of nature (as selected by God and instantiated in our world) necessarily include disturbances along the road.[59] Crises evoked by disturbances are necessary means to produce variability and thus enable new high-level configurations of order. Complexity theory may thus prompt theology to rethink its inherited idea of teleology in a manner that appreciates the long-term positive effects of avalanches. States of 'harmonious' equilibrium are recurrently punctuated by 'catastrophic' avalanches—and both equilibrium *and* catastrophes are governed by the same underlying principles of complexity. The instability of complex systems seems to be the inevitable price to be paid for the immense creativity in evolution. As pointed out by Per Bak in the last sentence of *How Nature Works*, 'The self-organised critical state with all its fluctuations

---

59. Niels Henrik Gregersen, 'Beyond the Balance: Theology in a World of Autopoietic Systems', *op cit.*

is not the best possible state, but it is the best state that is dynamically achievable'.[60]

Redescribed theologically, evolution is not a risk-free thing, but includes the labour of nature. The groaning and suffering of creation is thus not to be seen as specifically designed by a malicious, all-determining God. Setbacks and suffering are part of the package deal of participating in a yet unfinished creation. However, there is also a principle of grace built into the whole process (Gregersen, 2001b). There is, taken on a whole, a surplus of life-intensity promised to those who take up the chances of collaboration.

Life is not only a fight for survival, a zero-sum game, where one part only wins if the other part loses. As pointed out by Robert Wright in his book *Nonzero*, there is a 'non-zero-sumness' built into the structure of the world. 'In non-zero-sum games, one player's gain needn't be bad news for the other(s). Indeed, in highly non-zero-sum games the players' interests overlap entirely'. For complexity is the evolution of co-evolution, in which co-operation plays an inextricable role. In the eloquent words of Robert Wright,

> biological evolution, like cultural evolution, can be viewed as the ongoing elaboration of non-zero-sum dynamics. From alpha to omega, from the first primordial chromosome up to the first human beings, natural selection has smiled on the expansion of non-zero-sumness (Wright 2000, 252, cf 5).

It is not difficult to re-describe in religious terms this world of non-zero-sumness: Both a demand and a promise is built into the fabric of reality: Only those who are prepared to lose their life will gain it; eventually, they will not gain it over against others, but in the company with others. In this roundabout way, the world can be said to be designed for self-organisation, including both the demand of giving up established pathways of evolution, and the promise of

---

60. Per Bak, *How Nature Works: The Theory of Self-Organized Criticality*, *op cit*, 198.

becoming more than we would have been without going through the travail of risky self-organisation.

After all, at least a Christian theology should be familiar with the Gospel of John's view of the divine Word or Logos as penetrating all that is and which remains the generative Pattern of all patterns of life (John 1,3-4). It is this universal Pattern which is assumed by Christians to have made manifest its everlasting urge in the life story of Jesus Christ. Christians see the historical figure of Jesus as the prime parable of God exactly because he gave up his own existence in order to produce further life. For 'unless a grain of wheat falls into the earth and dies, it remains just a single grain; but if it dies, it yields much' (John 12,24).

On this view, it is to be expected that the creation of order includes the experience of setbacks and death as part of God's way of giving birth to new creations. Self-sacrifice as well as self-productivity are built into the structure of the world: a world designed for self-organisation.

The Cloning of Human Cells: An Australian Response to the Scientific Issues from an Ethical and Theological Perspective

John W White, Fraser Bergersen, Graeme Garrett,
Patricia Ewing, Jonathan Clarke

References in the text marked with an asterisk are included in a glossary at the end of the chapter.

Introduction

This paper arose in the first instance from a request made by the Anglican Synod of the Canberra & Goulburn Diocese (2001) to develop an essay in response to current biomedical research into cloning. The synod had no trouble in reaching a common mind on the question of cloning complete human persons. In agreement with many other scientific and secular utterances, it rejected the possibility outright and urged the Commonwealth Government to legislate to this effect. However, on the contentious issue of research into the cloning of human tissues, the synod was more uncertain. The need for greater clarity about the current state of scientific knowledge and the possible benefits and dangers involved with it was widely felt. Accordingly, the synod invited us to prepare a document that could be used as a focus for discussion in local churches and as a guide to policy formation for the wider church as it struggles to come to terms with this dramatic research from an ethical and theological perspective.

These origins account for the style and aims of the paper, and also for (at least some of) its limitations. As a committee, we had neither the time nor the resources to engage fully with all work relevant to this topic. The field is developing with astonishing speed. Almost every week brings news of unexpected discoveries. Faced with this difficulty, and mindful of the purpose of the paper, we have tried to provide an overview of the basic scientific developments, on the one hand, and an indication of the ethical and theological considerations that Christian faith can bring to the debate in Australia, on the other.

We focused our consideration of the scientific issues concerning cloning on four reports.

- the (February 1998) Royal Society's report *,Whither Cloning,* which was pivotal in forming British public opinion and the subsequent British legislation;[1]
- the (December 1998) report of the Australian Health Ethics Committee of the National Health and Medical Research Council, *Scientific, Ethical and Regulatory Considerations Relevant to Cloning of Human Beings,*[2]
- the (February 1999) Australian Academy of Science's position statement on human cloning, *On Human Cloning,* and the April 2001 report, *Human Stem Cell Research,*[3]
- the (August 2001) Andrews Committee report, *Human cloning.*[4]

The current debate

As already hinted, it is important to draw a distinction between the cloning of complete animals, such as was achieved with the sheep

1. *Whither Cloning* (January 1998) is a statement prepared by a group of Fellows chaired by Professor RB Heap and endorsed by the Council of the Royal Society. See http://www.royalsoc.ac.uk/.
2. This report, by the Australian Health Ethics Committee of the NHMRC, was presented to the Commonwealth Minister for Health and Aged Care on 16 December 1998.
3. The web reference for the full text of the Australian Academy of Science position statement on human cloning is http://www.science.org.au/academy/media/clone.pdf; and for the full text of the Australian Academy of Science position statement on stem cell research is http://www.science.org.au/academy/media/stemcell.pdf.
4. Human cloning House of Representatives Standing Committee on Legal and Constitutional Affairs, August 2001. See, 'Inquiry into scientific, ethical and regulatory aspects of cloning', Submissions Volume 5 (261–286, 683-783), www.aph.gov.au/house/committee/laca/index.htm.

named Dolly, and the cloning of animal parts such as DNA[*5] and cells. While whole human beings have not (as yet) been cloned, cloning of human DNA and cells is routinely undertaken in laboratory research.

Human cloning

There is now significant public awareness about human cloning. In part, this is one consequence of an announcement in July 2001 by Italian doctor, Professor Severino Antinori. At a meeting of the United States National Academy of Sciences, Dr Antinori confirmed that, despite all objections on both scientific and moral grounds, he was preparing to clone about 200 children from a group of 1300 volunteer couples. He proposed that, at a secret location in the United States, he would use the same cell nuclear transfer techniques (CNT*) which produced the cloned sheep Dolly in 1997. Crucially, there appears to be no United States national law or policy to inhibit Professor Antinori's intentions despite strong urgings for caution from the scientific community concerning the risks entailed.[6]

More recently, a biotechnology company in Massachusetts, Advanced Cell Technology, claimed to have cloned a human embryo* to the six cell stage using CNT. The objective was to transfer human DNA to a human egg* to confirm whether human tissue was capable of being transplanted without rejection in the laboratory.[7] This process is termed 'therapeutic cloning'. Although the science expressed in this report[8] has been criticised, the report has contributed to the high public profile of the cloning issue.[9]

While there are currently no proposals in Australia to imitate such experiments, the Australian scientific community has considered the approach that it might take to any work of that kind in this country. On 16 December 1998 the Australian Health Ethics Committee of the

---

5. Terms marked with an asterisk are further defined in the glossary at the end of the paper.
6. *New Scientist*, 19 January 2002: 9; *The Weekend Australian Magazine* 16–17 February 2002, 17–19.
7. Monday, 28 November 2001, abcnews.com.
8. JB Cibelli *et al*, *J Regen Med*, 2 (2001): 25–31.
9. *Nature*, 415 (2002), 109.

National Health and Medical Research Council (NHMRC) published its report, *Scientific, Ethical and Regulatory Considerations Relevant to Cloning Human Beings*. In its investigations, the committee received no support for the application of any technique with the aim of intentionally cloning an individual human being.[10]

In February 1999 the Australian Academy of Science published the discussion paper, *On Human Cloning*. And in September 1999 it hosted the international forum, Therapeutic Cloning for Tissue Repair. The discussion paper addressed ethical and moral implications of the newly developed possibility of using adult cell DNA to create a clone in an enucleated* egg by CNT. This report and its successor on embryonic stem cells (ES)* join with reports of the Royal Society and the Australian Parliament (the 'Andrews Committee' 2001) in analysing the potential for medical treatments based on cloning technology. While wishing to find enabling pathways for this kind of research, albeit under strict regulation, all *oppose* the cloning of people as proposed by Professor Antinori.

Stem cell* cloning

Given no credible support in the scientific community for the cloning of human beings, the production and use of human embryonic 'stem cells' is currently the most contentious issue from a religious point of view. The cloning of stem cells presents the possibility of the development of all tissue types for therapeutic use. However, it raises sharply the question of the status of the early human embryo, for example those embryos 'available' from unused in vitro* fertilisation procedures.

---

10.   AHEC Report, Executive Summary E2, iv. The Committee affirmed the UNESCO Declaration on the Human Genome and Human Rights, in particular Article 11, which states that: 'Practices which are contrary to human dignity, such as reproductive cloning of human beings, shall not be permitted. States and competent international organisations are invited to cooperate in identifying such practices and in determining, nationally or internationally, appropriate measures to be taken to ensure that the principles set out in this Declaration are respected.'

The science

The Australian Academy of Science defined *cloning* as: 'production of a cell or organism with the same nuclear genome as another cell or organism'.[11] The Academy chose this definition to reduce ambiguity in public discussion, to guard against legislative misinterpretation, and to underpin any regulatory or licensing guidelines.

Following their lead, we make a sharp distinction between *reproductive cloning* to produce a human fetus* by nuclear replacement, and *therapeutic cloning* to produce human stem cells, tissues and organs. Cloning of human cells and of human DNA (genes) are routine procedures in many laboratories, as is the cloning of human skin, and will not be discussed here. Also, we shall not discuss embryo-splitting, sometimes called 'twinning', the natural form of cloning that can lead to two or more identical fetuses.

Recent developments

The major scientific advances of the past four years in the field of cloning have been:

(i)   the cloning of mammals from adult cells,

(ii)   the establishment of cultures of 'all purpose' (totipotent*) cells, human embryonic stem (ES) cells with the potential to grow into many different cell types,

(iii)   the demonstration that human fetal nerve stem cells can develop into multiple and appropriate nerve cell types following transplantation (into experimental animals),

(iv)   the identification of growth factors which can direct the development of totipotent stem cells to any of the types of tissue found in the human body,

(v)   research on pluripotent* mesenchymal* stem cells (cells from bone marrow of adults which do not carry markers on their surface that lead to rejection) which may differentiate into bone, fat, or possibly muscle.

These findings provide new opportunities for research in cellular and developmental biology and, taken together, suggest that future

---

11.   *On Human Cloning* (Australian Academy of Science, 1999), 4. See website: http://www.science.org.au/academy/media/stemcell.pdf

possibilities may exist for self-compatible tissue and organ repair in humans.

(i) Cloning mammals from adult cells
The Australian Academy of Science has commented:

> . . . the cloning of 'Dolly' the sheep from the nucleus of an adult somatic cell in 1997 was the first example of production of viable offspring by transfer of a cell nucleus from an *adult* mammal into an unfertilised, enucleated egg. This was not the first time a sheep had been produced by nuclear replacement. In 1996, two genetically identical sheep were cloned by nuclear replacement using cells from nine-day embryos as the nuclear donors. This earlier report did not create alarm or much surprise; indeed, Willadsen had shown a decade earlier that viable offspring could be produced by fusion of enucleated eggs from sheep with separated eight-cell stage blastomeres (any one of the cells into which the fertilised ovum divides). 'Dolly' was different from earlier clones because she was derived from an adult mammary gland cell. This experiment, now replicated in an experimental mouse model and in cattle, has important scientific and ethical implications. These include the potential for better understanding the process of cell differentiation and its reversal, and of aging.[12]

The availability of this cell nuclear transfer method for producing totally compatible embryonic stem cells clearly has important potential as a therapeutic tool, and equally presents the most important challenge ethically. Nevertheless, the Academy concluded: 'In accordance with international opinion . . . reproductive cloning to

---

12. *Ibid*, 8.

produce human fetuses is unethical and unsafe and should be prohibited.'[13]

Why clone humans?
Why, then, would attempts be made to fully clone human individuals? Denis Alexander has suggested seven different reasons.[14] They range from the medically serious to the quite bizarre.

- As a way of overcoming infertility due to absent or dysfunctional gametes*. By using nuclear transfer, the donor nucleus could come from a somatic cell from either partner, generating a child clone with respect to one of the parents, but not to both.
- As a source of completely compatible transplantation tissue.
- To replace a child who has been lost through disease or by accident. (In this scenario a couple who can no longer have children lose their only child but arrange for the child's cells to be cultured following death—or even as an insurance before death. By nuclear transfer the child's DNA is then used to fertilise the mother's egg (or a donor egg) generating a replacement child, of identical sex and physical appearance.)
- The duplication of individuals with particular talents or abilities.
- To enable homosexual couples to have children sharing the genes of one of them. In the US lesbian partners are already having children following in vitro fertilisation using donor sperm, whereas male homosexual partners have, more rarely, paid a surrogate to carry a child procreated using a donated egg.
- Out of curiosity, possibly allied with a scientist's or doctor's ambition to create the first human clone
- In a cultic context (such as the Raelians).

Theoretical scenarios are one thing, but it is important to formulate a considered response to an actual situation. In this regard, Ian Wilmut, leader of the team that cloned Dolly, warns:

---

13. *Ibid*, 17.
14. *ISCAST Bulletin*, 35, http://www.iscast.org.au/bulletin/.

How can all the potential hazards be identified and
quantified so that we know in advance what the
risks would be if anyone did attempt to clone a
human being? They can't. Human cloning will
always represent an experiment and experimenting
on children is wrong. There are times when human
curiosity should forever remain unsatisfied.[15]

But such caution, as we have seen in the case of Antinori, is not
shared by everyone. Alexander thinks that humans *will* be cloned
somewhere once the technology is perfected. This being so, he
argues, it is vital that we make the point now that the resulting
children will be true human beings, children of God, and deserving
of the full protection of the law. He writes:

> . . . clearly if human clones are ever born, then God
> will love them as much as any other human being.
> Likewise Christians should be the first people to
> display acceptance and practical compassion
> towards cloned children.[16]

In the light of all this, we are of the opinion:

That the cloning of humans even to the fetal stage be unlawful.

*(ii) The establishment of cultures of human embryonic stem (ES) cells with
the potential to grow into many different cell types*
Though only discovered less than three years ago, sixty-four lines of
human embryonic stem (ES) cells derived from 'spare' in vitro
fertilisation embryos have now been propagated in cell culture.
Current legislation in the United States of America allows ES
experimentation, although not the production of new lines by the
CNT method.

---

15.   I Wilmut, K Campbell and C Tudge 'The Second Creation', *Headline*
      (2000)
16.   Denis R Alexander, 'Cloning Human—Distorting the Image of God?',
      Cambridge Papers, volume 10, number 2 (June 2001).

As these totipotent stem cells have the possibility of development into all tissue types, one avenue towards therapy is to 'tissue type' cells to potential patients for compatibility in much the same way as blood groups must be typed before transfusion. Questions remain concerning the number of different types that would have to be grown in vitro to make this a feasible and inexpensive option for therapy. While further research is required, it has been predicted that a large number would be required to secure 100 per cent matching to the patient, and to obviate the need to use immunosuppressive drugs. Moreover the embryonic stem cells must themselves be free from the genetic defect causing the disease in the first place.[17]

The alternative, production of human embryos by CNT specific to a patient's own immune system, would obviate the tissue typing problem of stem cells produced from the blastocyst*, assuming that development to that stage were possible. The feasibility of this for humans is not yet proven and there may be legal impediments in some countries.

(iii) The demonstration that human stem cells can develop into multiple and appropriate nerve cell types
In regard to this development, the Academy of Science has stated:

> Mouse ES cells are widely used in medical research to introduce new genes into specialised strains of experimental mice. Ongoing research at the University of Adelaide has applied knowledge gained from study of early mouse embryogenesis to direct mouse ES cells into homogeneous populations of differentiated cells. Soluble factors have been identified that convert ES cells homogeneously into primitive ectoderm, which can in turn be coaxed specifically into either ectoderm or mesoderm*. These germ* layer equivalents go on to form neural stem cells and neurons, and blood and muscle cells respectively. Purification of the soluble factors has permitted their functional and molecular charac-

---

17. *Scientific American*, 286 (2002): 27.

terisation. These factors have the ability to control differentiation* and dedifferentiation in a way that suggests ES cells do indeed have important therapeutic prospects in both tissue repair and as a vehicle for delivery of gene* therapy.[18]

Fetal nerve stem cells were the first human cells to be shown to develop into multiple cell types. This work has now been extended to show that human embryonic stem cells also can develop in this way without the production of any fetal forms. That is, nothing has been seen in cell culture that resembles even the earliest stage of a fetus.

Human ES cells developed in a joint initiative between the University of Singapore and Monash University have resulted in the world's second demonstration that ES cell lines can be derived from human blastocysts. The ES cells will differentiate into a range of cell types, either spontaneously or in response to specific culture conditions and factors. These cell types have characteristics of neuronal ganglia, lung epithelia, gut tissue, muscle cells, bone and cartilage, among others. The research challenges are to identify and characterise the factors and conditions that maintain, expand and direct the lineages of the cell lines to drive exclusive differentiation of cells into desired tissue types.

(iv) The identification of growth factors which can direct the development of totipotent stem cells to any of the four types of tissue found in the human body
The Australian Academy of Science report explains:

> Non-human primate ES cells were not isolated in rhesus and marmoset monkeys until fifteen years after the first isolation of ES cells in mice. The reagents such as interleukin 6 that maintain mouse ES cells in their proliferating and undifferentiated state do not work in primate ES cells; new experimental embryology systems and reagents

---

18.   *Human Stem Cell Research* (Australian Academy of Science, 2001), 11–12.

needed to be developed. The mouse is a good experimental model in some respects, with short generation times. Researchers at the University of Adelaide have found factors that control different-tiation and de-differentiation of mouse ES cells.[19]

(v) Research on pluripotent mesenchymal stem cells: cells from bone marrow of adults which do not carry markers on their surface that lead to rejection. These cells may differentiate into bone, fat or possibly muscle.
Pluripotent means that the cells are not capable of developing into all tissue types. The possibilities of these cells in the context of totipotent stem cells have recently been reviewed in detail and this review is an important resource for reflection on the scientific issues.[20]

Why are embryonic stem cells important?
The Royal Society's update on stem cell research summarises the British position:[21]

- Degenerative diseases and serious injuries to organs and tissues may be treated through stem cell therapies.
- Research on human embryonic stem cells will be required to investigate all of the potential therapies because other cell types, such as adult stem cells, may not have the same breadth of applications.
- The proposed legislative controls will be sufficient to prevent reproductive cloning while still allowing the development of therapeutic applications of cloning technology.
- New regulations under the 1990 Human Fertilisation and Embryology Act, which would allow research on human embryonic stem cells,

19. Professor Peter Rathgen, private communication.
20. *Nature* 414 (2001): 87–131.
21. *Stem Cell Research and Therapeutic Cloning: An Update* (London: The Royal Society, 2000).

are scientifically necessary to realise fully the potential of stem cell therapies.

In Australia there is much scientific and public interest in these experiments and some of the best research is being done in Melbourne, Adelaide and Sydney. *The Sydney Morning Herald*, for example, illustrates this with the headline 'Created in the Lab: Cells for Brain Repairs', and follows:

> . . . An Israeli research team has taken a step towards using human embryo tem cells to repair brain damage . . . The scientists convert human ES cells into pre cursor brain cells in the laboratory before injecting them into the brains of baby mice . . . They found the new cells migrated into many areas and grew into three different kinds of brain tissue, including neurons . . . Human ear cells can form all 220 types of tissue in the body. The research could lead to treatments for Parkinson's disease, motor neurone disease, heart failure and diabetes.[22]

The work is now published.[23]

Possible alternatives to embryonic stem cells

As a consequence of the way in which these cells are derived, some concerns have been expressed about the use of embryonic stem cells for therapeutic purposes. Alternatives under investigation include:

- reversal of differentiation of adult cells,
- isolation of dispersed stem cells in adults,
- culture of primordial germ cells.

The first of these methods has recently been reported as tested in Los Angeles (USA) and by PPI Therapeutics (Scotland) using cow cells. The method is to transfer cytoplasm* from an egg cell into ordinary adult cells. The egg cytoplasm seems to turn the specialised adult cells back into an undifferentiated state.

---

22. *The Sydney Morning Herald*, 1 and 2 December 2001, 3.
23. *Nature Biotechnology*, 1 December 2001.

Additional ways involve parthenogenesis where, under the influence of a chemical agent, the egg cell develops an additional set of maternal chromosomes* and then develops as if it had been fertilised. Some insects and birds reproduce that way but in mammals, having two sets of maternal chromosomes causes such severe problems that parthenogenic embryos never develop into a normal fetus. Nevertheless a recent patent to Advanced Cell Technology (USA) describes the production of embryonic stem cell–like cells from parthenogenic monkey embryos. These stayed undifferentiated for four months when placed with mouse 'feeder cells' and differentiated into skin and heart cells when the 'feeders' were removed. When produced from a woman there could be a close immunological match.

All of the above methods are in a relatively early stage of understanding though there is certainly promise in the work. The moratorium on CNT proposed by the Andrews Committee in Australia reflects a view that some of these methods might be achievable in a period of the order of three years.

In the light of all this, we are of the opinion:

That research on both embryonic stem cells and the alternative approaches should be permitted subject to strict guidelines.

The ethics

These startling advances in biotechnology raise ethical and moral problems which the whole community needs to think through and then act upon. In this context we can only hope to sketch some of the ethical issues involved.

The grounds for rejection of the cloning of people are for the most part philosophical and practical and have been widely debated. At the foundation of many of these philosophical views lie convictions about human life such as those famously expressed by Immanuel Kant.

> Every human being has a legitimate claim in respect
> from his fellow human beings and is in turn bound
> to respect every other. Humanity itself is a dignity;
> for a human being cannot be used merely as a

means by any human being . . . but must always be
used at the same time as an end. It is just in this that
his dignity (personality) consists, by which he raises
himself above all other beings in the world that are
not human beings . . . and so over all things.[24.]

This appreciation of the intrinsic dignity and value of each human
being, put in the context of contemporary biomedical technology, is
often interpreted as strongly encouraging the therapeutic aspects of
the science, but just as strongly forbidding any disrespectful
manipulation of human life for selfish ends by the same science.

The reasons for cloning humans already considered are by no
means uniformly rejected or accepted. Different individuals and
different traditions come to different conclusions on these complex
and diverse matters. This relativism of views is one of the grounds on
which some critics argue for a 'fail safe' position and reject all
cloning-related activities as being the first steps on a 'slippery slope'
to the commodification of human life.

Some would prefer that the possibility of human cloning had
never been discovered, or at least had been suppressed. However,
this is as unrealistic as it was for Brutus to speculate about Caesar:

> Fashion is thus; that what he is, augmented,
> would run to these and these extremities,
> And therefore think him as a serpent's egg
> Which hatch'd, would, as his kind,
>   grow mischievous,
> And kill him in the shell.
> (*Julius Caesar* Act 2, Scene i)

Additional, and at present, strong reasons of procedure add
weight to this rejection, at least for reproductive cloning. The first is
safety. Dolly was the single product of 277 attempts to get cell

---

24. Immanuel Kant, *The Metaphysics of Morals* (first published 1797),
    translated and edited by Mary Gregor (1996), 209. See the discussion
    by D Beyleveld and R Brownsword, 'Human Dignity, Human Rights,
    and Human Genetics', *Mod L Rev* 661 (1998): 665–667.

nuclear transfer to succeed to the extent of a live birth. Dolly now has premature arthritis and perhaps other ailments. A recent report says, 'Nearly all animal cloning experiments to date have suffered high rates of fetal and neonatal mortality . . . The abnormality rate is around 30 per cent.'

On the other hand, a new CNT procedure by the company Infigen claims to have surmounted some of these difficulties[25] and it is now suggested that mice cloned from somatic cells do not exhibit the 'imprinting abnormalities' thought to be the cause of many of the previous cloning failures.[26]

The second group of objections relates to implications about the status of donors and surrogates. Again, the Kantian notion of human beings as ends not means is central here. Can human beings or their reproductive systems ever be considered as commodities? And to what extent would use of a human egg or even human DNA contravene the Kantian principles?

Other 'in principle' objections to cloning people involve matters such as the threat to the essential privacy and integrity of the individual produced, and considerations related to the potential which the method holds for eugenic manipulation. There seems to be uniform international agreement that CNT procedures should not affect the 'germ line', that is should not alter the transferred DNA from the donor so as to genetically alter the inheritance of the cells produced. A long way in the future, the possibilities for eliminating genetically transferred conditions (such as diabetes) may suggest a revision of this attitude.

The theology

Background
The encounter of faith with scientific discovery is, of course, far from a new experience for the church. It reaches back at least to the unhappy confrontation between the Roman Catholic Church and the ideas of Galileo and Copernicus about the earth moving around the sun. In more recent times, advances in genetics, cell biology and

---

25. *Chemistry and Industry*, 17 December 2001, 785.
26. *Science* 295 (2002): 297.

experimental methods such as microinjection techniques have been at least as profound and disturbing. Examples include the discovery of the double helix, description of the human genome* and those of an ever increasing number of other species, the possibilities springing from the cloning from adult cells (the Dolly experiment), and the discovery of human embryonic stem cells and their totipotency. These advances have changed the practice of medicine in many areas and will have an increasing impact on the way in which it develops in the future.

The ethical problems raised confront the church with a challenge. Our job as thinking and believing people is to understand as best we can what modern biomedical science implies and to respond to it in the light of the revelation of God given in scripture and the tradition of the church. It is not a question of discarding one in favour of the other. On the one hand, science continues to advance, theories change and human understanding of the world deepens. But, on the other, there remains the profound revelation of the nature of God, the sanctity of life, and the ambiguity of the human heart, given to us through the wisdom faith. Living with and between these two great gifts at times produces tension. But we believe it can be a creative tension if tackled with faithful and open minds.

The contribution of theology to the biotechnology debate will be considered through four fundamental doctrines of the church: the belief in creation, the meaning of the *imago dei* (image of God), the reality of sin, and the significance of redemption.

Creation
In common with the Islamic tradition, the Judaeo-Christian faith understands God as creator of all things. This affirmation underpins to all else that is said about God. The Nicene Creed summarises Christian theology of creation in its opening sentence: 'We believe in God, the Father, the almighty, maker of heaven and earth, of all that is, seen and unseen.' (cf Genesis 1, Isaiah 40:28–31, 44:24–26, Psalm 89:24–26, 90:1–2, 146:5–6. Also John 1:1–12, Colossians 1:16ff, Revelation 4:11). Thus the creed firmly asserts that the world centres on God, not on human beings.

In dealing with the world—which for our purposes means dealings with biological entities and their components—we are handling things which are not in the first instance ours. All things belong first to God and, as creatures of God, reflect in their own ways the being and glory of God (Psalm 19:1). To exist at all entails a dignity, mystery and integrity that calls for respect and honour. Beings are not just so much stuff that we are free to treat in whatever way suits our interests.

Accordingly, a theological perspective on the world as God's *creature* has implications for the way biological entities may be manipulated. Actions which are fundamentally disrespectful of life, for example cruelty to animals in experiments, or the treatment of human genetic material as a commercial commodity, deserve to be seriously questioned.

The image of God
The most profound scriptural statement about human beings is that they are created in God's own image (*imago dei*). 'So God created humankind in his image, in the image of God he created them, male and female he created them.' (Genesis 1:27) Whereas this fundamental constitution of human beings is often distorted or disfigured in us (this is the meaning of 'sin', of which more in a moment), Jesus Christ is seen in the New Testament to be the undistorted and unsurpassable reflection of the being of God in human existence (cf 2 Corinthians 4:4, Colossians 1:15, Hebrews 1:3). This theology of the human person has been the subject of extensive debate throughout Christian history. But whatever else may be true, if human beings are created in the image of God, they possess and express qualities of being that are (no doubt in a time-bound and creaturely way) analogous to the qualities and being of God. Qualities such as life, freedom, intelligence, will, love and the capacity to relate all define what it means to be human, and all are founded in the life and nature of God as Creator. This has two important ethical implications.

Dignity
Theologically conceived, the *dignity* of the human person (and, by extension, the human community) is not instrumental but intrinsic. In other words, human beings are not valuable only because of what they achieve, do, possess, or contribute to society, still less to the

economy. They are valuable because of what they *are* in themselves, God's creatures made in God's image. Following Kant, this means, that human beings must always be treated as *ends* and never only as *means*. A theology of the human person therefore raises questions about any cloning techniques that turn human beings (in whole or in part) into utilitarian or even manufactured objects, at the mercy of the power and interests of some other person or group.

This view of dignity also impinges on the debate about when human life begins. Conservative (mainly Roman Catholic) theology argues that human life begins from the moment of conception and therefore human dignity must be affirmed of the embryo from the moment of fertilisation. This position is highly critical of any interference with or termination of the development of the embryo, since it is regarded as possessing all the rights and dignity we should afford a being made in God's image. Any manipulation of the embryo for purposes other than nurture along its natural path toward full human development is seen as a violation of a God-given value and therefore to be resisted strongly.

Clearly the Catholic approach is a significant challenge to almost any embryonic experimentation. While in our view this position is too extreme, its importance nonetheless is that it confronts us squarely with the question of the intrinsic dignity and integrity of the human organism from the outset. Such moral and theological seriousness is an important part of the context of all experimental actions on human life at whatever stage.

Other theological traditions adopt a more developmental approach, understanding the formation of human personhood as a process rather than a one-off completed act. As early as the high Middle Ages, for example, St Thomas Aquinas followed the Aristotelian idea of a *process* from conception to birth of humans.[27] He saw it in three stages—the 'vegetative' (living but not feeling) stage, the 'sensitive' stage (this emerges when the baby begins to kick inside the womb) and finally comes the stage sometime before parturition of the 'animate soul' (when the fetus is fully human). Aquinas' own perception of staged human development was: 'The

---

27. See Norman Ford, *When Did I Begin?* (Cambridge: Cambridge University Press, 1997).

embryo has first of all a soul which is merely sensitive, and when this is removed, it is supplanted by a more perfect soul, which is both sensitive and intellectual.'[28]

In the light of contemporary science, this may be seen as a rough depiction of a highly complex process. But it does allow for a more open-ended theology of human gestation. An immediately fertilised human egg may be seen as a human being in potential, but not in full actuality. Therefore what may be appropriate in terms of human manipulation of the process of 'hominisation' (the emergence of a human being) at one stage of development may not be acceptable at another. Somewhere between fertilisation of the egg and birth of the baby a stage is reached where human qualities are sufficiently established to demand recognition of the biological, moral, spiritual and legal status of a being human.

In our judgment, theology alone is not competent to determine this point. Scientific, moral, legal and common-sense considerations are also required. However, from this more open perspective on a theology of the image of God, not only is there no compelling reason to forbid the use of embryo research for beneficial ends, there may be strong reasons to celebrate and support it.

While caution is in order, the position taken by the Human Fertilisation and Embryology Act of 1991 in the United Kingdom is a useful guide at this point. That act forbids the culture of human embryos beyond the first fourteen days, and also forbids the replacement in the uterus of any embryo used for research.[29]

---

28. Thomas Aquinas, *Summa Theologica*, volume 1, first part Q76, translated by Laurence Shapcote (Chicago: Encyclopaedia Britannica Inc, 1991), 392.

29. 1991 Human Fertilisation and Embryology Act (HFE)
-1998 HGAC/HFEA recommends licences be issued for human ES research.
-2000 House of Commons votes for human ES cell research.
-2001 House of Lords votes yes
-2001 European Parliament says stop UK.
Nature 414 (2001): 838, reported: 'Among the major scientific nations, Britain emerged in 2001 as an enthusiastic supporter of ES-cell research, amending its law to allow ES cells to be isolated from human blastocysts—the hollow ball of cells that forms after some five days of embryological development—for research into regenerative medicine.'

It is worth noting that this position has been urged by the Church of England. Addressing the House of Lords on 28 April 1999, the Bishop of Oxford (the Rt Revd Richard Harries) stated:

> The Church of England's Board for Social Responsibility, which I chair, is totally opposed to the cloning of embryos for reproductive purposes. On research using nuclear replacement technology for therapeutic purposes, there is greater division of opinion . . . I take a developmental view of the human person and believe that the recommendation of the Warnock Report, now enshrined in law, that the formation of the primitive streak* 14 days after conception as that clear point beyond which all research should be banned . . . Before that point, in the very early cluster of cells, it is not yet clear which will develop into a distinct individual. Furthermore . . . it is a fact that in nature itself as many as three-quarters of the eggs which are fertilised are lost anyway in the normal course of events, most before they implant in their mother's womb about a week after conception.[30]

Human creativity

Second, the creation of humankind in the image of God implies that we share one of the most fundamental characteristics of God—the power of creation itself. Humans are endowed with the capacity to discover the 'new', to give expression to what has not yet been. Of course, human creativity is creaturely. God creates *ex nihilo* (out of nothing). By contrast, human beings interact with a world already created by God. We, therefore, are at best *co-creators* with God. Art, music, science, technology, friendship, politics, language, indeed every human activity, reflects this co-creative capacity to some degree or another.

The achievements of science are among the most impressive examples of the creative operation of the image of God in

---

30. See Hansard, House of Lords, 28 April 1999.

humankind. The era of biotechnology holds promise of being one of the greatest of all cocreative adventures of the human spirit yet undertaken. It has already disclosed breathtaking wonders and powers marked by beauty and the possibility of good. Where it is undertaken in conformity with the principle of humankind's dignity as created in the image of God, this work deserves theological celebration and even the praise of God! Like all things human, however, it can be pursued unethically, or even for depraved ends. At this point of the discussion, the church has a significant contribution to make.

Sin

The idea that humankind is made in the image of God, and invited to be coparticipants in the divine actions of creation, is certainly an important interpretation of human dignity, freedom and goodness. It is fundamental to any theological anthropology based on scripture. But by itself it tells only part of the story. The same capacity to reflect the being and nature of God includes the possibility of using our human powers for ends that distort or even oppose the purposes of God.

Freedom (creativity) is a divine gift. And it is *really* given to human beings. But, as we know, it is often used for selfish, destructive and violent ends. The scriptures call this 'sin', the abuse of the divine image. The story of the state-sponsored execution of Jesus, who is regarded by the New Testament writers as the most transparent presence of the image of God in all history, demonstrates how destructive human action, thought and imagination can be. Jeremiah's words: 'The heart is devious above all else; it is perverse—who can understand it?' (Jeremiah 17:9, cf. Romans 3:23) may sound harsh. But in the face of war, torture, rape, greed, injustice, oppression, violence, terrorism and the like, they begin to seem like nothing less than the sober truth. The great theologian Reinhold Niebuhr once quipped that the only empirically demonstrable doctrine of the Christian creed is that of (original) sin.

All use of human creativity is ambiguous. Biological science is no exception. The possibilities for good are very clear: diagnosis of illness, repair of injured or diseased tissues, prolongation of healthy life, reversal or prevention of genetic defects, organ transplants, and so on. We can celebrate the divine image reflected in such work. But greedy, manipulative and violent uses of the same technology can occur. Manufactured body parts (and even whole persons) for economic, political or military gain, the use of fetuses as factories for human 'spare parts', the development of procedures for so-called 'designer babies', cross species hybridisation, wanton genetic modification of food crops and so on, are dangerous and at the limit immoral.

A theological understanding of the sinful capacity of human beings encourages us to be vigilant in choosing ethical guidelines and taking policy initiatives for the development of this new science and technology. The potential for good is shadowed by the possibility of evil. In being attentive to the first possibility we need to be careful that we are not unmindful of the second.

Redemption
From the beginning of the biblical witness, God is revealed as a God of redemption, concerned with the suffering, sickness and violence of the world. According to scripture, God comes near in healing, saving and peace-giving. Moses' encounter with God at the burning bush sets the stage for the Judaeo-Christian understanding of God as saviour:

> Then the Lord said, 'I have observed the misery of my people who are in Egypt; I have heard their cry on account of their taskmasters. Indeed, I know their sufferings, and I have come down to deliver them . . .' (Exodus 3:7)

This redemptive mission of God is comes to a climax in the life and work of Jesus Christ. In the synagogue at Nazareth, Jesus announced the purpose of his life with the words:

> The Spirit of the Lord is upon me, because he has anointed me to bring good news to the poor. He has sent me to proclaim release to the captives and recovery of sight to the blind, to let the oppressed go

free, to proclaim the year of the Lord's favour (Luke
4:18–19, cf Isaiah 61:1–11).

God's concern for those who suffer and are oppressed (whatever
form the affliction might take) is undeniable in the scriptural
narrative. Human cooperation with God as redeemer is an invitation
and imperative of the Gospel. The church's involvement with
healing, hospitals and medical research is long and honourable. The
biotechnical revolution represents a radical new development of this
dimension of human participation in the healing work of God.
Within appropriate limits it is to be welcomed and supported.
In the light of all this, we are of the opinion:

*That our churches be encouraged to become informed about and join in the
national debate on bioethical questions, with the particular intention of
bringing to bear the insights of the Christian tradition on the matter.*

The law
One way in which to manage an environment where humankind has
a tendency to immoral and self-destructive behaviour is through the
law. This is a significant issue in regard to the science of human
cloning. It is, of course, possible at law to proscribe certain kinds of
cloning. It is also possible, however, to legislate to enable particular
kinds of cloning.

International responses
The Royal Society has suggested reasons for 'enabling legislation'
rather than 'forbidding legislation'. This view has influenced the
Parliament of the United Kingdom. In November 2000, the Royal
Society prepared a report on stem cell research and therapeutic
cloning. It concluded that:

> . . . it is very unlikely that scientists will be able to
> answer within the next 10 years all of the
> outstanding questions about stem cells and it might
> be several decades before we achieve a full
> understanding of how the specialised state of cells is
> achieved and maintained.

Scientists still need to discover how stem cells from non-embryonic sources can be extracted, kept alive in the laboratory, multiplied for extended periods of time and directed to form specific types of specialised cells. Scientists might never be able to overcome all of the hurdles blocking the path to the therapeutic use of adult rather than embryonic stem cells.[31]

The 1997 UNESCO Universal Declaration on the Human Genome and Human Rights states:

Practices which are contrary to human dignity, such as reproductive cloning of human beings, shall not be permitted.[32]

Australia

The Australian Academy of Science papers summarise the Australian and international legal attitudes to human cloning and stem cell research to the year 2001. The cloning of individual human beings is prohibited by state legislation in Victoria, South Australia and Western Australia. It is also prohibited by NHMRC Ethical guidelines on assisted reproductive technology.[33]

The Andrews report provides recent legal appraisal in Australia. The conclusions of that committee (August 2001) included:
- a ban on the cloning of human beings,
- a moratorium of three years on application of cloning techniques in humans to give adequate time for public discussion and development of a national approach for oversight of ethical and safety issues,

---

31. http://www.royalsoc.ac.uk.
32. Cited in Scientific, Ethical and Regulatory Considerations Relevant to Cloning of Human Beings, NHMRC 16 December 1998, 1.
33. *Ethical Guidelines on Assisted Reproductive Technology* (Sydney: AGPS 1996).

- a majority opinion that research on embryos should be permitted, but only on embryos surplus to assisted fertility programs. A national licensing body would regulate such research.[34]

In the light of all this, we are of the opinion:

That these aspects of the Andrews Committee report and recommendations be endorsed.

Conclusions

In accord with international opinion and the recent Andrews Committee report to the Australian Parliament, we believe the church should reject the use of CNT methods to produce clones of people. There is no real support for reproductive cloning either in Australia or internationally.

However, we do support the exploration of alternative therapeutic pathways to ES cells. We are convinced of the potential of cloning techniques for therapeutic purposes, in particular the possibilities of human embryonic and other stem cells for human tissue repair. While we acknowledge that the issue is complex and that opinions differ, we believe there are good philosophical and theological arguments in support of the derivation of human embryonic stem cells from 'surplus' in vitro fertilisation embryos, and also the purposeful use of CNT to produce those embryos for experimental purposes aimed at new therapies for human disease.

We conclude that, as with the debate on the acceptability of in vitro fertilisation twenty years ago, there is a sustainable position theologically and philosophically to allow both CNT procedures and the derivation of human embryonic stem cells using them. However, this should be done under strictly licensed conditions so as to permit scientific inquiry to proceed towards therapeutic goals without abuse of the dignity of human life. In this respect we accept (while acknowledging opposition to) the arbitrary fourteen-day period from

---

34. A full statement of the Report can be found at: House of Representatives Standing Committee on Legal and Constitutional Affairs, 'Inquiry into Scientific, Ethical and Regulatory Aspects of Cloning', Submissions volume 5 (261–286, 683-783)
www.aph.gov.au/house/committee/laca/index.htm.

fertilisation as the limit of the time in which it should be permissible for the human embryo to be the subject of experimental cloning procedures. Though this timeline is later than fertilisation itself, we consider the moment of penetration of the sperm into the ovum as equally arbitrary from the point of view of the existence of a new human being. We are not convinced of a theological or philosophical basis for seeing that process as instantaneous.

In the light of all that has been said we encourage the people of God, with due caution in the face of human sinfulness, to celebrate and affirm the God given nature of such remarkable scientific developments as we have seen unfold in the last few years. We need not fear science, but rather see it, when rightly pursued, as an aspect of God's revelation and a participation in God's creative and redemptive purposes in the world.

Glossary and explanatory notes
(Adapted from Alexander)
References in the text to this glossary are marked with an asterisk.

Blastocyst: A cluster of cells following early cleavage of the fertilised egg, consisting of outer cells that have the potential to form placenta and an inner cell mass with the potential to form an embryo. The first signs of the embryo appear as the 'primitive streak', about 14 days after fertilisation.

Chromosomes: DNA structures in the nucleus of a cell. Chromosomes carry the heredity factors, genes, and are present in constant numbers in each species. In humans, there are forty-six (twenty-three pairs) in each cell, except in the mature ovum and sperm where there are twenty-three single chromosomes. A complete set of twenty-three is inherited from each parent.

CNT: See Nuclear replacement

cloning: Production of a cell or organism with the same nuclear genome as another cell or organism (see also Reproductive cloning, Therapeutic cloning, and Explanatory cotes)

Cytoplasm: The contents of a cell other than the nucleus. Cytoplasm consists of a fluid containing numerous structures, eg mitochondria that carry out essential cell functions.

differentiation: The process cells undergo as they mature. Differentiated cells have distinctive characteristics, perform specific functions and are less likely to divide.

Diploid: A cell with a full set of genetic material, consisting of chromosomes in matching pairs. A diploid cell has one chromosome from each parental set. Most animal cells have a diploid set of chromosomes. The diploid human genome has forty-six chromosomes.

DNA: Deoxyribonucleic acid, found primarily in the nucleus of cells arranged into chromosomes (some DNA is also found in mitochondria). DNA carries coded information for making all the structures and materials that the body needs to function.

Ectoderm: Outermost layer of embryo in early development.

Egg: The mature female germ cell, also called the ovum or oocyte.

Embryo: the developing human organism from the time of fertilisation until the main organs have developed, eight weeks after fertilisation. After this time the organism becomes known as a fetus.

Embryonic stem (ES) cell line: Cultured cells obtained by isolation of inner cell mass cells from blastocysts or by isolation of primordial germ cells from a fetus. ES cells cannot give rise to an embryo if placed in the uterus.

Enucleated egg: An egg from which the nucleus has been removed.

Fertilisation: The process whereby male and female gametes unite, beginning when a sperm contacts the outside of the egg and ending with the union of the male and female nuclei to form the zygote.

Fetus: The term used for a human embryo after the eighth week of development until birth.

Gametes: The sperm and egg cells, which contain single copies of each chromosome.

Gene: Genes are defined sequences in DNA, carried on the chromosomes and are responsible for the inherited characteristics that distinguish one individual from another. Each human individual has an estimated 100,000 separate genes. See also Explanatory note.

Genome: The complete genetic make up of a cell or organism.

Germ cell: A reproductive cell precursor that will eventually give rise to a sperm or ovum. All other body cells are somatic cells.

In vitro: In glass, referring to a process or reaction carried out in a test-tube or culture dish.

Mesoderm: Middle germ-layer of embryo.

Mesenchymal stem cells: Cells from bone marrow of adults, which do not carry markers on their surface that lead to rejection. These cells may differentiate into bone, fat or possibly muscle.

Nuclear replacement (cell nuclear transfer or CNT): A technique that involves placing the nucleus from a diploid cell into an egg from which the nucleus has been removed.

Nucleus (*pl* nuclei): The central protoplasm of the cell that contains the chromosomes.

Pluripotent: A cell or embryonic tissue capable of producing more than one type of cell or tissue.

Primordial germ cells: Precursor reproductive cells in an embryo or fetus.

Primitive streak: A dark, thickened longitudinal band that forms at one end of the embryonic disc, consisting of a surface layer of ectoderm overlying a thickened mass of mesoderm cells. It marks the future longitudinal axis of the embryo.

Reproductive Cloning: The production of a human fetus from a single cell by asexual reproduction. See also Explanatory note.

Somatic cell: Any cell of an embryo, fetus, child or adult not destined to become a sperm or egg cell.

Stem cell: An undifferentiated cell, which is a precursor to a number of differentiated (specialised) cell types. Stem cells may be totipotent, pluripoten, or committed to a particular cell lineage (eg neural stem cell).

Therapeutic cloning: Applications of cloning technology which do not result in the production of genetically identical fetuses or babies such as the use of stem cells as a therapy for medical disorders

Totipotent: Capable of giving rise to all types of differentiated cell found in that organism. A single totipotent cell could, by division, reproduce the whole organism.

Acknowledgements
We would like to thank Dr Denis R Alexander, Editor, *Science and Christian Belief*, Cambridge UK, Mr Richard Refshauge, Chancellor of the Diocese of Canberra and Goulburn, Bishop Tom Frame, Bishop to the Armed Forces and the Revd Peter Grundy for their comments on this paper.

Authors

Dr Fraser Bergersen
Fraser John Bergersen, AM, DSc, FAA, FRS, is a microbiologist and Visiting Fellow at the School of Biochemistry and Molecular Biology, Faculty of Science, Australian National University. He was, for forty years, a Chief Research Scientist, CSIRO Division of Plant Industry, Canberra, and is a member of the Canberra Baptist Church.

Dr Jonathan Clarke

Jonathan Clarke is a member of St Matthews, Wanniassa. His work as a geologist has given him an interest in understanding how science and technology are to be best understood and used from a Christian perspective. Jonathan is on the board of ISCAST, the Institute for the Study of Christianity in an Age of Science and Technology (iscast.org.au) and is editor of the ISCAST Bulletin.

Mrs Patricia Ewing

Patricia Ewing, BAppSci MLS, MAppSci. Patricia has worked in medical research (immunology, molecular biology and protein chemistry), IVF, and clinical pathology. She is currently employed by ACT Pathology at the Canberra Hospital.

Dr Graeme Garrett

Graeme Garrett is the Pat Wardle Senior Lecturer in Theology at St Mark's National Theological Centre in Canberra. He is a priest in the Diocese of Canberra & Goulburn. His major interests are contemporary theology, preaching and social ethics.

Professor John White, Chairman

John W White, CMG, FAA, FRS, is chairman of the board of ISCAST (Institute for the Study of Christianity in an Age of Science and Technology) and president of the Royal Australian Chemical Institute. He is a professor of Physical and Theoretical Chemistry in the Research School of Chemistry at the Australian National University's Institute of Advanced Studies, where he has been since 1985.

A Process-based Model for an Ontology of Activity

Richard Campbell

Abstract

The paper proposes a process-based model for an ontology that encompasses the emergence of increasing complex systems. Starting with a division of processes into those that are stable and those that are fleeting, it is built through a series of exclusive and exhaustive disjunctions. The crucial distinction is between those cohesive and stable systems that are energy wells, and those that are far-from-equilibrium. The latter are necessarily open—they can persist only by interaction with their environments Further distinctions, developed by means of the notions of self-maintenance and error detection, lead to the identification of complex biological organisms that are flexible learners. This model provides a nonreductive model for understanding human beings as both emergent and yet embodied. In particular, it provides a way of characterising action as 'metaphysically deep', not an ontological embarrassment within an otherwise physicalist world. How are we to understand ourselves and the world? I sketch here a metaphysical model as a radical alternative to the reductive microphysicalist picture generally assumed by popular writers and philosophers alike.[1]

1.   I am indebted to Mark Bickhard, Cliff Hooker and Wayne Christensen
     for the ideas that I have assembled in this paper.

Processes

Contemporary physics tells us that *there are no fundamental particles.* Quantum field theory shifts the basic ontology of the universe from microparticles to quantum fields. If nothing is fundamentally a substance-like particle, that suggests that all things have to be conceived fundamentally as *processes* of various scales and complexity, having causal efficacy in themselves. What have seemed to be particles are now conceptualised as particle-like processes and interactions resulting from the quantisation of field processes and interactions, and those are no more particles than are the integer number of oscillatory waves produced by plucking a guitar string. Each of these so-called things is a quantised field process. The world consists of *organised fields* in process—all the way down, and all the way up.[2]

Upon that basis, this paper builds up, step by step, a model of ontological kinds, through a series of disjunctions. Articulating the model in this way might give the appearance of being *a priori*, but that is only superficial. The selection of these disjunctions is informed by the outcomes of many empirical investigations. Unlike the *a priori* dogmatism of physicalists, this model is empirically grounded.

Stability

Processes exist *only* in some organisation or other. Some organisations of process are fleeting, such as Newton's legendary falling apple. Others are stable, or at least relatively stable—indeed, some persist for eons. These simple observations yield another crucial disjunction: *either the organisation of a process is stable relative to its environment, or it is not.* That distinction is the first step in this model.

---

2. See, for example, Mark Bickhard, 'A Process Model of the Emergence of Representation', in *Emergence, Complexity, Hierarchy, Organisation, Selected and Edited Papers from the ECHO III Conference*, edited by GL Farre and T Oksala (Espoo, Finland: Acta Polytechnica Scandinavica, Mathematics, Computing and Management in Engineering Series number 91, 3–7 August 1998), 263–270, and his 'Autonomy, Function and Representation', *Communication and Cognition*, special issue on Artificial Intelligence, 17 (2000): 111–131.

Cohesion

Some processes are stable in certain ways, but not in others. In particular, some groups of processes manifest stability in ways that are sufficient to demarcate them from their environment as integral systems, whereas others exhibit certain sorts of stability, but do not constitute cohesive systems. Consider a group of gas molecules: it assumes whatever shape and condition its containing environment imposes, and it will simply disperse if it is not constrained by a closed container. Whilst most gases are chemically stable, the group of gas molecules does not manifest any overall integration: a quantity of a gas has no internal cohesion. But there are many kinds of processes that do, and that consequently are stable not only over time but also against perturbation. Accordingly, the next step is to distinguish, amongst processes that manifest some sort of stability, *those that constitute cohesive systems from those that are not.*

A *cohesive* system is one in which different elements are held together by dynamical bonds between them, which have the effect of individuating the system from its environment.[3] Accordingly, wherever we find such a system, we are able to identify and reidentify it. That is what licenses our calling it an entity. What makes components into a cohesive system—into an identifiable entity—are the internal bonds that constrain the behaviour of its constituent subprocesses in such a way that the totality behaves dynamically as an integral whole. These bonds arise from, although they are not reducible to, features of those quantum processes that constitute all of the components of a system. For example, the molecular bonds in the crystal lattice of a rock cause the rock as a whole to behave as a unified system under a large range of interactions—if it is kicked with moderate force, it moves relative to the ground. Contrast what

---

3. The notion that systems can be individuated in a principled way has been dismissed as ad hoc, arbitrary and observer-relative. But there are many causal properties that can serve as a basis for principled specifications of system identity that are not observer-dependent. See JD Collier, 'Supervenience and Reduction in Biological Hierarchies', *Canadian Journal of Philosophy*, supp volume, *Biology and Philosophy* (Calgary: University of Calgary Press, Calgary, 1988), and WD Christensen and Mark H Bickhard, 'The Process Dynamics of Normative Function', *The Monist*, 85(1) (2002): 3–28.

happens when a pile of sand is kicked—the causal interactions between the grains of sand do not form bonds strong enough for the pile to behave as an integral system when it is kicked. Consequently, it scatters.

Of course, any system coheres only within a limited range of conditions. Hit the rock hard with a hammer and it will fracture, its cohesion will be disrupted. The cohesion conditions of any individual entity can be specified physically (for example, a rock is cohesive within a specifiable range of temperature and external forces). Whether a given system is cohesive with respect to the forces to which it is subject is a determinate matter. Now, the property of cohesion generates further causally significant properties. The internal bonds that cause the particles in a rock to hold together generate its mass, which is a holistic property. Likewise, it is the cohesion of a kite that allows it to fly, because the integrity of the kite's structure acts to sum the forces of the small interactions of air particles against it, generating a net lift force.

However cohesive systems (ie entities) are formed, they typically manifest properties that are different from those of their internal subprocesses. Some of these new properties result from an aggregation of the properties of the processes that are their constituents. For instance, the mass of a table is the aggregate of the mass of its four legs plus the mass of its top. They in turn are the aggregates of the mass of their constituent molecules. In such cases, the properties of the macro-level combination can be explained by an exhaustive and exclusive decomposition of the system into its proper parts. Nevertheless, it is important to note that more is involved in being a cohesive and causally effective aggregate than simply the arithmetical sum (that is, a bare conjunction) of its constituents. The components have to *stick together*, somehow or other, in order to effect a difference. And sticking together requires internal bonds.

Now, although certain properties of cohesive systems can be explained as resulting from aggregations of their internal parts, some systems are such that some of their properties cannot be so explained. There are at least four different conditions under which a system property may be an aggregate of the properties of its proper parts. I do not have space to elaborate them here. But the failure of system properties to satisfy one or more of these conditions provides precise and distinct senses in which they can be said to be 'more than the sum of the parts' of that system. It is evident that there are many macro-entities whose properties cannot be understood at all in terms of aggregation. These nonaggregative properties are crucial to causal emergence. Contemporary science now understands a good deal more about how different kinds of bonds organise their constituent processes into systems of significantly different kinds. Not all cohesive systems result from static bonding as rocks do—others, such as living cells involve more dynamical relationships.

Yet even in the case of rocks, many of whose properties *can* be explained by aggregating the properties of the molecules it is made of, those microcomponents themselves exhibit properties that cannot in turn be derived by aggregation of any kind from their internal subprocesses—they are emergent. Yet those components are also stable, cohesive systems. A molecule of silica, for example, also exhibits cohesion, but it has emergent properties—unlike the properties of a rock itself.

The crucial difference is between those systems whose cohesion is produced by bonds that have aggregative effects and those whose cohesion is produced by dynamical bonds that have nonaggregative, nonlinear effects. Combinations of the latter kind bring into being new quantum fields with novel properties. The key point is that the fusion involved produces new unified wholes, with causal powers that cannot be derived by simply referring to the separate causal powers of its constituents, considered apart. It is the role of the empirical sciences to explicate more precisely the ways in which these bonding processes produce unified entities with novel properties, but the general phenomenon they seek to explicate is not hostage to any particular scientific theory. What is ontologically significant is that, in these cases of nonlinear unification, the properties of the whole are somehow 'more' than the arithmetical sum of its parts—such system properties, and the causal powers of such a system, are *emergent*. Emergence should no longer be viewed as a dubious metaphysical mystery, but as explicable in terms of nonlinear functions.

It follows that there is a simple link between cohesion and emergence: whenever a complex of processes organises itself into a new cohesive system by forming internal bonds that involve nonlinear forces, the resultant entity has emergent properties and powers. The result is the familiar picture of a multilayered model of the world as stratified into different levels, in a micro-to-macro hierarchy. The Cartesian model of two substances—mind and matter—has long been outdated, but the usual response is to reject just one (usually mind). Thereby materialism, or physicalism as this philosophical position is more often called these days, simply perpetuates the Cartesian framework. I call it a 'one-legged' version of Cartesianism. We need a new model of Nature that genuinely moves beyond Cartesianism altogether. In this new model of Nature, entities, characterised by their distinctive properties and processes, *emerge* out of the processes that constitute the entities, properties, and processes of the levels below it. At the bottom is a level consisting of quantum fields, or whatever our best physics in the future tells us are the basic constituents out of which our world is generated. As we go up the levels, we successively encounter atoms, molecules, cells, multicellular organisms, human beings, social groups and institutions etc.

Energy-well and far-from-equilibrium stability
The next step focuses on those cohesive systems whose dynamical bonds generate nonlinear (that is, nonaggregative, emergent) properties. The processes that constitute cohesive, relatively stable systems do not all operate in the same way—in fact, the resultant entities form a range that can be characterised by the two fundamental types that provide its end points. These two types of entity manifest ontologically different forms of stability. They are: (1) energy well stability, and (2) far-from-equilibrium stability.

'Energy wells' are cohesive process systems that persist at or near thermodynamic equilibrium, and whose organisation can be disrupted only by an input, from external sources, of a critical level of energy. Typically, such a disruption of their organisational structure can only be brought about by a higher level of energy than they typically encounter in their ambient environment. Hence they are very stable, cohesive and robust.

Atoms are straightforward examples: they are a furious process of electron waves around an even more furious dance of quarks and gluons. In general, atomic processes are strongly cohesive and can be destabilised only by being bombarded by a great deal of external energy.

Combinations of such stable 'energy well' processes exist at the macroscopic level, yielding new, larger entities. For example, where different kinds of atoms interact in certain stable ways, they produce molecules with significantly different properties from those of the kinds of atoms that are their constituents. The organisational structure of hydrogen and oxygen atoms are such that two electron waves belonging to hydrogen atoms can come to participate in the outer 'shell' of an oxygen atom to produce a molecule of a new stable compound, H_2O. The resulting molecule of water has very different properties from the kinds of atoms that are its constituents. Strictly speaking, the constituent atoms of hydrogen and oxygen no longer exist. The configuration of their quantum fields has actually *changed* as a result of this fusion of their respective configurations, considered separately. They have been replaced by a new field, with quite new properties.[4]

The distinctive and most original feature of the model being articulated here, however, is its extended account of the *second* kind of cohesive and stable organisation with emergent properties. The phenomenon of far-from-equilibrium stability poses a significant puzzle: How is it possible? How could an organised process that is not in thermodynamic equilibrium not only persist for some significant period without moving to equilibrium, but also exhibit a robust form of cohesion in the face of environmental changes? That is the ontologically revealing question to ask.

The most primitive kind of stable process of this kind is a system that is kept going artificially, entirely by external means. In a chemical bath, for instance, interesting processes can persist because external pumps maintain a flow of the required chemicals from external reservoirs into the bath, while other pumps remove waste products. Until such a system is switched off, or runs out of chemicals, the chemical processes within the bath are sustained, but their stability is completely dependent upon its environmental

---

4.   For a more detailed discussion of such fusion, and of how it is to be understood in terms of the *replacement* of property instances, see Paul Humphreys, 'Aspects of Emergence', *Philosophical Topics*, 24 (1996).

conditions: the pumps and the supplies contained in the external reservoirs. Such a chemical bath is, of course, a human artefact. As we will shortly see, there are more significant instances of far-from-equilibrium stability that occur naturally.

But what enables any far-from-equilibrium system to survive are the ways its intrinsic processes keep interacting with its ambient environment. Its very persistence depends upon external supplies. In short, the stability of far-from-equilibrium processes is a function of their being *necessarily open* processes.

Self-maintenant systems

A chemical bath like that just described contributes nothing to the persistence of the conditions on which it depends for its own continuance. But there are many other relatively stable far-from-equilibrium systems that do. Here is the next exclusive and exhaustive disjunction invoked by the model: *such systems either contribute to the persistence of the conditions on which they depend, or they do not.* In terms of the development of the model, a candle flame is a familiar example that exhibits this distinctive difference from our simple chemical bath. For a candle flame is a process that makes several active contributions to its own persistence. It maintains its temperature above the combustion threshold, it vaporises wax into a continuing supply of fuel and, in usual atmospheric conditions, it induces convection currents, thus pulling in the oxygen it needs and removing the carbon dioxide produced by its own combustion.

Processes like this tend to maintain themselves—they exhibit *self-maintenance*. That provides another way of expressing this disjunction: *either relatively stable far-from-equilibrium systems are self-maintenant, or they are not.* The ability to be self-maintaining is an *emergent causal power* of the organisation of the candle flame, it cannot be explained simply as the physical resultant of the causal properties of its distinct constituents. Of course, in one sense its persistence is also dependent on its external conditions: when the candle flame has burnt all its wax, or it is deprived of oxygen, it ceases to be. But so long as the boundary conditions are fulfilled—so long as its external requirements for fuel and oxygen continue to be satisfied—it continues to contribute to its own persistence. It succeeds in maintaining its own process of burning. The ability of a complex system to do this is a holistic property of the system itself. That is one reason why its being self-maintenant cannot be explained in terms of the causal properties of its constituents.

So long as those processes keep the system operational, it will retain its integrity. But once they break down, either because of some fatal disruption from outside or because of aging, the system immediately begins to disintegrate. Some components will decay faster than others—in a dead body, bones last longer than muscles—but there is no sense in which a living body and the corpse left by its death are the *same* body. The former was an integral, self-maintaining system, the latter is *already* in the process of decomposing. That is implicit in the fact that these systems are far-from-equilibrium. Thus, decay proves to be the inescapable dark side of the processes crucial to this ontology.

Recursively self-maintenant systems
A further level of complexity is exhibited by systems that can maintain stability not only within certain ranges of conditions, but also within certain ranges of *changes* of conditions. That is, they can switch to deploying *different* processes depending on conditions they detect in the environment. A relatively simple example is a bacterium, which has the ability to swim up a sugar gradient, but which tumbles if it finds itself to be swimming down a sugar gradient. This lozenge-shaped bacterium has detectors at both ends. When the one at its 'front' detects a higher amount of dissolved sugar than does the one at the 'rear', the bacterium keeps swimming. If not, it tumbles. As a result, it is able to swim towards a source of dissolved sugar.

These two kinds of activity—swimming and tumbling—are different ways for the bacterium to act appropriately to its environmental conditions. These two ways of acting are 'appropriate' in the sense that each contributes to its self-maintenance in the differing circumstances. The bacterium's ability to detect sugar-gradients, and to respond by switching between its two modes of behaving, means that it thereby maintains its own ability to be self-maintenant—it is able to switch between activating one or other of its self-maintenant processes as the environment changes. That is, by means of its internal activity, it exhibits *recursive self-maintenance*.

For a process to be recursively self-maintenant, it must contain within itself some sort of infrastructure that can make the relevant shifts in the system's own internal processes. A bacterium can switch between swimming and tumbling because, although it is a single cell, it nevertheless contains internal subprocesses that can be activated in response to what yet other internal subprocesses detect in its environment (specifically to differentials in the sugar levels detected at its 'front' and 'rear'). A switching mechanism is the simplest form of infrastructure that can perform this function. More complex organisms contain more elaborate infrastructure that enables continual adjustment to detected variations in their environmental conditions—this is both more complex and more subtle than simple switching.

A relatively stable and cohesive organisation of processes that contains within itself sufficient complexity to work in ways that ensure (within limits) its own viability is an *autonomous* system. For the model, that is the significant difference between a candle flame and a bacterium. The complexity that enables the former to be self-maintenant is not internal to the flame itself: those conditions are provided (principally) by the candle and the atmosphere. A candle flame is therefore not autonomous. By contrast, a bacterium is—it strikingly provides for some of its own viability conditions. All biological organisms contain infrastructure of this sort, which enable them to adjust to environmental variation. More than that, the stable structural relationships that cause the components of the system to bind together are not static, as are the bonds that form rocks. Rather, they are constituted by dynamic relationships that continually *recreate* the system itself. Typically, their constituents are replaced many times over during the life of the organism itself. The integrity of such cohesive systems of processes arises from self-generating, self-reinforcing processes.

This concept of an autonomous system, which maintains its own integrity though either internal switching or adjustment, yields the next exclusive and exhaustive disjunction through which the ontological model can be elaborated: *some stable far-from-equilibrium processes are recursively self-maintenant, while others are not.* Those systems are autonomous that satisfy the former disjunct.

These considerations entail an ontology radically different from that standardly offered by physicalism. Biological systems—including human bodies—are *not* substantial entities ('things' in the strong sense) whose constituents are cells (smaller things), which are in turn (after a few more reductions) constituted out of fundamental particles. Like candle flames, but in ways that are much more complex and sophisticated, biological systems are necessarily open, organised action systems, in *essential* interactions with their environments. Unlike candle flames, through their internal control of such interactions they are able to maintain their own viability conditions and to control their own reproduction. The ontological consequence is that we cannot say what they *are* without taking those interactions into account.

Now, any recursively self-maintenant system is, in at least a minimal sense, goal-directed. Of course, to *describe* it as 'goal-directed' requires an observer. A bacterium does not *know*, in any sense other than a fanciful projected metaphor, that it is seeking sugar. Nevertheless, its characteristic way of switching between swimming and tumbling manifests a directedness, a 'towardness', that can reasonably be described as goal-directedness.

At this stage, speaking of goal-directedness carries no implication of consciousness, let alone self-consciousness, on the part of the system itself. Nevertheless, to call such systems 'goal-directed' is neither question-begging, nor anthropomorphic. This concept can be built up from the simple concepts of concepts of 'flow' and 'control'. In the kind of process-based metaphysics I am sketching here, *everything* is in motion. The ancient intuition of Heraclitus that 'everything flows' is confirmed by contemporary physics. That processes 'flow' is the simplest yet most fundamental thing that can be said about them.

By *control* is meant a relationship between two processes such that the outcome of the first affects the course of the second.[5] That is, the

---

5.   The following account is based on MH Bickhard and RL Campbell, 'Some Foundational Questions concerning Language Studies: With a Focus on Categorial Grammars and Model-theoretic Possible World Semantics', *Journal of Pragmatics*, 17 (1992): 401–433, and MH Bickhard: 'Autonomy, Function and Representation', *op cit.*

outcome of the first exerts a selection among the possibilities available to the second process. It modifies *how* the second flows, like a stick in a fast-flowing stream modifies the pattern of the water flow.[6] An interactive system shows itself to be a control structure by its manifest ability to test for whether it is in some relevant state, and to switch its own subsystems so as to bring itself into, and maintain itself in, that state. Thereby, it keeps directing itself towards that state as the outcome of its own internal processes. This goal-directedness is what licenses, indeed requires, the use of action verbs to describe the behaviour of such a system. We can, and must, speak of what it is *doing*. When the goals selected by the testing, switching and directing subsystems of an interactive system contribute to the *continued existence* of the system itself, it is a self-maintaining system.

Error-detection

These minimal notions of goal-directedness and signalling are enough to justify the observation that the system can go wrong. It can make a mistake. Further, attributing that mistake to the system itself is something that makes sense in terms of the system's own operations. Of course, a bacterium does not have the *concept* of error, because bacteria do not have concepts of any kind. But strictly in terms of the operations of the organism, as described thus far, the interactive model can make sense of the organism's acting in error. That is, it is possible that the organism might discriminate something in its environment that causes it to switch into a procedure that happens *not* to be appropriate in that environment. When it does so, it has manifestly made a mistake.

What justifies the phrase 'not appropriate' here is the fact that the chosen procedure does not contribute to the organism's self-maintenance. For example, it might receive no nutrients. A bacterium will swim up a saccharine gradient as well as a sugar gradient, but

---

6. The simile comes from WD Christensen and CA Hooker, 'An Interactivist-Constructivist Approach to Intelligence: Self-directed Anticipative Learning', *Philosophical Psychology*, 13 (2000): 11. Note that this notion of 'control' is quite minimal. The English verb 'to control' is often used to express a quite different, much richer concept, which implies goal-directedness—that is *not* implied at this stage.

when it does so, it is *in error*. In the kind of case envisaged, the indicated action is not apt for that kind of situation. The appropriateness in question is a *practical* matter.

On this account, an organism can *be* in error even though it does not have the *concept* of error and does not *know* that it is in error. The next step by which the model is enriched focuses upon those more complex organisms that *can discover for themselves* that some procedure is erroneous, even though they still are not complex enough to have such a concept. This provides the next significant disjunction for the elaboration of the interactive model: *either recursively self-maintenant systems have an ability to detect that some action they have performed has been in error, or they do not.*

Systems as complex as a frog not only have the ability to detect error, they also have evolved an ability to enact one potential interaction when alternative possible interactions are indicated at the same time. Suppose a frog sees a fly and at roughly the same time sees the shadow caused by a hawk flying by. There is no need to ascribe to the frog the ability to compare fly-representations with hawk-representations in order to explain what happens next. Most likely it will jump into the water rather than flick its tongue at the fly. All that is required to explain its jumping is that these two potential actions be indicated *to* and *for* the frog by its detection of environmental differentiations, and that its internal processes enable it to select (in some sense) between them.

Flexible learning

Here again, there is an important distinction. A frog's 'selecting' to jump into the water, because it has detected a hawk hovering overhead, rather than to flick its tongue at a fly it has also detected, need be no more than its having an ability to discriminate between these two affective stimuli and its having an instinctual tendency (developed through evolution) for its reaction to the larger shadow to be the more dominant. After all, these two types of action have very different implications for the frog's ability to keep on being self-maintaining! It is another matter if an organism is capable of *learning*, through conditioning, that some stimulus indicates favourable outcomes, even though a stimulus of that kind would normally be neutral so far as its instinctual responses go. A psychologist's rat, for example, is able to learn which way to turn at the corners of a maze, and to press the blue bar to get food, rather than the red bar (which yields nothing). This rat has learnt which action to favour. It is not too far-fetched to say that it has learnt to *assign value* to what it discriminates and that it has acquired the ability to evaluate the likely outcomes of alternative potential actions.

So, where an organism has the ability to learn which kinds of action yield rewards, and to select amongst potential actions on the basis of that learning, it seems reasonable to say that in a minimal sense it can 'evaluate' these potential interactions. On that basis, we have to say that a frog does not *choose* to jump into its pond when a hawk is hovering nearby. But a rat can anticipate and evaluate the projected outcomes of certain simple potential actions.

The kind of learning involved here is *practical* knowledge—what is learnt is *how* to achieve significant goals. A rat has no theoretical knowledge of why pressing the blue bar should produce food! The maze has been contrived, of course, by a psychologist. But even in the case of much significant human learning, the connections that explain why choosing a certain course of action tends to be a way to produce good outcomes are often not immediately obvious. Even when we have direct informational pathways for evaluating action, we are often ignorant of the underlying processes that serve as effective signals indicating that some potential action would be appropriate at this time.

The need to select amongst alternative goals, such as between a frog's selecting to eat or to save its life by jumping into the water, is not the only kind of selection that complex organisms need to make. As the concept has been introduced so far, goal-directedness has been narrowly conceived as involving a specified routine of determinate tasks, which tend to bring about a particular outcome. But the more highly developed an organism is, the less there is a unique routine of specific actions that the organism must perform if it is to attain a given end. As organisms become more highly developed, learning becomes increasingly self-directed, and behaviour becomes increasingly flexible. In these instances most of the normative directedness constraining the organism's behaviour are not uniquely associated with a specific set of tasks. There may be numerous *alternative specifications of task-routines* that have the potential to fulfil those same norms. This is so despite the fact that some would perhaps attain that goal more efficiently and more effectively than others would.

In order to deal with these latter cases, the phenomenon of the directedness of action has to be recognised as broader and as encompassing more than performing particular task-specifications uniquely determined by a precise goal. Let us reserve the term 'goal-directedness' for *specific* goals, associated with particular task-routines. Then the broader notion of generalised goals can be described as involving *generic norms*, which typically do not determine a unique task specification. An indefinite number of outcomes might satisfy them, and there might be indefinitely many alternative task specifications that could yield one or other of those outcomes.[7]

Generic norms in this sense are holistic: they relate to an open-ended range of possible tasks, all of which might satisfy (more or less well) the viability conditions of the organism. These conditions are what the organism, as a whole, must satisfy somehow, if it is to persist as an integral system. Consequently, in order to satisfy its generic norms, it has to *select* amongst an open-ended range of potential actions, all of which are to some extent functionally indicated by what it has detected in its environment. A hungry cheetah, for example, has to select which prey to stalk and chase, taking account of the facts that it can be injured by large and dangerous animals, that different potential prey deploy different flight-and-fight strategies, that it has a limited amount of energy to expend etc. etc. There are no simple and reliable signals that indicate suitable prey, comparable to the role that carbon dioxide plays for mosquitoes.

---

7. This highlights another deficiency of the etiological approach to explaining functionality. Etiological theories explain proper functions though evolutionary selection of task specifications, whereas in higher organisms there is not a unique and determinate set of tasks necessary to the attainment of its goals. For a more detailed discussion, see WD Christensen and CA Hooker, 'Self-directed Agents', forthcoming in *Naturalism, Evolution, and Intentionality*, edited by J McIntosh, a special supplementary volume of the *Canadian Journal of Philosophy*.

Richard Campbell

To satisfy their generic norms, higher level organisms have to be *flexible agents*. They must have the ability to learn from the outcomes of previous actions which of the potential actions available to it in a given situation is more likely to succeed. That is, they must have become adept at evaluating the likely outcomes of alternative potential actions, and be able to adjust their behaviour accordingly. Nor do they simply select some specific task routine and switch into it. Rather, any significant action is likely to involve a continual process of appraising and evaluating, of selecting and adjusting—all of which calls upon their previous experience of which actions are most appropriate in which kinds of situation.[8] Flexibility and adaptability thus depend upon learning. For a cheetah, this means that it has to learn, through experience, the many interrelated factors involved in successful hunting, including available cover, stalking distance, prey speed and agility, as well as its own capacities for interaction.

This yields the next significant disjunction in the elaboration of the model: *either those recursively self-maintenant systems that can detect that some action they have performed has been in error have an ability to learn from the outcome of their actions, or they do not*. Higher organisms are recursively self-maintenant systems that can not only detect error, but can also learn from their mistakes and adjust their behaviour through anticipating the likely outcomes of the potential interactions indicated to them by their environmental differentiations. They are 'flexible learners'. The model thus constructed is schematically presented in Figure 1 below.

Human beings are much more complicated than bacteria, mosquitoes, frogs, rats and cheetahs. Nevertheless, many of our abilities have been developed following the same principles. The dynamic model sketched here has unfolded the underlying processes

---

8. For this reason, the tendency amongst psychologists to divide learning into conditioned responses, on the one hand, and cognitive learning, on the other, is too simple-minded. The learning that feeds into this continual selecting and adjusting of motor action is still practical, not theoretical as the cognitivists would have it, but it is too norm-governed to fit into the causal models of stimulus-response conditioning.

of our self-development. We cannot say what constitutes a human being just by adverting to the cellular components of our bodies. That complex organisation of processes that is me extends from my past, and projects into my future, and reaches outside the envelope of my skin. Humans are also *necessarily open* processes. Deprive me of interactive exchanges with my environment, and I will soon die. And then the corpse remaining from my former body will begin to rot.

Furthermore, much more is involved in the emergence of fully human beings than just the biological evolution of our bodies. The step from candle flames to even the simplest biological organisms introduces recursive loops as the activity of the system as a whole has an effect on the internal operations of its constituent processes. Likewise, the development of our distinctly human abilities involves the multifarious activities of human sociality. Our individual abilities and traits are significantly affected by the social contexts, institutions, and cultures into which we are born. The emergence of the properties and powers of these social entities—and how they in turn affect the behaviour of the people who live within them—are probably even more complicated than the emergence of lifeforms from chemical systems. Nevertheless, I venture that the appropriate accounts will follow the logical 'shape' of the model outlined here. This model provides a nonreductive schema for understanding human beings as both emergent and yet embodied. In particular, it provides a way of characterising action as 'metaphysically deep', not an ontological embarrassment within an otherwise physicalist world.

Figure 1: The model for an interactive ontology

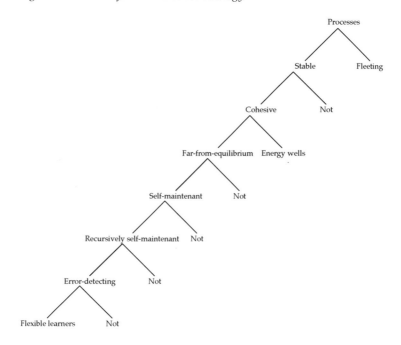

Part Three

Cosmology

The Absence of God or a Surer Path to God? The Origin of the Universe in Science and Theology

David Wilkinson

Introduction

My role here is to give some kind of overview and introduction to some of the questions that we will be discussing together. In this I want to take seriously not only the academic context but also the way that the questions of science and religion work out in the context of popular culture. This is important not only in teaching these issues, but also we must recognise that the way the dialogue of science and religion is *communicated* has an extremely important bearing on its content.

For example, in the area of cosmology two popular writers have in large part dominated the public perception of science and religion. When Stephen Hawking's *A Brief History of Time* was launched in 1988 it captured the public imagination in a way that would keep it on the bestseller list for well over three years. It had an initial print run of only 40,000 but ten years later in 1998 it had sold over ten million copies worldwide, been reprinted fifty times in hardback and translated into more than thirty-three languages.

It has spawned an industry of spin-offs and has made Hawking into a cult personality. So much so that the publication of his recent *The Universe in a Nutshell* and Hawking's sixtieth birthday celebration were high-profile media events. Why the popularity? No doubt in part the popularity is due to Hawking's own remarkable personal story. Yet that alone does not explain the whole story. Part of the popularity is that Hawking is engaging in the big questions about God and the universe. Carl Sagan, somewhat unfairly, in a foreword to *A Brief History of Time*, called it 'a book about God . . . or perhaps about the absence of God . . . The word God fills these pages . . . a universe with no edge in space, no beginning or end in time, and nothing for a Creator to do.'[1]

In contrast, Paul Davies has popularised cosmology with the conviction that 'science offers a surer path to God than religion'.[2] He is fascinated by the intelligibility of the Universe and the anthropic balances in the law and circumstance of the universe that make intelligent life possible.

Is cosmology a surer path to God or is it about the absence of God? To explore this question we will review a number of issues that have current importance in the relationship of cosmology and religion, both in the academic and popular contexts. In this we see some remarkable questions being raised and a serious conversation about God taking place. It may not prove God or indeed disprove God, but it does provide a fruitful dialogue about God.

The size of the universe

To say that the universe is big is perhaps stating the obvious! Yet just how big it is, is a non-trivial fact about the universe. The Hubble Space Telescope and a new generation of ground-based telescopes have been able to see objects further away than many people ever imagined. In the galaxy cluster Abel 2218, we see galaxies some two billion light years away. Indeed, these galaxies typically containing 100 billion stars act as a gravitational lens and allow us to see galaxies some five times further away. Recently, an object has been photographed which is 11.5 billion years away, or to put it another away we are seeing it only 0.5 billion years after the big bang.

When we consider such a vast universe of at least 100 billion galaxies spread over twelve billion light years, it inspires awe as well as some important theological questions. Pascal felt swallowed up by

---

1. SW Hawking, *A Brief History of Time* (London: Bantam, 1988). The book which started it all off!

2. P Davies, *God and the New Physics* (Harmondsworth: Pelican, 1983), ix. Davies' engaging attempt to use science as a path to God. See also, by the same author, *The Cosmic Blueprint* (London: Heinemann, 1987), *The Mind of God* (Harmondsworth: Penguin, 1992) and *About Time: Einstein's Unfinished Revolution* (Harmondsworth: Penguin, 1996).

the infinite spaces and the contemporary writer Danah Zohar speaks of fear at the vastness of the universe.

For theology, the size of the universe poses some questions about creation and indeed the Creator. Some of the earliest speculations on the existence of extraterrestrial life emerged as astronomers began to realise the size of the universe. Richard Bentley (1662–1742) in England and Christiaan Huygens (1629–1695) in Holland suggested that in such a large universe there would be stars and galaxies that human beings would never see. Therefore if the heavens declare the glory of God (Psalm 19:1) then there would have to be other intelligent life elsewhere in the universe to see God's glory. Today the theology may not be as important but the size of the universe is still a major motivation in the belief in extraterrestrial intelligence.

Alongside this, there is question about the Creator of such a vast universe. It is simply why did God create such a vast universe? Intelligent life could exist with one planet and one star so why the creation of billions? Now of course, there is an important scientific answer, that is that in a big bang universe you need a long time to make enough carbon in stars for human life that means a universe which expands over billions of years. Yet if there is a Creator why such a mechanism? An important insight that the Christian tradition can give here is that the Creator is a God of grace, that is extravagant generosity. The size of the universe is a reflection of God's extravagance in creation and creation always needs to be understood in this light.

First cause?

The past few decades of cosmology have been built on the big bang. This is where the theological issues have been largely focused. Within the scientific community, it is generally agreed, on the basis of the redshift of galaxies, the observation of the microwave background radiation and the theoretical prediction of the observed hydrogen-to-helium ratio, that the origin of the universe is well described by the model of the hot big bang, with the universe expanding from a singularity some twelve billion years ago.[3] Of course no scientific model is without its problems, and the big bang leaves certain questions unanswered. Questions such as the age of the universe and the nature of the dark matter that is necessary for galaxy formation are at present unresolved. Although the model of the big bang has needed some careful refining, it has stood up remarkably well to over thirty years of scrutiny and new observations.

We are fascinated with the question, 'What happened at the first moment?' Cosmology uses its knowledge of the physical laws to reconstruct a model of what happened in the past. In this it has been extremely successful with our current models describing the universe well back to a time when it was only 10^{-43} seconds old. Now that is a very small fraction of a second, but it is not zero. At that point our current theories break down, due to an inconsistency between general relativity and quantum theory. Current scientific theory is unable to give a description of the initial conditions of the expansion of the universe. This is extremely frustrating to scientists. In a famous quote Robert Jastrow captures the mood:

> For the scientist who has lived by his faith in the power of reason, the story ends like a bad dream. He has scaled the mountains of ignorance; he is about to conquer the highest peak; and as he pulls himself over the final rock, he is greeted by a band of theologians who have been sitting there for centuries.[4]

If our current laws of physics break down then some will immediately say that we need God to 'fix' the initial conditions of the universe. If science is unable to describe the initial moments is this where God comes in to set the universe off? To put it another way, if the universe began with a big bang then who lit the blue touch

---

3. See T Ferris, *The Whole Shebang: A State of the Universe(s) Report* (New York: Touchstone, 1998). Much praised review by an American journalist of modern cosmology.
4. R Jastrow, *God and the Astronomers* (New York: Norton, 1978), 116.

paper? This temporal version of the cosmological argument has a long and distinguished history. In 1951, Pope Pius XII stated:

> Thus with that concreteness which is characteristic of physical proofs, it [science] has confirmed the contingency of the universe and also the well-founded deduction as to the epoch . . . when the cosmos came forth from the hands of the Creator. Hence, creation took place in time. Therefore, there is a Creator.[5]

Even the distinguished Oxford mathematician Edward Milne closed his book on the expansion of the universe with the words, 'The first cause of the universe is left for the reader to insert. But our picture is incomplete without him.'

This remains a popular argument within the public mind. Why is this? Partly it is due to the application of everyday common sense to cosmology. Our experience of cause and effect encourages us to think of the origin of the universe in this way. Further, many people including professional astronomers, present the big bang in terms of a huge explosion. In attempting to popularise the big bang in this way you inevitably leave the door wide open to the question of who set off the explosion, along with questions as to what is it exploding into? We need to remember that the term 'big bang' was coined by Sir Fred Hoyle to disparage the theory, which he did not like. The term stuck, but the model really refers to a rapid expansion of space-time rather than a huge initial explosion. This is a classic example of the importance of communication in the perception of the science and religion debate. How can a model that is described primarily in the language of mathematics be communicated to the general public or indeed theologians without the use of mathematics and in a way that is not going to lead to misleading conclusions?

Of course, the problems of proving God in this way are well known. The logic of proving God as first cause is suspect because of the nature of time and also whether in fact you can apply

---

5. Quoted in SL Jaki, *Cosmos and Creator* (Edinburgh: Scottish Academic Press, 1980), 19.

cause/effect to the universe as a whole. Theologically such an attempted proof also runs the risk of a god of the gaps[6] and the result of a deistic creator who simply starts the universe off and then goes into retirement. Such a god is not the God of the Christian tradition, who is the one who upholds the whole physical process at every point over the whole twelve billion years.

Such an attempted proof also shows an ignorance of contemporary science. It is here that Hawking's work is of prime importance. What Hawking does is to suggest a possible way of uniting quantum theory and gravity (the realm of general relativity) to describe the beginning of the universe. He suggest the use of Euclidean space-time where:

> It is possible for space-time to be finite in extent and yet have no singularities . . . at which the laws of science broke down and no edge of space-time at which one would have to appeal to God or some new law to set the boundary conditions of space-time.[7]

One of the results of this is to put it bluntly is that he describes how the blue touch paper of the big bang lights itself. The core of Hawking's theory, in John Barrow's phrase, is that 'once upon a time there was no time'.[8] Hawking is saying that the universe does have a beginning but it does not need a cause, for in the theory the notion of time melts away. Hawking's universe emerges from a fluctuation in a quantum field. No cause as such is necessary.

It must be stressed that there are many scientific difficulties with Hawking's theory and it is not widely accepted. There are other proposals on how to deal with the problem of the laws breaking down. In addition, Hawking actually does not have a full theory. He makes his suggestions on the basis of this is what the theory would

---

6. CA Coulson, *Science and Religion: A Changing Relationship* (Cambridge: Cambridge University Press, 1955), 7.
7. SW Hawking, *A Brief History of Time, op cit*, 135–136.
8. JD Barrow, 'Universe Began in No Time at All', *The Observer*, 7 May 1993.

look like if he had a full theory. Further it is difficult to know whether quantum theory can be legitimately applied to the whole universe.[9]

Hawking however is confident. In his most recent book, *The Universe in a Nutshell,*[10] he describes the new field of p-branes and M-theory, which may provide the way to combine quantum theory and gravity. Yet this is Hawking's 'holy grail'. Fourteen years ago he predicted such a theory might be possible in the near future but he has still not got an accepted and consistent ultimate 'theory of everything'.

With those words of caution, I suggest that Hawking should be welcomed by theologians. He helpfully questions the cosmological argument in temporal form. The universe may have a finite age but it does not follow that one can use a cause/effect argument on the universe to prove a Creator God. This moves us away from the god of the gaps and deism to see the whole universe as the result of God's continual creating and sustaining. He is at much at work at the first 10^{-43} seconds as at any other time. A scientific description of that moment in time does not invalidate it as being the activity of God as any other event.[11]

Hawking questions a deistic god of the gaps. The biblical understanding of the Creator God is very different and so Christians need not feel threatened by such scientific progress in cosmology. The cosmologist Don Page points out that the Judaeo-Christian view claims that:

> God creates and sustains the entire universe rather
> than just the beginning. Whether or not the universe
> has a beginning has no relevance to the question of
> its creation, just as whether an artist's line has a

9. See R Penrose, *The Emperor's New Mind* (Oxford: Oxford University Press, 1989), an engaging book by one of Hawking's close collaborators, and JD Barrow, *Theories of Everything* (Oxford: Clarendon Press, 1991).

10. S Hawking, *The Universe in a Nutshell* (London: Bantam, 2001). Hawking's new sequel to *A Brief History of Time*.

11. D Wilkinson, *God, Time and Stephen Hawking* (Crowborough: Monarch, 2001). Updated version of popular introduction to these issues.

beginning and an end, or instead forms a circle with no end, has no relevance to the question of its being drawn.[12]

In all of this, however, cosmology raises questions that it cannot answer. If it is wrong to follow a god of the gaps approach, it is valid to ask what is the origin of the laws of physics themselves? If, as Hawking would suggest, the universe emerges as a quantum fluctuation, we need to ask where quantum theory itself comes from? Where does the pattern of the world come from and how is it maintained? This is not a god of the gaps argument as science itself assumes these laws in order to work. There is a long tradition stretching back to Newton who saw the laws of the universe as work of the divine lawgiver. Kepler was 'carried away by unutterable rapture' as the correlation between orbital periods and mean diameters, which showed that the planets moved in elliptical orbits, was disclosed. Once again the Christian will argue the Creator God is the natural answer.

In addition, we can ask, 'Why is the universe intelligible?' Einstein once said that the most incomprehensible thing about the universe is that it is comprehensible. Yet why should this be the case, that the mathematics of our minds resonates with the mathematics of the universe? It is remarkable that Hawking should be able to pursue a mathematical solution to the initial conditions of the whole universe and have some hope that one day it will be written on a T-shirt! Some writers, including John Polkinghorne, suggest that the natural answer is that there exists a Creator God who the basis of the order in the universe and the ability of our minds to understand it.[13]

Purpose?

Alongside questions as to why the universe is intelligible, there is an even more fundamental 'why' question. That is, why the universe at all? Hawking himself states, 'Although science may solve the

---

12. D Page, 'Hawking's Timely Story', *Nature*, volume 333 (1998): 742–743.
13. See JC Polkinghorne, *One World* (London: SPCK, 1986), and *Faith, Science and Understanding* (London: SPCK, 2001).

problem of how the universe began, it cannot answer the question: Why does the universe bother to exist? I don't know the answer to that.'[14] The philosopher Leibniz had asked many years ago why is there something rather than nothing?' This is not to resurrect the first cause argument, it is to recognise that the purpose and meaning of the universe lie beyond science. The Christian will argue they find a natural answer in a personal God.

This questions the so-called conflict approach, which sees scientific and theological descriptions in competition. This conflict approach is hugely popular. On one hand, there are many popular science books that adopt this approach with science as the ultimate victor.[15] They claim that once you have a scientific description of the nature and evolution of the universe then that is all you need. On the other hand, equally popular but in a very different constituency are the books of seven-day creationists who also adopt the conflict approach. However, in their conflict a scientific reading of Genesis 1 always wins.[16]

---

14. SW Hawking, *Black Holes and Baby Universes* (London: Bantam, 1993), 90. A collection of lectures, essays and papers covering technical subjects and Hawking's personal life and his views on religion.

15. For example P Atkins, *Creation Revisited* (New York: Freeman, 1992) (an atheistic interpretation of creation written by an Oxford chemist and populariser of science), R Dawkins, *The Blind Watchmaker* (Harmondsworth: Penguin, 1988), R Dawkins, *The Selfish Gene* (Oxford: Oxford University Press, 1989), R Dawkins , *River out of Eden* (London: Weidenfeld and Nicholson, 1995), C Sagan, *Cosmos* (London, Abacus, 1983), D Dennett, *Darwin's Dangerous Idea: Evolution and the Meanings of Life* (New York: Simon and Schuster, 1995), EO Wilson, *Sociobiology: the New Synthesis* (Cambridge, Mass: Harvard University Press, 1975).

16. HM Morris and GE Parker, *What is Creation Science?* (San Diego: Creation-Life Publishers, 1982), HM Morris, *Scientific Creationism* (Edinburgh: Christian World Publishers, 1974), JC Whitcomb and HM Morris, *The Genesis Flood* (Grand Rapids: Baker, 1961) and C Mitchell, *The Case for Creationism* (Grantham: Autumn House Ltd, 1995).

It is wrong to underestimate the force of this approach either in the area of popular science or in conservative Christianity. The popularity can stem from a number of reasons. First, such a conflict approach is more attractive to the media, whose style of presentation is attracted to argument. Second, a conflict approach simplifies a very complex interaction of science and theology, allowing the scientist or the theologian to communicate with confidence in areas that they know little about. Thus, Dawkins brilliance in writing about biology contrasts with his total naivety in theology, just as some creationists are embarrassingly ill informed about what modern science actually says. As the rate of expansion of knowledge continues and by necessity education becomes specialised in certain areas, there is a particular danger of the attractiveness of conflict models.

In the light of this it is interesting to note a number of studies in the last decade on how young people see science and religion.[17] Kay and Francis studied 729 pupils who were sixteen years and over in Scotland.[18] They identified a strong sense of scientism, that is the belief that science is the only source of truth. It was stronger amongst males than females. In addition, Kay and Francis suggest that this scientism excludes all other truth possibilities and consequently depresses or prevents the development of a positive attitude toward Christianity. They conclude, 'Part of the problem rests with the misapprehension scientism generates about the nature of Christian belief concerning origins. Scientism presumes Christianity is creationist, and therefore dismisses it. Scientism is unable to see how Christians hold variant positions on origins and that not all of these are incompatible with the pursuit of science.' Similar findings also came out of a study by Kay of 4,484 pupils in the eleven to sixteen-year-old age group in fifty-five schools in the UK.[19] He finds that

---

17. H Reich, *British Journal of Religious Education*, 11, number 2 (1989): 62–69.
18. WK Kay and LJ Francis, *Drift from the Churches* (University of Wales Press, 1996).
19. WK Kay, 'Male and Female Conceptualisations of Science at the Interface with Religious Education', in *Christian Theology and Religious Education*, edited by J Astley and LJ Francis (London: SPCK, 1995).

boys who are interested in science are inclined to see science and religion in conflict, while he does not see the same correlation in girls. If girls reject religion it appears to be on grounds unconnected with science. Girls are able to hold the religious positions in a more complementary way than boys who are more attracted to the conflict hypothesis.

From such studies, a number of practical suggestions arise in the communication of the dialogue between cosmology and theology. One is the importance of the churches encouraging and affirming science. This has a major effect in young people holding together science and religion as complementary accounts of the same truth rather than conflicting accounts. Current cosmology is an open door for the churches to do this, for as we have seen it has been raising questions that invite a theological conversation. Second, our educational process at all levels needs to help people to understand the nature of science as well as its results. Overemphasis on its results encourages a view that science is always successful and always secure. A critical realist view of science will help both scientists and theologians to engage in dialogue. Third, a cross-disciplinary dialogue must be encouraged at all levels to resist the danger of over-specialisation of knowledge. In this educational strategy, cosmology can be very helpful. It is the type of science that is both accessible to most people, while the theological questions are very clear.

Anthropic balances?

The last few decades have seen a growth in an understanding of the extraordinary anthropic balances in the law and circumstances of the universe that make it possible for carbon-based intelligent life to exist. Some such as Paul Davies and Sir Fred Hoyle have used such insights to argue for an intelligent designer behind the universe.[20]

A recent book on these anthropic balances makes interesting reading for the person who is interested in the theological questions. Sir Martin Rees, the current British Astronomer Royal, is one the world's leading cosmologists and astrophysicists. He details the fine-tuning of six numbers in the universe that make life possible. These

---

20. P Davies, *The Mind of God* (New York: Simon & Schuster, 1992) and F Hoyle, *The Intelligent Universe* (London: Michael Joseph, 1983).

numbers represent the ratio of the electric force and the gravitational force, how firmly atomic nuclei bind together, the amount of material in the universe, the cosmological constant, the ratio of energy needed to disperse an object to its total rest mass energy and the number of spatial dimensions in the universe.[21]

These numbers are just right and Rees sees that they need explanation. He is not convinced with the argument that they 'just are'. To argue against this, he quotes the philosopher John Leslie, who said that if you were in front of a firing squad and fifty marksmen all missed you, you would not say, 'Well, that's just the way it was.' You would seek some reason for such an extraordinary event. Then Rees is not convinced by these numbers being evidence of a Creator God. However, this is dismissed without any real argument. His own answer is that the anthropic principle selects this universe out of many. That is, we see the fine-tuning of these numbers because in another universe where the numbers are different we would not be in existence to see them. This he calls 'compellingly attractive' and 'a natural deduction from some (albeit speculative) theories'.[22]

Rees is a wise and guarded commentator on such issues. Yet his response to anthropic balances is very interesting. First, he as a cosmologist is so struck by them that he thinks it is necessary to explore an explanation. Second, he dismisses the theological response without any real engagement. Third, his preferred explanation raises the question of whether it is science or metaphysics. Some will argue that the belief in other universes is a natural consequence of a certain inflationary theories of the early universe. Therefore although we might never know that they are there in terms of passing information from one universe to ours, they have a scientific status. Others argue that other universes are simply metaphysical speculation to be dealt with as a philosophical rather than scientific explanation.

Both the cosmologist who wants to use the anthropic principle with other universes to explain the anthropic balances, and the

---

21. M Rees, *Just Six Numbers: The Deep Forces that Shape the Universe* (London: Weidenfeld and Nicholson, 2000). Clear and lucid introduction to modern cosmology by the current Astronomer Royal.
22. M Rees, *op cit*, 150.

theologian who wants to use anthropic balances to argue for the existence of God needs to be aware of this discussion. It cautions both not to go too far. Certainly the theologian will want to resist the temptation to use anthropic balances to go back to the design argument proof of the existence of God. The possibility of other universes echoes David Hume's classic critique of the design argument that there may be another explanation. While this stops any sense of proof, it does not stop a revived natural theology that speaks of pointers rather than logical proofs. Anthropic balances are consistent within the Christian claim of a Creator God who wills the universe to be fruitful in terms of human life, and may for some be both aesthetic and scientific pointers to a Creator.

The search for extraterrestrial intelligence
It is worth in this overview picking up one other area where the dialogue between cosmology and theology has an important outlet in popular culture. That is in the speculation about and the search for extra-terrestrial intelligence.[23]

Paul Davies sees it as a key issue:

> Even the discovery of a single extraterrestrial microbe, if it could be shown to have evolved independently of life on earth, would drastically alter our world-view and change our society as profoundly as the Copernican and Darwinian revolutions. It could truly be described as the greatest scientific discovery of all time . . . it is hard to see how the world's great religions could continue in anything like their present form should an alien message be received.[24]

---

23. D Wilkinson, *Alone in the Universe? The X-Files, Aliens and God* (Crowborough: Monarch, 1997). Examination of the scientific arguments for extraterrestrial intelligence and the theological implications.
24. P Davies, *Are We Alone?* (London: Penguin, 1995), xi.

On scientific grounds the arguments for extraterrestrial intelligence are at present inconclusive. The universe is a large place and to say that there must be other suitable planets for life out there is a strong argument to use in the public mind. However, there are other arguments, which are a little more difficult to communicate, but are very strong against. First, we have been searching the skies for a significant amount of time and we have seen nothing. Second, although the universe is a big place there is a 'Goldilocks Principle' that specifies a large number of conditions for things to be just right for intelligent life. Third, it is a long and very sensitive process to go from amino acids to intelligent self-conscious life. We might be surrounded by life in our galaxy but it might all be bacteria. Fourth, as Fermi pointed out in the 1950s, 'If they existed they would be here.' Fermi's point was that if intelligent life was developing easily throughout the galaxy one race would have colonised the galaxy by this time in the galaxy's twelve billion-year history.

None of these arguments is conclusive. Cosmologists, struck by just how big the universe is, tend to be more sympathetic to the existence of extraterrestrial intelligence. Biologists, struck with the complexity of the development of human life and the sensitivity of such a process to the environment are more sceptical.

On the theological side, Davies is right to raise the questions but is a little too melodramatic in terms of his conclusions. As we have seen, Christian theologians were some of the first to speculate about other life in the universe. This was in part due to the fact that the uniqueness of human beings was maintained by relationship with God rather than by place in the universe. That is the earth did not have to be at the centre of everything to make human beings special. They were special due to God's gift of relationship in creation and redemption.

One of the areas that would need to be addressed if other intelligent life were discovered would be the Christian understanding of incarnation. The limited amount of thinking in this area has gone in two directions. Some have argued that the incarnation on earth is once for all, while others have suggested that God would be incarnate in 'little green flesh'. This may sound overly speculative, but the discussion raises some important questions on revelation, sin, redemption and the particularity of the Christian gospel.[25]

It seems to me that we need as scientists and theologians to take the search for extraterrestrial life seriously. It may be speculative but as I have argued elsewhere it demonstrates a looking for relationship, purpose, identity, security and salvation. As far back as 1949, Sir Fred Hoyle pointed out a motivation for believing in extraterrestrial intelligence, that is 'the expectation that we are going to be saved from ourselves by some miraculous interstellar intervention'.[26] It opens up the possibility of another branch of the dialogue in the relationship of science and theology.

Conclusion

Is the origin of the universe about the absence of God or is it a surer path to God? I have argued that it is neither. Instead, the origin of the universe and life within it provides a fruitful interaction between science and theology, which is complex but also accessible to a wide audience.

Science asks us to think again about theology, for example in the images and models that describe the Creator. At the same time, science also raises questions that go beyond its own ability to answer and therefore invites theology into a dialogue.

Meanwhile theology has much to say. Richard Dawkins is scathing when he says, 'What has "theology" ever said that is of the smallest use to anybody? When has "theology" ever said anything that is demonstrably true and is not obvious?'[27] Yet he is also misguided. Theology questions scientism and gives a framework of creation that naturally explains intelligibility, the origin of the physical laws, anthropic fruitfulness and a sense of awe.

---

25. WN Pittenger, *The Word Incarnate* (London: Nisbet, 1959), EA Milne, *Modern Cosmology and the Christian Idea of God* (London: Oxford University Press, 1952), EL Mascall, *Christian Theology and Modern Science* (London: Longmans, 1956) and SL Jaki, *Cosmos and Creator* (Edinburgh: Scottish Academic Press, 1980).

26. F Hoyle, Monthly Notices of the Royal Astronomical Society, 109 (1949), 365.

27. R Dawkins, 'Writer Donates £1m to Strike Blow for Theology', *The Independent*, 18 March 1993.

In order for the dialogue to be fruitful, science and theology must be allowed to be themselves even if that complicates rather than simplifies the picture. Those who follow the conflict approach do not reflect on the complexity of the nature of science and religion. For example, Davies sees science as the 'surer path' because he dismisses revelation or religious experience. Yet this does not do justice to the main monotheistic religions of the world. From the Christian perspective, Sir Robert Boyd, Emeritus Professor of Physics at the University of London, in commenting on whether Hawking's theory would show us the mind of God, wrote, 'The missing data in Hawking's analysis of the "Mind of God" is the mind of One "who made himself of no reputation", whose love is unconditional and whose "name is above every name"'.[28] Scientists must take theology seriously and, at the same time, theologians must take science seriously.

---

28. R Boyd, *Science and Christian Belief*, volume 6, number 2 (1994): 143.

Time and Eternity as Scientific and Theological Problem

Mark Worthing

Introduction

In J R R Tolkein's *The Hobbit* there is a scene in which the unlikely protagonist, Bilbo Baggins, encounters the creature Gollum in a dark cavern and must win a riddling contest to keep from being eaten. At a critical stage of the contest Gollum puts forth this riddle:

> This thing all things devours:
> Birds, beasts, trees, flowers;
> Gnaws iron, bites steel;
> Grinds hard stone to meal;
> Slays king, ruins town,
> And beats tall mountains down.[1]

In the dark, frightened of being eaten and completely stumped Bilbo Baggins pleads for longer to solve the riddle calling out, 'Time! Time!' And of course, that is the answer. Like Bilbo Baggins we may feel rather in the dark and stumped with regard to our present topic. But for us, time is not the answer to the riddle—time is the riddle.

And time, I believe, is an appropriate riddle to grapple with at a conference on creation and complexity. We cannot speak meaningfully, either scientifically or theologically, about the creation, that is, the physical universe, without also speaking about time. Time is part of the very fabric of creation and must be taken into account in any theological reflection on the complexity of creation.

When we speak of creation and its complexity we refer usually either to the physical universe itself or to the origins of the universe. I would like to shift the focus slightly from either the created order or the origins of creation to the Creator. In what I will cover in this paper, even the more scientific and philosophical reflections, the

---

1.   JRR Tolkein, *The Hobbit, or There and Back Again*, 72.

creative and driving impulse has been my own reflections on the Christian doctrine of the Trinity. A foundational insight, and one that I did not immediately or easily grasp as a theologian, is that the understanding of the Trinity, not as the simultaneous and static existence of three persons, but as the dynamic and mutual relationship between Father, Son and Spirit, suggests a complexity within God that has, to borrow scientific jargon—non-trivial implications for our understanding of that which flows forth from the being of God into the creative activity of God.

If theologians had from the beginning worked from a confession of the Trinitarian God and the eternality of this God toward an understanding of time, the debate over time and eternity in theology may have followed a very different path. As things occurred, however, the tendency all too often was to deduce an understanding of eternity as either timelessness or unending time from our conceptions of time. Not surprisingly, therefore, attempts to extrapolate a theology of eternity from a classical, linear understanding of time have tended toward a suppression of the complexity of the time/eternity problem.

Similarly, theories of time among the natural sciences have also exhibited a tendency to cling to classical, linear understandings in the face of growing indications that time is far more complex than we are wont to accept.[2]

Classically, the distinction between space and time has always been that of the distinction between being and becoming. But if time is about becoming—a relentless transformation of all reality—then it is perhaps one of the more poignant ironies of science that neither time itself nor our ideas about time appear particularly open to transformation. But our ideas of time must allow for the transformability of all reality—including time. Anything less not only ignores the fundamental complexity and dynamic nature of time, it also excludes teleology from science and viable eschatology from Christian thought.

---

2.   Cf Chris Isham, 'Creation of the Universe as a Quantum Process', in *Physics, Philosophy, and Theology: A Common Quest for Understanding*, edited by R Russell, W Stoeger and G Coyne (Vatican City: Vatican Observatory, 1997), 389.

The development of the idea of time in theology and science

For early Christian thinkers there were two sources that were influential in their understanding of time: the Hebrew and Greek scriptures, and Greek philosophical thought, particularly that of Plato.

In contrast to Greek philosophical thought, which tended to view time as circular, the Hebrews portrayed time as a line that had a beginning and end. On each end of this line stood God, lord of the beginning, lord of the end, and lord of all that occurred between these points. Humans existed with pasts that could not be revisited and futures that were yet to come. Only God transcended in any sense this linear progression of time. For the Lord, a thousand years was as a day and a day as a thousand years. Whatever time was and whatever constraints it imposed, the experience of time for God was clearly distinct from the human experience of time.

The New Testament is filled with the language of time, with a wide array of words employed to express time related concepts. Most prominent are *hemera* (day) *hora* (hour) *kairos* (season or decisive moment) *chronos* (time) *aion* (age). But of all these, Oscar Cullmann has suggested that 'the two ideas that most clearly elucidate the New Testament conception of time are those usually expressed by *kairos* ('a point of time') and *aion* ('age'). While *kairos* refers to a definite point in time, and *aion* to a duration of time, both significantly are used to 'characterise that time in which redemptive history occurs'. And in all cases it is not human actions but God who determines that a certain decisive moment or age is one in which God acts salvifically.[3] The best known of this class of New Testament texts is Galatians 4:4: 'But when the time [*kairos*] had fully come, God sent his Son, born of a woman . . . to redeem those under the law.' God chooses the decisive moment in our time to enter our space in physical form.

Given the tradition of linear time and its connection with the physical world within the Judeo-Christian tradition it is not surprising that a fundamental breakthrough in the understanding of

---

3.   Oscar Culllmann, *Christ and Time: The Primitive Christian Conception of Time and History*, translated by F Filson (London: SCM Press, 1962), 38f.

time came from a Jewish and a Christian thinker reflecting on the theology of creation.

Philo of Alexandria saw that the existence of time and matter were bound together. In 'On the Creation' he wrote:

> Before the world time had no existence, but was created either simultaneous with it, or after it; for since time is the interval of the motion of the heavens, there could not have been any such thing as motion before there was anything which could be moved; but it follows of necessity that it received existence subsequently or simultaneously. It therefore follows also of necessity, that time was created either at the same moment with the world, or later than it.[4]

Unfortunately, Philo was not consistent in following through the logic of his own ideas. For while seeming to recognise the relationship between time and physical processes, he leaves open the possibility of time being created *after* the creation of the material world. It was left to the fifth century Christian theologian, Augustine of Hippo, to put forward what has generally been considered the first essentially correct understanding of time. In *The City of God* Augustine wrote:

> For if eternity and time are rightly distinguished by this, that time does not exist without some movement and transition, while in eternity there is no change, who does not see that there could have been no time had not some creature been made, which by some motion could give birth to change—the various parts of which motion and change, as they cannot be simultaneous, succeed one another—and thus, in these shorter or longer intervals of duration, time would begin? . . . Then

---

4.   Philo of Alexandria, *The Works of Philo*, translated by CD Yonge (Peabody, Massachusetts: Hendrickson, 1993), 5.

assuredly the world was made, not in time, but simultaneously with time.[5]

Augustine left no doubt that as soon as there is matter, there is process and there is time. His conception of eternity, however, as that in which there is no change, was indicative of a problem in relating time and eternity in Christian thought that has continued down to the present time.

In taking this particular view of eternity Augustine was closely following the thought of Plato, who held that eternity bears no relation to time, and therefore for Augustine there could clearly be no time in God's eternity.

A more flexible model had been put forward by Plotinus, who suggested that eternity is not opposed to time but is its presupposition. Eternity encompasses all of life whereas through the medium of the soul we experience time as the dissolution of this unity into a sequence of separate moments that refer to the eternal totality.[6] While Boethius and later Karl Barth built on the approach of Plotinus it was the model of Plato that Augustine followed and with him much of the Western intellectual tradition for the next 1,500 years.

It was this tradition that produced Isaac Newton, who not only gave us the epitome of a classical understanding of space but also produced a definition of absolute time. Wrote Newton:

> Absolute, true and mathematical time, of itself, and from its own nature flows equably and without regard to anything external, and by another name is called duration: relative, apparent and common

5.   Augustine, *The City of God*, translated by Marcus Dods (New York: Random House, 1950), XI.6, 350.
6.   See Wolfhart Pannenberg, *Systematic Theology*, volume 1, translated by G Bromiley (Grand Rapids: Eerdmans, 1991), 403f.

time, is some sensible and external . . . measure of
duration by the means of motion.[7]

Newton postulated an absolute time composed of individual
instants conceived of as substances existing independently of other
things and possessing an independent ontological status.[8]

It was within this context that the next major turning point in the
scientific understanding of time occurred. Beginning with a series of
papers in 1905, Albert Einstein put forward his theory of special
relativity, culminating with the 1915 appearance of his theory of
general relativity. With this one theory Einstein revolutionised the
way we think of space and time. Einstein showed that there is not
only no absolute space, but also no absolute time, because all of the
laws of science are the same for (or relative to) each observer. This
means that it is possible for two separate observers to experience time
in the same manner, relative to their own positions, yet differently in
relation to each other. This is illustrated most famously by the
hypothetical 'twins paradox' in which one twin lives her life at sea
level, and the other on a mountaintop farther from the centre of the
earth's rotational spin and therefore moving at a faster speed relative
to her sea-level twin. The twin on the mountaintop, because of the
decreasing frequency of light waves the farther one is from the
earth's centre, would appear to age slightly slower than the twin at
sea level. Hence each observer's personal measure of time is relative
to his or her own position—and movement.

While this illustration is well known to most today its implications
are quite far-reaching. The actual affect of such an experiment would
be barely measurable—and would certainly have no meaningful
impact on the life of either twin. But the notion of absolute time had
been found to have a chink in its armour. Time is no longer perceived
as absolute but relational. As Harold Schilling put it: '[Time] has a
unique relationship to space, which is also relational; and together

---

7.   Isaac Newton, *Principia Mathematica*, cited in John Yates, *The
     Timelessness of God* (New York: University of America Press, 1990),
     59.
8.   Cf John Yates, *The Timelessness of God* (New York: University Press
     of America, 1990), 59.

they constitute an indissectable continuum, space-time, of which each is a component complemen-tary to the other.'[9] Surprisingly, however, the implications of relativity theory for our functional conception of time have been less radical than one might expect. As Christ Isham observed: 'In spite of their differences, the spacetimes of Newtonian and relativistic physics share the property of being fixed, background structures within which the material content of the universe has its being.'[10] While the notion of absolute time was passing from our technical vocabulary the classical, linear view of time as a fixed given remained stubbornly entrenched.

The rise of quantum mechanics would shake the theoretical foundations of the classical conception of time even further. But again, the implications of these new developments in physics were not applied to time in as radical a fashion as they were to our understanding of space.

The current situation with regard to the scientific understanding of time

We should not suppose it unusual that despite the revolutions in physics of the twentieth century the classical view of time continues to predominate. Our everyday experience of time is inescapably linear. We experience and think of time in terms of past, present and future. Time is sequential and directional. One moment succeeds another. Past moments can never be returned to and future moments remain unknown. Time is one-directional and is often spoken of as having a beginning and end. This view of time has served us very well. It corresponds to our everyday experience. But what if time is more complex than it appears? Even some of our most noted time heretics have merely stretched the conceptual boundaries of the existing classical view of time. Einstein's curvature of space-time amounts merely to an elongation or shortening of time relative to different observers and their respective motion. Stephen Hawking at one time considered the possibility of the arrow of time reversing and invokes imaginary time in an effort to avoid an absolute beginning of

---

9. Harold Schilling, *The New Consciousness in Science and Religion* (London: SCM, 1973), 120f.
10. Chris Isham, *op cit*, 389.

the universe.[11] And Frank Tipler suggests a stretching of time in a final never-ending moment at the end of a collapsing universe.[12] But all these ideas, as radical or even as unlikely as they appear, are only intelligible within the framework of a classical, linear understanding of time.

Yet continuing reflection on the implications of relativity theory, emerging quantum insights, and increasing awareness of our reliance on a particular Platonic-Augustinian conception of time are causing questions to be asked about the nature of time that are, to say the least, difficult for us to even conceptualise. After Einstein's linkage of space and time into a single four-dimensional structure it is only logical that we should apply the insights of relativity theory and quantum mechanics to time with the same revolutionary rigor as has been the case with space. The failure in many cases to do so only underscores the difficulties involved in even beginning to grasp the questions that arise.

For instance, can time split, as do universes in the MWI of quantum theory? Can it loop? Does it have multiple access points? Is its relationship to space a constant? Are there the equivalent of black holes in time? Could all time be condensed/collapsed similar to matter in a closed universe? If not, then have we really accepted the full implications of Einstein's unification of space-time as a single structure? Paul Davies suggests the scope of the question when he writes:

> What has not been appreciated until this century . . .
> is the close connection between gravity and the
> nature of space and time. It is a connection which
> implies that overwhelming gravitational collapse

---

11. Cf Stephen Hawking, *A Brief History of Time* (New York: Bantam Books, 1988), chapters 8 and 9.

12. Cf Frank Tipler, 'The Omega Point as *Eschaton*: Answers to Pannenberg's Questions for Scientists', *Zygon*, 24:2 (June 1989): 217–253, and 'The Omega Point Theory: A Model for an Evolving God', in *Physics, Philosophy, and Theology*, edited by R Russell, W Stoeger, and G Coyne (Vatican City: Vatican Observatory, 1988).

amounts to much more than a crisis of matter—it is a crisis in the very structure of existence.[13]

If time itself is not capable of transformation/evolution, is the whole concept of time ultimately just an illusion? How would non-linear conceptions of time be expressed mathematically? What will be the impact for our understanding of time of a long-awaited correct quantum theory of gravity given the already accepted impact of gravity upon space-time? What would curved time look like?

The possibilities raised by such questions are difficult to imagine for they suggest characteristics of time that are not part of our everyday experience. Perhaps the situation could be illustrated in the following way.

We are all familiar with the standard use of timelines to portray the linear flow of time from past, through the present and toward the future.

past	present	future

But what if this portrayed only one aspect of time? If we could back up and gain a wide angle view, so to speak, of time, are there other possibilities for how time might be portrayed, with our experience of a linear progression of time only one aspect of a much larger and more complex picture of time? Could it be that we are living in a sort of temporal 'flatland' and that the landscape of time may look very different as seen from the perspective of an omniscient observer.[14]

---

13. Paul Davies, The Edge of Infinity: Beyond the Black Hole (Harmondsworth: Penguin, 1994), 11f.

14. 'Many and strange are the universes that drift like bubbles in the foam upon the River of Time. Some—a very few—move against or athwart its current; and fewer still are those that lie forever beyond its reach, knowing nothing of the future or the past.' Arthur C Clarke, *The Nine Billion Names of God* (New York: Signet Books, 1974), 94. Opening lines of 'The Wall of Darkness'.

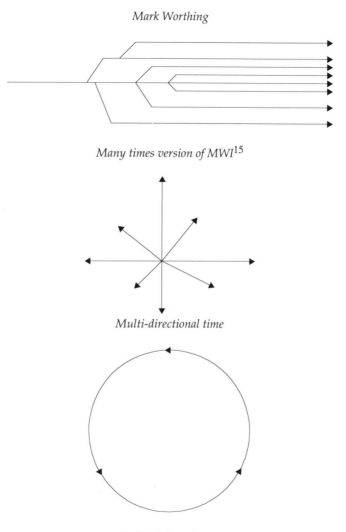

Many times version of MWI[15]

Multi-directional time

Cyclical view of time

---

15. Sometimes science fiction, unfettered by logical restrictions, provides the most intriguing and amusing examples of science imagination. David Brin, himself trained as an astronomer and engineer, wrote a short story called the 'River of Time', in which time continues to split with people sharing somehow a common space but different times. Cf D Brin, *The River of Time* (New York: Bantam, 1987), 282ff.

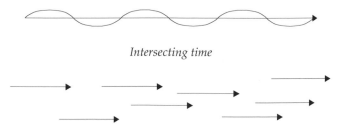

Intersecting time

Independent time 'chunks' embedded into common space

What will come out of emerging rethinks on time in the sciences is impossible to predict. What we might reasonably expect, however, is a view of time emerging that recognises greater complexity is the various components and relationships of time. Given the already accepted influence of gravity on time, the eventual appearance of a correct theory of quantum gravity will likely have a profound impact upon our understanding of time. Alternately, it is possible that things might occur the other way around and a rethink of time might open the way for a quantum theory of gravity. Our understanding of time, in many ways, is still very classical and linear and the implications of the linkage of time and space into a unified space-time are not always fully appreciated. Perhaps it has been the failure of our thinking on time to keep pace with other implications of quantum theory that has prevented us from a breakthrough in this area.

Theological reflections

These questions and models are for physicists, cosmologists and mathematicians to resolve. But what about theology? The answers to these questions would be of great consequence for theology. But theology also has its own particular time dilemmas. Does time have its origin at the creation of the physical world? What is the relationship between time and eternity? What is eternity? What is the relationship between the Trinitarian God of Christian faith and time? These specifically theological problems are not unrelated to those in the natural sciences. Again, the failure to recognise the full complexity of time is a common thread. It has been rightly observed that the 'complexity [of time] is not least of all to be seen in the fact that philosophy, theology and natural science all have different answers to the problem of time and indeed, pose the problem itself in different ways'.[16]

Science and theology may pose the problem of time in different ways but the initial step toward progress for both may be very similar. I would suggest that like science, theology must look afresh at the question of time and begin to think outside the square, as it were, if progress is to be made on longstanding dilemmas. The parameters of that square were set for us by Augustine. They are:

1. Time is bound to the material world.
2. Time has an absolute beginning at creation.
3. A dichotomy exists between time and eternity.
4. Eternity is timeless.

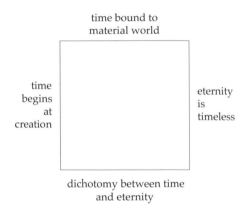

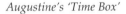

Augustine's 'Time Box'

Within the confines and limitations of this square we have sought to answer questions about the relationship between God and time, divine freedom and human freedom, theodicy, and the possibility of Christian escha-tology within an open, closed or even accelerating

---

16. Mike Sandbothe, 'Die Verzeitlichung der Zeit. Grundtendenzen der moderne Zeitphilosophie und die aktuelle Wiederentdeckung der Zeit', in *Glaube und Denken. Jahrbuch der Karl-Heim-Gesellschaft* (Brendow, 1994), 132.

universe. Despite the application of the most clever and well-meaning logic to these problems, Christian thinkers often find themselves backed into some very awkward corners. My suggestion is that a radical rethink on the nature of time on the basis of the doctrine of the Trinity and with a recognition of the complexity of the nature of time could provide new possibilities for approaching a number of related theological problems.

1. Time does not depend upon the existence of matter for its being. If this thesis is correct it has two additional implications. What I am suggesting, therefore, is that Augustine got it wrong on at least three counts in his understanding of time and eternity. First, time is not an expression only of physical properties but is also an expression of thought and relationship. Hence secondly, time, while taking on a new expression at the creation of the material world does not find its absolute beginning but existed already as an attribute of the Trinitarian God whose inner Trinitarian relationships and thoughts were not simply static. And thirdly, if time is an attribute of the Trinitarian God, then eternity is not 'timeless'. Importantly, if time does not depend on matter for its being, then there is nothing left of Augustine's time box and a whole new world is opened up for theological reflection.

2. Time itself is not static but is open to transformation. The creation of the material world did not entail the creation of time but the transformation of time, as it now also expressed process and becoming at the level of the material. Eschatologically, if we take seriously the Christian belief in the transformation and renewal of the heavens and the earth, then we must also consider the transformation of time. As a youth growing up in a Baptist church in America we used to sing 'Amazing Grace' quite often. One day I remember the pastor stopping us and saying that the line, 'when we've been there ten thousand years' didn't adequately express eternity. That was fair enough. So from that time on he suggested we sing instead, 'when we've been there ten million years.' Of course, this is no more adequate than 10,000 years. One big number had simply been replaced by an even bigger one. The concept of eternity was not timelessness, but one of a never-ending continuation of time. I would suggest that neither timelessness nor a never-ending continuation of time is biblically or theologically adequate. Instead, I believe that

time, like the physical creation, will somehow be transformed as God becomes all in all (1 Corinthians 15:28). As a theologian, that is my expectation. What I would look to science for is not verification of my theological views, but rather indications of the transformability of time.

If we begin with our understanding of time, which is conditioned by the entire history of Western thought, and try to reason our way to an understanding of eternity, we should not be surprised that our conclusions are unsatisfying. From the perspective of theology, it is sounder to begin with the Trinity itself. If time is an expression of becoming and exists as soon as there is relationship then the dynamic inner Trinitarian relationship and three-way flow of love suggests that time is not created by God with the physical universe but is an attribute of the eternal God. Karl Barth made a significant step in this direction when he spoke of an 'order and succession' and a 'before and after' in the triune being of God.' For Barth, the fact there is nothing of what we would traditionally understand of time in God 'does not justify us in saying that time is simply excluded in God or that his essence is simply a negation of time'.[17]

The problem we may encounter here, however, is that if we fail to distinguish between God's time (or eternity) and our own temporality then, as Pannenberg warns, we run the danger of making God into a finite being like ourselves if God 'at every moment of his life looks ahead to a future that is distinct from the present and sees the past fading away from him. This is to limit his present on both sides'.[18]

Pannenberg himself draws the distinction between God's experience of time and a creaturely experience of time as follows:

> In distinction from creatures, who as finite beings are subject to the march of time, the eternal God does not have ahead of him any future that is different from his present. For this reason that which has been is still present to him. God is eternal

17.   Barth, *Church Dogmatics* II/I, translated by G Bromiley and TF Torrance (Edinburgh: T&T Clark, 1957), 615.

18.   Pannenberg, *Systematic Theology*, volume 1, 405.

because he has no future outside himself. His future is that of himself and of all that is distinct from him. But to have no future outside oneself, to be one's own future, in the fellowship of Father, Son, and Spirit, is the free origin of himself and his creatures.[19]

Pannenberg's approach to the problem of time and eternity is one of the most fruitful to come out of theological reflection. Yet I believe there is more work to be done. The problem and possibility of the transformation of time itself remains to be fully dealt with. And if time is transformed then we should also expect to experience time in a manner in continuity with God's experience in the eschaton. Will then all time also be present to us?[20] What influence will emerging scientific views of time have on our theological understanding of time and eternity? Also, the complexity of time remains to be taken fully into account. This will likely provide increased possibilities for understanding the relationship of the Trinitarian God with the salvific past and eschatological future of free creatures made in this God's own image. But alas—we remain regrettably bound to a linear experience of time—and time, indeed, has run out for further reflection on these matters.

I conclude with another quote from Augustine on time from his *Confessions*.

---

19. Pannenberg, *op cit*, 410.
20. Barth contends that 'God's eternity in its eternal Now embraces and contains all parts of time and all things in itself simultaneously and at one moment'. (*Church Dogmatics*, II/I, *op cit*, 614.). Some refer to this possibility as Bob Russell's library. Bob Russell is well known for describing eternity as being able to face a vast library self of books with each book representing another moment in time. As we progress through the books page by page we remember what has come before but cannot return to it and we have no knowledge of what lies ahead. But in eternity we will have access equally to all the volumes.

What is time? I know well enough what it is, provided that nobody asks me; but if I am asked what it is and try to explain, I am baffled.[21]

---

21. *Confessions* 11.14.

The End of it All: Cosmology and Christian Eschatology in Dialogue

David Wilkinson

Introduction

In contrast to the beginning of the universe, very little dialogue has taken place between science and religion with regard to the end of the universe. Yet current scientific speculation on the future of the earth and the universe is a hot topic in contemporary science, and raises some important questions for Christian eschatology, that is thinking about the end.

Another fascinating contrast is that contemporary science rather than encouraging an optimistic view of the future, which was prevalent at the end of the nineteenth century, paints a rather pessimistic view of the future. In this paper we review these sources of 'cosmic pessimism' and then pose some questions for Christian theology.

A pessimistic view of the future?

Destruction of the environment
The use of global resources, such as food in the face of growing population, deforestation and the overuse of fossil fuels, has received a great deal of interest in recent years with the growth of environmental concern. Coupled with such issues of global pollution as the dumping of waste and global warming and the destruction of the ozone layer, the situation if continued becomes serious.[1]

The recent report of the Scientific Assessment Group of the Intergovernmental Panel on Climate Change, uniting most of the world's atmospheric scientists, concluded that if the current situation of the emission of greenhouse gases continues then models predict an average increase in temperature for the earth of between 1.5 and 6 degrees in the next century. The implications of this for sea-level

---

1. RJ Berry, editor, *The Care of Creation* (Leicester: IVP, 2000).

changes, ecosystems and population movement are severe. For example it will create some 150 million environmental refugees over the next 100 years.

Some react to this with warnings that the earth will become uninhabitable within the next century, others look to technology in order to control these consequences.

Terrestrial mass extinction

Hollywood movies such as *Deep Impact*, costing around $100 million, from Steven Spielberg's Dreamworks studio, and *Armageddon*, starring Bruce Willis, concern comets heading for the earth threatening 'an extinction-level event'. Tidal waves destroy New York, humanity takes to deep caves to survive and astronauts are dispatched on a last-ditch attempt to avert disaster.

Such scenarios are not solely the area of science fiction. The impact of the twenty-one fragments of comet Shoemaker-Levy on Jupiter in 1994 demonstrated the possibility and indeed seriousness of such impacts. Scars existed in the Jovian atmosphere for more than a year.[2]

In 1991 and 1994 asteroids passed within 100,000 km of earth, which is about half the distance between the earth and the moon. The impact of an asteroid only a mile wide would lead to tidal waves or a crater twenty miles wide depending on whether it impacted on sea or land. The accompanying explosion would be the equivalent of two million Hiroshima-sized bombs. Indeed, it is widely held that an impact by a comet or asteroid led to the extinction of the dinosaurs some sixty-five million years ago. In fact the dinosaurs are not the only species that seem to have been wiped out within a short time in the fossil record. Such mass extinctions happen roughly every thirty million years. We have shown elsewhere that all such extinctions cannot be caused by cometary impacts, so other mechanisms such as enhanced volcanic activity may be responsible.[3] Yet the danger from comets or asteroids remains real.

---

2.   P Barnes-Svarney, *Asteroid: Earth Destroyer or New Frontier?* (New York: Pelnum Press, 1996), 125–127.
3.   ME Bailey, DA Wilkinson and AW Wolfendale, 'Can Episodic Comet Showers Explain the 30 Myr Cyclicity in the Terrestrial Record?',

A collision with a comet is entirely possible every 250 million years on average. We also now know of some 2,000 asteroids whose orbits cross the orbit of the earth, and therefore potentially could cause catastrophic environmental conditions for human beings. Smaller asteroids not leading to extinction events may be expected every 0.3 million years, while larger ones capable of mass extinction every 100 million years.

Such a serious possibility has recently led to serious political discussion on how the earth may be protected.

The end of the sun
Whether or not a comet hits, we know for certain that in 5 billion years, the earth will be uninhabitable. The sun will come to the end of its available hydrogen fuel and will begin to swell up, its outer layers swallowing up Mercury, Venus and the earth. It will then lose its outer layers and the centre will become a white dwarf, an object of high density about the size of the earth. Without the heat and light of the sun none of the remaining planets will be habitable.

At this point, it is envisaged that human beings will have moved away from the earth to colonise the galaxy, finding new stars and inhabitable planets. It may be worth noting in passing that this may not be as easy as it sounds. There are good arguments for believing that the earth may be unique in its environment.[4] However, human beings seem capable in the future of living on vast space stations or even engineering planetary atmospheres for their own benefit.

Yet terraforming (as scientists call it) a neighbouring world is not the only exit strategy. Donald Korycansky of the University of California at Santa Cruz and his collaborators suggest that earth could be edged out of harm's way with a gravitational slingshot, a trick long used to boost the speed of planetary probes. The earth would be the spacecraft, grabbing orbital energy from a passing asteroid. That would increase the earth's speed and enlarge its orbit.

Record?', *Monthly Notices of the Royal Astronomical Society*, 227 (1987): 863–885, and AW Wolfendale and DA Wilkinson, 'Periodic Mass Extinctions', in *Catastrophes and Evolution*, edited by SVM Clube (Cambridge: Cambridge University Press, 1989), 231–239.
4.   D Wilkinson, *Alone in the Universe?* (Crowborough: Monarch, 1997).

David Wilkinson

Repeated every few thousand years, Korycansky argues that such flybys could stretch earth's habitable lifetime by billions of years.

The end of the universe

A decade ago, cosmologists saw two possible futures for the universe.[5] The universe was believed to be slowing down in its expansion. Therefore, it could reach a point where the force of gravity acts on the matter of the universe to reverse the expansion force of the big bang, collapsing the universe back to a point of infinite density—a big crunch.

In such a scenario, a maximum size will be reached in not less than another twenty billion years (the current age of the universe is of the order of ten billion years). As the universe shrinks, the galaxies will merge, the sky as seen from any surviving planet will become as bright as the surface of the sun, stars will explode, and protons and neutrons will be reduced back to a quark soup before the universe either disappears in a quantum fluctuation or reaches a state of infinite density known as a singularity.

However, a second scenario was also on offer. Scientists argued that there might not be enough matter in the universe to make this happen. If this was the case, the universe expands forever becoming more and more a cold, lifeless place full of dead stars. This is called heat death, which Arthur Bloch likened to a giant stew cooling for billions of years so that soon the carrots will become indistinguishable from the onions!

For a number of years, both observers and theorists struggled to decide between these two possibilities. The key was thought to be how much matter there was in the universe, and this was difficult because gravitational studies of the local movements of galaxies indicated a large amount of unseen matter, that is dark matter. This form of matter that did not emit light was present but its nature was unknown.

---

5.   JN Islam, The Ultimate Fate of the Universe (Cambridge: Cambridge University Press, 1983), F Close, *End: Cosmic Catastrophe and the Fate of the Universe* (London: Simon & Schuster, 1988), and P Davies, *The Last Three Minutes: Conjectures about the Ultimate Fate of the Universe* (London: Weidenfeld & Nicolson, 1994).

However, since 1998 the picture has totally changed. Cosmology has undergone a massive revolution stemming from the work of those who wanted to see how the rate of expansion was changing in order to decide between big crunch and heat death. In this work they discovered something that nobody expected.

Two groups were at the forefront of this research. The Supernova Cosmology Project was headed by Saul Perlmutter, a physicist at Lawrence Berkeley Laboratory in California. At the same time, the High-Z Supernovae Search involved an international team headed by Brian Schmidt of Australia's Mount Stromlo and Siding Springs observatories and Adam Riess of the Space Telescope Science Institute in Baltimore, Maryland.

The principles of their work and their results were much the same although Perlmutter has tended to receive more media attention.

To see how the universe is expanding one must look at distant objects that emitted light much earlier in the universe's history. If one knows the intrinsic brightness of these objects then a comparison of their intrinsic brightness and the brightness of them as you measure from earth will give you the distance. This 'standard candle' method then allows you to compare their redshifts (which gives you their recession velocity) and distances in order to see how the universe was expanding in the past compared to now.

The key is therefore to find such standard candles that you can see at large cosmological distances. The two groups used supernovae explosions as these standard candles. For a few days, supernovae explosions of a certain type shine nearly as brightly as a whole galaxy. In particular, type Ia supernovae, which are the explosions of white dwarfs onto which matter has fallen from a companion star, can be used as standard candles over cosmological distances.

Now type Ia supernovae are not all exactly the same brightness. However, by studying the way the supernovae brighten and fade this uncertainty can be reduced so that distances can be known to within an error of seven per cent, which is equal to the best of astronomical distance indicators.

The main problem however with these standard candles is that there are not a lot of them, and they fade very quickly. They are quite rare—the last one seen in our galaxy was in 1006! However, by surveying lots of galaxies you multiply the chances of seeing them.

The technique was developed to survey a million galaxies in a typical night's observing and from that find more than ten supernovae.

The results announced in 1998 were completely unexpected. Far from the universe slowing down, the results indicated that the expansion of the universe was actually speeding up. This sent a shock wave through the scientific community. Observers tried to check the result and theoreticians began to ask what was causing such acceleration. As time has gone on the evidence has accumulated to show that the acceleration is real.

What does this mean? One possibility is that the data is misleading. For example, for some reason supernovae may be fainter in the past, and therefore look further away. That seems unlikely but remains a possibility. Or perhaps the predictions of general relativity, on which the expanding universe is based, are wrong. This would be unexpected because of the success of general relativity in so many other areas. If both of these options are rejected, then one is forced to the conclusion that some unknown type of material or force throughout the universe is accelerating its rate of expansion. It is this final conclusion to which most scientists have been drawn.

This new force therefore controls the expansion of the universe even though it has no discernible effect on scales less than a billion light years, that is we do not see its effects in our local stars and galaxies. To put it another way it seems that the combined amount of visible matter and dark matter is less than half the content of the universe. The rest is 'dark energy' with a totally unexpected feature, that is it does not attract like gravity but repels. Due to this repulsion force the universe is accelerating in its rate of expansion.

The evidence for dark energy has two unexpected bonuses. Measurements on the microwave background radiation seem at present to point to the total energy density in the universe equalling the critical density, which is more than the combination of matter and dark matter. The inclusion of dark energy allows cosmological models to fit with the microwave measurements. Second, this accelerating expansion naturally explains the apparent problem over the age of the universe and the oldest stars. In the mid-1990s evidence seemed to indicate that the universe was younger than the age of some of the stars within it. However, with the universe accelerating in its expansion rate the age of the universe is nearer to twelve billion years rather than 10 billion years, and this solves the problem.

What is this dark energy? Einstein in applying general relativity to the universe had suggested a cosmic repulsion, represented by his introduction of a 'cosmological constant' into the equations, in order to achieve a static rather than contracting universe. He rejected such a suggestion as his 'biggest blunder' yet physicists have returned to it.

Some have suggested that the vacuum itself can exert a force for it is a seething mass of particles and antiparticles. The difficulty of this vacuum energy is that it is completely inert, maintaining the same density for all time. This means that the cosmological constant would have to be fine-tuned at the beginning of the universe. This is an example of an anthropic balance, that is something in the law and circumstance of the universe that is 'just right' for the existence of life. Some distinguished cosmologists such as Sir Martin Rees and Steven Weinberg pursue an anthropic explanation for this fine-tuning, involving the concept of many universes and the fact that our existence selects for us this particular universe.

Others have suggested a new idea known as quintessence, which refers to a dynamical quantum field that gravitationally repels. The advantage of quintessence over the vacuum energy is that quintessence may interact with matter and evolve with time, so might naturally adjust itself to reach the present day value without the need for fine-tuning. The further advantage to cosmologists is that quintessence compared to the vacuum energy, may undergo all kinds of complex evolution. Theorists however are only speculating at this point. Some suggest that quintessence springs form the other dimensions required by string theory.

Those who suggest quintessence do so not only for scientific reasons. Ostriker and Steinhardt write:

> As acceleration takes hold over the next tens of billions of years, the matter and energy in the universe will become more and more diluted and space will stretch too rapidly to enable new structures to form. Living things will find the cosmos increasingly hostile. If the acceleration is caused by vacuum energy, then the cosmic story is

complete: the planets, stars and galaxies we see today are the pinnacle of cosmic evolution. But if the acceleration is caused by quintessence, the ending has yet to be written. The universe might accelerate forever, or the quintessence could decay into new form of matter and radiation, repopulating the universe . . . the universe had once been alive and then died, only to be a given a second chance.[6]

It is interesting that they are looking for some hope in this cosmic picture. As we shall see they are not alone in such speculation.

More precise measurements of supernovae over longer distances may be able to separate quintessence from the vacuum energy, and indeed differences in the acceleration rate produce small differences in the microwave background radiation that the MAP and Planck spacecraft should be able to detect in the near future.

It is probably at this point that we need to recall a word of caution from one of the world's most distinguished cosmologists, James Peebles. He wrote recently that 'the theory of the accelerating universe is a work in progress. I admire the architec-ture, but I would not want to move in just yet'.[7]

Yet at the same time we should not underestimate the importance of these findings. 'If you thought the universe was hard to comprehend before,' says University of Chicago astrophysicist Michael Turner, 'then you'd better take some smart pills, because it's only going to get worse.'

So what will be the future of a universe made up of five per cent ordinary matter, thirty-five per cent exotic dark matter and sixty per cent dark energy? T S Eliot was right: 'This is the way the world ends. Not with a bang but a whimper.' When the universe is 10^{12} years old, stars cease to form, as there is no hydrogen left. At this stage all massive stars have now turned into neutron stars and black holes. At 10^{14} years, small stars become white dwarfs. The universe becomes a

---

6.   JP Ostriker and PJ Steinhardt, 'The Quintessential Universe', *Scientific American*, January (2001): 51.

7.   PJE Peebles, 'Making Sense of Modern Cosmology', *Scientific American*, January (2001): 54.

cold and uninteresting place composed of dead stars and black holes. According to some theories of particle physics, protons themselves should decay at 10^{31} years. All that would be left would be some weakly interacting particles and a low-level energy background.[8]

A theological view of the future?
Theologians have responded in different degrees to these pictures of the future. Much work has been done in recent years on the destruction of the environment, both theologically and practically.[9] Perhaps because of this, interest has been deflected away from other questions about the future. For example, Moltmann's *God in Creation* demonstrates an environmental perspective but does not go further.[10]

Very few have taken seriously mass extinctions and the end of the sun, one of the exceptions being the philosopher John Leslie.[11] However, Leslie is not concerned too much with theological issues as with assessing the so-called 'Doomsday Argument' developed by physicists Brandon Carter and Richard Gott. This suggests that the human race will not survive for very much longer, for if it did then we would be living at an extraordinarily early epoch in human history. This itself poses huge theological questions that have not been addressed.

Other questions have been rarely addressed. The existence of mass extinctions raises the question of why there is so much waste in the

---

8. FC Adams and G Laughlin, 'A Dying Universe: The Long Term Fate and Evolution of Astrophysical Objects', *Reviews of Modern Physics* 69 (1997): 337–372.

9. See for example S McFague, *Models of God: Theology for an Ecological, Nuclear Age* (London: SCM, 1987), H Rolston III, Environmental Ethics (Temple University, 1989), L Osborne, *Stewards of Creation: Environmentalism in the Light of Biblical Teaching* (Oxford: Latimer House, 1990), G Prance, *The Earth under Threat: A Christian Perspective* (Iona: Wild Goose Publications, 1996), CA Russell, *The Earth, Humanity and God* (London: UCL Press, 1994), and R Frost and D Wilkinson, *A New Start: Hopes and Dreams for the New Millennium* (London: Hodder, 1999).

10. J Moltmann, *God in Creation* (San Francisco: Harper and Row, 1985).

11. J Leslie, *The End of the World* (London: Routledge, 1998).

creative process. The end of the sun raises the question of whether human beings are destined to be cosmic travellers, seeking out new planets capable of supporting life.

More seriously, very few theologians have taken seriously the scenarios for the end of the universe. It cannot be argued that this is because the scientific picture is very recent. The scenarios of heat death and big crunch have been with us in outline since the work of Einstein and Hubble in the 1920s. In fact, as early as 1854 Hermann Helmholtz gave a lecture on the implications of the 'running down' of the universe predicted by the second law of thermodynamics.[12]

It is an area where scientists and theologians need to work together but an area where there is a degree of mutual cynicism. The theologian Daniel Hardy writes, 'It is partly due to the widespread avoidance of direct engagement with creation and eschatology by theologians . . . that scientists and those of a speculative turn of mind have turned to such wider issues.'[13] Meanwhile the cosmologist Frank Tipler in his writing about the end of the universe wants to 'rescue eschatology from the hands of theologians who with a few exceptions . . . are quite ignorant of it'.[14] Likewise, in a series of lectures given at New York University in 1978, the physicist Freeman Dyson stated his purpose as, 'I hope with these lectures to hasten the arrival of the day when eschatology, the study of the end of the universe, will be a respectable scientific discipline and not merely a branch of theology'.[15] Here are challenges from the scientific community that theologians need to take seriously.

Why is there such a lack of theological enthusiasm to deal seriously with the end of the universe? First, gazing into the future is perceived to be very difficult and subject to a great deal of risk. The origin of the universe is often presented as a solid scientific fact, and

12. M and IF Goldstein, *The Refrigerator and the Universe* (Cambridge, Massachusetts: Harvard University Press, 1993).

13. DW Hardy, 'Creation and Eschatology', in *The Doctrine of Creation*, edited by C Gunton (Edinburgh: T&T Clark, 1997), 112

14. FJ Tipler, *The Physics of Immortality* (London: Weidenfeld & Nicolson, 1994), xiii.

15. FJ Dyson, 'Time without End: Physics and Biology in an Open Universe', *Reviews of Modern Physics*, 51/3 (1979): 447.

therefore theologians feel that they are on more solid ground. This may be illusory, as any models of the origin of the universe share with predictions about its future the assumption that the laws of physics apply at any time in the universe's history and one's model is only as good as the evidence on which it is built. Of course, the evidence of the redshift, the microwave background and the helium abundance in the universe forms a strong basis for the big bang model, allowing us to be more confident about the origin rather than the future. However, the future is not totally unknown. The long lifetime of the universe and a future of futility either in heat death or big crunch are as firm scientific conclusions as the big bang.

The second reason is a reason shared with theological work concerned with the origin of the universe. That is that there is an inherent difficulty in discussing the beginning and end of the universe from inside it. Arthur Peacocke has pointed out that the beginning and end of the universe are not events in history, but are the framework for history itself, and that the scientific method was never designed to deal fully with these issues. This recognition should lead to a degree of humility, but does not mean that it is useless to engage with the beginning of the universe. Indeed, for the Christian theologian, belief in the universe as creation means that the beginning and end of the universe are appropriate topics for theological work.

Third, theological work on the end of the universe has suffered from the theological excess of former years. Predictions of the end of the world, hell and damnation preaching, and the absurdity of some theological speculation have given eschatology a bad name. Work on the origin of the universe may seem safer, although the spectre of seven-day creationism is always in the background. Yet the existence of theological excess indicates the need for good theology in this area rather than silence. Theology needs to reclaim and explore the relationship between eschatology and the physical universe.

Fourth, it is difficult to see initially how work on the end of the universe has any practical value. Does it really matter whether the universe will end in 100 billion years? Does it have anything to say to questions of justice or Christian lifestyle? The strength of the revival of interest in Christian eschatology has been the way that theologians such as Moltmann have earthed the future in the past and present, with a moral implication for human response. It is difficult to see how this may be the case concerning events which are predicted billions of years in the future. However, we shall see that the end of the story always is important.

Hardy is one of the few theologians who have attempted to address the question of the end of the universe, in relation to both science and the doctrine of creation. Criticising Tipler's speculations about immortality (although perhaps not under-standing them fully), he suggests that theology must provide a combined account of creation and eschatology that would consist of 'the successful integration of current understanding of cosmology (the structure and dynamics of the universe) with theology (normative conditions of the structure and dynamics of the universe grounded in normative authority)'.[16]

He then outlines the lines on which the account might proceed. They may be summarised as:

1. Creation keeps the universe from ending, but also brings it to an end.

2. Covenant is a way to view the dynamics of the created universe with two aspects—obligatory and promissory.

3. These dynamics result from a radical gift/self-promise on the part of God, in which God gives to the other (universe, world, humanity) varying capacities for finitude, full possibilities of development, and redemption in the face of evil.

4. This action of God requires worship, and in this creation and eschatology return glory to God.

This is a helpful starting point but Hardy is somewhat disappointing in applying this to the scientific picture of the end of the universe. Indeed, after pleading for integration of the current understanding of cosmology he does not interact with it at all. Hardy needs a number of bridges between theology and cosmology in order for the integration to proceed.

The other theologian to take these issues seriously is Pannenberg. In 1981 in his questions to scientists, he asked,

---

16. DW Hardy, *God's Ways with the World* (Edinburgh: T&T Clark, 1996), 157.

> Is the Christian affirmation of an imminent end of
> this world that in some way invades the present
> reconcilable with scientific extrapolations of the
> continuing existence of the universe for billions of
> years ahead? . . . Scientific predictions that in some
> comfortably distant future the conditions for life
> will no longer continue on our planet are hardly
> comparable to biblical eschatology.[17]

It is interesting that this is a question he poses to the scientific community. However, Pannenberg could have equally addressed this question to the theological community.

In what follows I attempt to outline some of the specific theological questions raised by the scientific picture of the end of the universe. They may become bridges between scientists such as Tipler and theologians such as Hardy. It is the conviction of the paper that the scientific picture of the end of the universe is significant and needs to be taken with theological seriousness. I therefore pose six questions to both scientists and theologians.

What does the end of the universe mean for the doctrine of creation?
The futility of the end of the universe has been taken seriously by a number of philosophers and scientists. In a famous quote, Bertrand Russell laments:

> The world which science presents for our belief is
> even more purposeless, more void of meaning . . .
> that all the labours of the ages, all the devotion, all
> the inspiration, all the noonday brightness of human
> genius, are destined to extinction in the vast depth
> of the solar system, and the whole temple of man's
> achievement must inevitably be buried beneath the
> debris of a universe in ruins—all these things, if not

---

17. W Pannenberg, 'Theological Questions to Scientists', *Zygon*, 16 (1981): 65–77.

quite beyond dispute, are yet so nearly certain that
no philosophy that rejects them can hope to stand.[18]

Steven Weinberg is an American cosmologist who has made
outstanding and fundamental contributions to the development of
the subject during this century. Primarily because of the picture given
by science about the end of the universe, he states, 'The more the
universe seems comprehensible, the more it also seems pointless'.[19]

Christian theology needs to take this seriously. Can the universe
be understood as creation with this picture of the end? How
significant is the end of the story to the understanding of the whole?

This can be illustrated in the area of natural theology. A great deal
of work concerned with creation, especially in the area of science and
religion has concentrated on aspects of design.[20] These accounts see
the anthropic balances in the law and circumstances of the universe
as pointers to or at least consistent with the belief in a Creator God.

The danger of this is that it stresses the beautiful aspects of
creation rather than the reality of creation. David Hume criticised the
design argument for highlighting the good things in creation while
not taking into account evil. The same criticism could be made of
modern restatements of the design argument in the area of modern
cosmology.

One of the leading proponents of such an argument is the
physicist Paul Davies. In an interview I pressed him on the apparent
futility of the end of the universe.[21] He responded by restating the

---

18. B Russell, *Why I Am Not a Christian* (New York: George Allen and
    Unwin, 1957), 107.
19. S Weinberg, *The First Three Minutes* (London: Andre Deutsch, 1977),
    154.
20. See, for example, DA Wilkinson, 'The Revival of Natural Theology in
    Contemporary Cosmology', *Science and Christian Belief*, 2, number 2
    (1990): 95–116, P Davies, *God and the New Physics* (Harmondsworth:
    Pelican, 1983), JC Polkinghorne, *Science and Creation* (London:
    SPCK, 1988), A Peacocke, *Paths from Science Towards God: The End
    of All Our Exploring* (Oxford: Oneworld, 2001), and DA Wilkinson,
    God, Time and Stephen Hawking (Crowborough: Monarch, 2001).
21. D Wilkinson and P Davies, 'Surer Path to God?', *Third Way*, June
    1999.

importance of anthropic balances and indeed the possible existence of life throughout the universe. In his book, *Are We Alone?*, he concluded, 'For those who hope for a deeper purpose beneath physical existence, the presence of extraterrestrial life forms would provide a spectacular boost, implying that we live in a universe that is in some sense getting better and better rather than worse and worse'.[22] He seems desperate to avoid Weinberg's despair.

In contrast, a Christian understanding of creation can incorporate an end in futility. This is because such an end may not be totally unexpected within the tension that the creation is both good and fallen. Such a tension is seen within the biblical literature. Creation is good and beautiful, independent of our presence within it and ability to observe it (Genesis 1, Job 38–39). Yet at the same time, the fall has had some corrupting effects on the creation. So that the earth is under a curse but it is also under covenant (Genesis 8:21, 9:8–17).

Such a tension might lead to you to expect a creation that exhibits at the same time both purpose and futility. This of course raises questions of how the fall in terms of human rebellion affects the physical universe. The questions have some parallel with questions concerning human death. In one sense human beings are destined to futility, they will all die. Resurrection does not immediately solve questions such as what is the purpose of death. Is death itself part of God's intention within creation?

In the same way, was the future of the universe ending in heat death or big crunch part of God's plan from the beginning and if so, why? The answer to such questions must however struggle with the tension of a good and fallen creation. Not holding in some way to that tension leads to extremes. Hardy is right to see creation as keeping the universe from ending, but also bringing it to an end.

Some have stressed too much the fallen aspects of creation, seeing it as totally futile. Thus Frank Tipler picks up on this and writes, 'As I understand biblical eschatology, once humankind have no further use for the physical universe, it is terminated.' Yet that is not biblical eschatology. The Old Testament through the earth being under covenant makes clear God's continuing purposes for the earth. In the New Testament the pictures are not of human beings escaping from

---

22. P Davies, *Are We Alone?* (London: Penguin, 1996), 52.

the earth to heaven, but that God should do something with the earth, so we can dwell on it in rest with God. God comes here rather than we go somewhere else. The incarnation itself is an affirmation of the value and goodness of creation.

At the other extreme, a view of the universe that sees everything as good may find it difficult to cope with the futility of the end. Some see the physical evolution of the universe as bringing about something better and better, identifying God's purposes totally and exclusively with this universe. Indeed, the physical evolution leads to spiritual evolution in an ever-upward spiral.

Christian eschatology wants to avoid either extreme and does so not only by reflecting on the doctrine of creation but also on incarnation and resurrection. If the incarnation affirms creation, then the resurrection not only vindicates the whole created order but it also points the way beyond it, as the first fruits of a new created order. The biblical picture sees that God's purposes are still with this creation but go beyond it. On this basis the universe which science presents incorporating both purpose and futility has some resonances with the biblical picture.

What has the end of the universe to say to the doctrine of new creation?
Moltmann comments, 'It is God's new beginning which brings this perverted world to its deserved and longed-for end'.[23] This is an important Christian insight that is often overlooked.

Initially, the biblical theme of God creating a new heaven and a new earth seems to link well with a present universe destined to futility. Just as God's purposes for the human person go beyond the futility of physical death, so God's purposes go beyond the present creation to new creation.

However, we need to be clear what we really mean by this, and the initial picture has a great deal more to it than we might at first realise. For example, a 1983 commentary on a passage from 2 Peter that we will examine below quotes a commentator who identifies the

---

23. J Moltmann, 'Is the World Coming to an End or Has Its Future already Begun?', in *The Future as God's Gift*, edited by D Fergusson and M Sarot (Edinburgh: T&T Clark, 2000), 131.

biblical verse literally with the scientific picture of the end of the universe:

> The solar system and the great galaxies, even space-
> time relationships will be abolished . . . All elements
> which make up the physical world will be dissolved
> by heat and utterly melt away. It is a picture which
> in an astonishing degree corresponds to what might
> actually happen according to modern theories of the
> physical universe.[24]

The commentator does not seem worried at all that the writer of 2 Peter would be astonished to be told that 100 billion years would have to pass before these events! In addition to parallels of swelling suns and the like, another difficulty is in the relationship of old creation and new creation. Some strands of biblical interpretation have seen the new creation coming after the total destruction of the old, with no continuity between the two apart from God himself and a number of 'saved souls'.

Yet the main biblical passages are a little subtler than this. First, new creation is a theme that appears in Isaiah 65–66. For example,

> Behold I will create new heavens and a new earth.
> The former things will not be remembered, nor will
> they come to mind. But be glad and rejoice forever
> in what I will create, for I will create Jerusalem to be
> a delight and its people a joy. I will rejoice over
> Jerusalem and take delight in my people; the sound
> of weeping and of crying will be heard in it no
> more. (Isaiah 65:17–19)

The passage speaks of the action of God of bringing about a place that is joyful, life fulfilling with guaranteed work satisfaction and environmental safety. The question is, does verse 17 suggest abolition and replacement of the old creation? The context however describes

---

24. B Reicke, quoted in M Green, *2 Peter and Jude* (Leicester: IVP, 1983), 138.

the new creation in terms of a renewed and reordered earth. Thus Westermann comments, 'The words, "I create anew the heavens and the earth" do not imply that the heaven and earth are to be destroyed and in their place a new heaven and earth created . . . Instead, the world, designated as "heaven and earth" is to be miraculously renewed.'[25] Watts follows the same line, taking the 'new heavens and new earth' language to represent 'the new order, divinely instituted which chapters 40–66 have revealed and in which the Persian empire has Yahweh's sanction and Israel is called to be a worshipping and a pilgrim people with Jerusalem as its focus'.[26]

Second, 2 Peter 3:10 has traditionally been used to justify total destruction of this creation, using the English translation:

> But the day of the Lord will come like a thief. The heavens will disappear with a roar; the elements will be destroyed by fire, and the earth and everything in it will be burned up. (2 Peter 3:10)

This 'burning up' has been identified in various scenarios ranging from the fireball of the big crunch to the utter destruction of the present cosmos by fire and replacement by a new one. On this view the present physical universe has no ultimate place in God's purposes.

However, as Bauckham has persuasively argued, the translation is somewhat misleading.[27] There is a divergence in the manuscripts and 'burned up' is not the only translation. The earliest and the best manuscripts suggest the earth and everything in it will be found out, that is exposed and laid bare. The writer is not speaking about destruction but purging. This passage is about God's judgment, not cosmological speculation.

Support for this comes from the way the verb is linked in the Old Testament to judicial and quasijudicial scrutiny (eg Exodus 22:8, Psalm 17:3 and Daniel 5:27). In the Old Testament, fire is used as a metaphor of judgment, which simply does not destroy but purifies

---

25. C Westermann, *Isaiah 40–66* (London: SCM, 1969), 408.
26. JDW Watts, *Isaiah 34–66* (Waco, Texas: Word, 1987), 354.
27. R Bauckham, *Jude, 2 Peter* (Waco, Texas: Word, 1983), 316–322.

(eg Isaiah 21–26, Malachi 1–4), and the language of dissolving or melting would fit in with the figurative use of the idea of fire refining impure metals.

Thus verses 7-12 are about God's act of judgment that will purge the created order of all evil. It is out of this act of judgment that a new heaven and a new earth come about (v13). Indeed, the parallel with the Flood (vv 5–6) suggests that although the event may be cataclysmic, there is still considerable continuity between the world before and after purifying judgment. As Bauckham comments, 'Such passages emphasise the radical discontinuity between the old and the new but it is nevertheless clear that they intend to describe a renewal not an abolition of creation'.[28]

The third passage concerning new creation occurs in Revelation 21 and 22:

> Then I saw a new heaven and a new earth, for the
> first heaven and the first earth had passed away,
> and there was no longer any sea. (Revelation 21:1)

Once again this has been interpreted as the total destruction of the old creation. However, this does not fit with what follows. The images are of a new Jerusalem coming down out of heaven presumably to the new earth (v 2) and the statement, 'see I am making all things new' (v 5). Beasley-Murray comments on this verse, 'The word order should be observed, "Behold, new am I making all things!" The emphasis is on the newness, which God imparts to his creation, and therefore to his creatures. He is not discarding them, but granting them to know the newness of life manifest in the risen Christ, and operative even in this age in all who are in Christ.'[29]

---

28. R Bauckham, 'Response to Ernest Lucas—The New Testament Teaching on the Environment', paper presented at A Christian Approach to the Environment, The John Ray Initiative, Brunei Centre, University of London, 20 February 1999.

29. GR Beasley-Murray, *The Book of Revelation* (London: Oliphants, 1974), 312.

Here we have again the renewal of the old by a radical transformation, not the abolishing of it to start again. Bauckham comments, 'The contrast between "the first heaven and the first earth" on the one hand, and "the new heaven and the new earth" on the other refers to the eschatological renewal of this creation, not its replacement by another'.[30]

The fourth passage, 1 Corinthians 15:35–49 also follows this line. In his imagery of seed and plant, Paul combines continuity and transformation. The old creation is not abolished but is transformed. The resurrection of Jesus provides the model for this. The New Testament sees the resurrected Jesus as the same Jesus but somehow different.

What is important in all of this is that the New Testament does not see new creation as God's 'second attempt'. John Polkinghorne summarises, 'The new creation is not a second attempt by God at what he had first tried to do in the old creation. It is a different kind of divine action altogether, and the difference may be summarised by saying that the first creation was *ex nihilo* while the new creation will be *ex vetere*. In other words, the old creation is God's bringing into being a universe that is free to exist "on its own", in the ontological space made available by the divine kenotic act of allowing the existence of something wholly other; the new creation is the divine redemption of the old.'[31]

This redemption of the old seems to be pictured in terms of a long process such as seed into plant as well as a specific event of judgment such as in the 2 Peter passage. What is common is that both are acts of God. There is no sense of creation progressing by itself—only God's actions can bring about a new creation.

The end of the universe envisioned by science can interact well with this. The ultimate fate of the universe is not an ever-upward spiral, indeed it needs to be saved from futility by an act of God. The only 'good ending' of the story is a transformation or renewal of the present universe. Ian Barbour argues that the biblical stories of the

30. R Bauckham, *The Theology of the Book of Revelation* (Cambridge: Cambridge University Press, 1993), 49.
31. J Polkinghorne, *Science and Christian Belief* (London: SPCK, 1994), 167.

end are symbolic expressions of trust in God.[32] The importance of trust in God for the future can be seen in the contemporary perspective of the end of the universe.

If the resurrection of Jesus gives us the best model of the new creation, we can tentatively ask how this new heaven and earth will exhibit both continuity and discontinuity with the present creation. How might we characterise this theological continuity and discontinuity in terms of the scientific view of the universe? It seems to me that within many aspects to be explored, two areas are the nature of space-time and the nature of matter.

In terms of space-time, many theologians have seen new creation as some timeless existence. Yet many contemporary theologians suggest that divine eternity should not be conceived of as sheer timeless-sness. Time is important for relationship and growth. The continuity may be that time is real in the new creation but the discontinuity is that time no longer limits us in the way that it does in this creation. In this creation time is associated with decay and growth, but in new creation might time be simply about growth?

In terms of matter what will be the nature of the new creation? The resurrection body of Jesus implies some form of physical embodiment that has the continuity with this creation of eating fish and seeing the marks of the nails. However, the risen and ascended Jesus does not need to eat fish to survive, and the marks of crucifixion are now marks of glory rather than suffering. Physical matter has been transformed. In this creation matter comprises energy and information pattern. How is that transformed in new creation? Is the information pattern embodied in a different way? Certainly, the Christian understanding of Eucharist points towards this continuity and discontinuity of matter, the bread and wine being a foretaste of the heavenly banquet.

What does the future of the universe say to the relationship of the earth to the universe?
In the movie *Annie Hall*, the young Woody Allen is so worried about the expansion of the universe that he cannot do his homework.

---

32. Ian Barbour, *When Science Meets Religion: Enemies, Strangers or Partners?* (London: SPCK, 2000).

'Someday it will break apart,' he moans, 'and that will be the end of everything.' But, his mother replies, 'You're here in Brooklyn! Brooklyn is not expanding!'

I suggested earlier that many contemporary pictures of the future, certainly in the popular arena, are concerned with the end of the world rather than the end of the universe. The question of the end of the world is much more immediate of course than the end of the universe. However, in the last three decades, work on the anthropic principle has demonstrated the close connection between the earth and the universe in the context of the origin of the universe. That is, the earth only exists because of very sensitive balances in the laws and circumstances of the early universe. This at the very least raises the question of the relationship of the earth and the universe in the context of their end. Indeed the 'doomsday argument' is based on the assumption that expansion into the universe is the inevitable future for human beings.

Much of the biblical material quite understandably pictures the end of the world rather than the end of the whole universe. How far can the biblical view of the earth or the world be extrapolated to all creation? Furthermore, how does God's act of redemption of human beings relate, if at all, to the whole universe?

One of the key passages in this is also a difficult one to understand:

> The creation waits in eager expectation for the sons of God to be revealed. For the creation was subjected to frustration, not by its own choice, but by the will of the one who subjected it, in hope that the creation itself will be liberated from its bondage to decay and brought into the glorious freedom of the children of God. We know that the whole creation has been groaning as in the pains of childbirth right up to the present time. (Romans 8:19–22)

What is the relationship of the rebellion and redemption of human beings to creation? Some have interpreted this in a very anthropocentric way, that we are at the centre of the universe and therefore our state determines the state of the rest of the universe.

The geneticist RJ Berry, writing with the environmental issue in mind, argues that Paul's point is that as long as we refuse to play the part assigned to us by God, that is to act as his stewards, then the entire world of nature is frustrated and dislocated. That is, 'an untended garden is one which is overrun by thorns and thistles'.[33]

In this he follows Cranfield who comments:

> What sense is there in saying that 'the subhuman creation—the Jungfrau, for example, or the Matterhorn, or the planet Venus—suffers frustration by being prevented from properly fulfilling the purpose of its existence'? The answer must surely be that the whole magnificent theatre of the universe, together with all its splendid properties and all the varied chorus of subhuman life, created for God's glory, is cheated of its true fulfilment so long as man, the chief actor in the great drama of God's praise, fails to contribute his rational part . . . just as all the other players in a concerto would be frustrated of their purpose if the soloist were to fail to play his part.[34]

Thus human disobedience means that the natural order cannot achieve its goal. The redemption of humans is a part of wider redemptive work.

Does this mean that humans have some part to play in the renewal of the cosmos as well as the renewal of the earth? It is easier to see how renewed human beings may join in with God's purposes of cleaning and caring for the environment. It is harder to see this in a cosmic perspective.

---

33. RJ Berry, 'Creation and Environment', *Science and Christian Belief*, 7, number 1 (1995): 39.

34. CEB Cranfield, 'Some Observations on Romans 8:19–21', in *Reconciliation and Hope: Essays on Atonement and Eschatology*, edited by R Banks (Grand Rapids: Eerdmans, 1974), 224–230.

What does the end of the universe mean for providence?
Models of providence have to take seriously the universe over its entire history, rather than just the present state of the universe.[35] Polkinghorne has em-phasised this in relationship to the beginning of the universe. Although those models of providence that picture the universe as God's body work reasonably well with a universe of its present structure, variety and life, Polkinghorne has pointed out that such models are weak in coping with the universe as a 'quark soup' in the first few moments of the big bang.[36]

We can raise the same weakness in relation to the end of the universe. At this point does God's body decay forever or die? Models that stress immanence too much at the expense of transcendence must take the end of the universe with seriousness.

Likewise, models that stress God's non-intervention in the universe are presented with an interesting question in terms of the end of the universe. For example, Wiles' model sees God simply sustaining the creative process of the universe, limiting himself not to act in the world in any particular way.[37] The question then arises, is God sustaining a process that will end in futility? The universe may seem creative and diverse at the moment, giving the human actors freedom to work out the drama as they wish. But what of the time when the universe is tending to destruction and the uniformity of heat death? Has God given the actors freedom to work out their own drama in a theatre that is destined for demolition?

An allied question concerning God's action in the universe concerns what is the purpose of God in creation. Arguing against new creation as God's second attempt to get things right, Gunton has suggested that that creation is to an end, which is that all that is within space time be perfected in praise of the creator. Redemption is then the 'achievement of the original purpose of creation'.[38] Moltmann views Christian eschatology not as ending but as beginning of new creation, when creation is finally taken up into life

35. D Wilkinson, 'The God of the Physical Universe' in *Science, Life and Belief,* edited by RJ Berry and M Jeeves (Leicester: Apollos, 1998).

36. JC Polkinghorne, *Science and Providence* (London: SPCK, 1988).

37. M Wiles, *God's Action in the World* (London: SCM, 1986).

38. C Gunton, *Christ and Creation* (Grand Rapids: Eerdmans, 1992), 57.

of Trinity.[39] But how do these theological concepts relate to the scientific picture for the future of the physical universe? Is the physical universe, sustained by God, simply a backdrop to the purposes of God in redemption and perfection?

What does the end of the universe mean for hope?
In one of the few books that deals directly with the end of the universe, Polkinghorne and Welker rightly point out, 'Scientific prognosis puts to theology the question of whether it is not, in fact, ultimate . . . despair that is the appropriate human attitude to the world in which we live. Theology's response is to replace despair with hope and joy.'[40]

Bauckham and Hart have recently examined what they suggest is one of the meta-narratives of the Western world, that is the belief in human progress.[41] In this, human history is pictured as a long march towards the Utopian goal.

A number of factors have contributed to such a myth. The Enlightenment confidence in human reason gave rise to the belief that once human beings were freed from authority, prejudice and superstition, they would achieve prosperity. The success of science and technology gave confidence to the human ability to shape not just the world but also the future. Education came to be seen in a central role, able to deliver not just knowledge but moral change. Models of biological evolution gave philosophical models of progress, that is just as the biological world had given rise to human beings, so human beings could evolve to bring about a better world.

On the basis of these things, the power and responsibility for creating the future are seen to be human. Humanity can deliver

39. J Moltmann, *The Coming of God: Christian Eschatology* (London: SCM, 1996).
40. JC Polkinghorne and M Welker, 'Introduction', in *The End of the World and the Ends of God: Science and Theology on Eschatology*, edited by JC Polkinghorne and M Welker (Harrisburg, Pennsylvania: Trinity Press International, 2000), 11.
41. R Bauckham and T Hart, *Hope against Hope: Christian Eschatology in Contemporary Context* (London: DLT, 1999).

Utopia, and this myth of human progress was able to replace trust in God.

Bauckham and Hart go on to show how such a myth has had its credibility shattered in the events of the twentieth century. War, torture, famine, poverty and the ecological crisis all undermine the belief of humanity able to achieve Utopia.

It is interesting to note against such a background that the myth of human progress appears quite strongly in some of the responses to the 'cosmic pessimism' of science. There are those who see science and technology not simply as the cause of environmental damage but in fact the way out of such problems. Nuclear technology (and then speculation about cold fusion) was sold as energy that would not use up fossil fuels. In the movies *Armageddon* and *Deep Impact* the world is saved by a combination of technology, human ingenuity and courage. Even within the scientific literature, the end of the sun is combated by terraforming in other solar systems.

The 'myth of human progress' is also a strong theme in the some of the responses to the despair of Stephen Weinberg. Two leading cosmologists, Freeman Dyson and Frank Tipler see technological progress as the way out of this despair at the futility of the universe.

Perhaps the most intriguing unknown, however, concerns the cosmic role played by intelligent life itself. As the physicist Freeman Dyson notes, 'It is impossible to calculate in detail the long-range future of the universe without including the effects of life and intelligence. Much of the earth has been trans-formed, for better and worse, by the presence here of an intelligent species capable of manipulating its environment for its own benefit. Similarly, advanced civilisations in the far future might be able to melt down stars and even entire galaxies to make gigantic campfires, or otherwise tilt the long-term odds in their favour. Life in the waning cosmic twilight might be jejune, but it could last a long time. Consider the marshalled resources of all the natural and artificial intelligences in the observable universe over the next, say, trillion years.'[42]

---

42. F Dyson, *Infinite in All Directions* (New York: Harper and Row, 1988).

In a heat death universe Dyson suggested that biological life would adapt first through genetic engineering to redesign organisms that could cope in such a universe. Then consciousness would be transferred to new kinds of hardware that would be able to cope with the ultra-low temperatures of a heat death universe, including for example a complex dust cloud. Such a cloud could maintain itself forever and collect an endless amount of information. Thus he concluded, 'life and intelligence are potentially immortal'.

As Davis has pointed out, such a view is depen-dent on a number of controversial assumptions.[43] First, conscious-ness is simply defined as a type of complex physical structure. Even if a computer or dust cloud could mirror the complexity of the human brain, would this infer consciousness? For example, could consciousness survive without any other consciousness to relate to? Second, Dyson's scenario is dependent on the survival of matter. If as some theories of particle physics predict, the proton does decay there will come a point when the universe will only consist of radiation, and the complex structures cannot be maintained.

Such an interest in immortality has been pursued also by Tipler.[44] In contrast to Dyson he pursues the future of humanity, or more strictly human intelligence, within a universe which collapses back to a big crunch.

Tipler has been one of the cosmologists at the forefront of thinking concerning the anthropic principle. Extending the anthropic principle into the future, he proposed with John Barrow what they called the Final Anthropic Principle, that is, 'Intelligent information processing must come into existence in the universe, and once it comes into existence it will never die out'.[45]

In order to get to this, Tipler first notices that although the present universe is ten billion years old, its future even in a closed model is at

---

43. JJ Davis, 'Cosmic Endgame: Theological Reflections on Recent Scientific Speculations on the Ultimate Fate of the Universe', *Science and Christian Belief*, 11 (1999): 15–27.
44. FJ Tipler, *The Physics of Immortality* (London: Weidenfeld and Nicolson, 1994).
45. JD Barrow and FJ Tipler, T*he Anthropic Cosmological Principle* (Oxford: Oxford University Press, 1986).

least another 100 billion years. He speculates about what might be possible technologically in such a long future. He suggests that although humans themselves might die, information processing would continue within computers. Indeed, our consciousness may be transferred to computers. As computers expand across space then information processing would increase. He argues that it is possible on such a model that a point will be reached when an infinite amount of information will have been processed, and 'life' has expanded everywhere in the universe.

This 'Omega Point' contains all the information of the universe and could change the nature of the universe itself. Life has achieved 'God-like' attributes. Immortality for Tipler is simply that there are an infinite number of thoughts before the big crunch. Such a picture is a long way from the Christian belief in resurrection and new life within a personal relationship with a Creator God.

Once again this scenario is dependent on a number of assumptions. First, Tipler's speculations are dependent on the universe being closed—in fact this is a particular prediction of his theory. As we saw earlier the present evidence is that the universe is not closed, in fact it is increasing in its expansion rate. Second, as with Dyson, can consciousness be so easily transferred to digital computers? Third, there seems little justification for believing that complex structures necessary for life could be maintained anywhere near the final state of big crunch.[46]

Nevertheless both Dyson and Tipler represent a cosmic version of the myth of human progress. They imagine that through scientific and technological development human beings will be able to achieve some sort of immortality. Yet what sort of immor-tality is achieved? It seems to be a desperate way of respon-ding to the futility of the universe.

I have argued elsewhere that such optimism in future technology and indeed a critique of it is a major feature of recent science fiction.[47] Within certain works of science fiction, in particular the *Star*

---

46. See GFR Ellis and DH Coule, 'Life at the End of the Universe', *General Relativity and Gravitation*, 26:7 (1994): 738.
47. DA Wilkinson, *The Power of the Force: The Spirituality of the Star War Films* (Oxford: Lion, 2000).

Wars movies of George Lucas, the myth of human progress is seen to be inadequate and hope is based on the belief in transcendence. It seems that Tipler is striving for such a thing in his 'Omega Point' theory.

Bauckham and Hart show that the Christian hope is based on the belief in transcendence. George Steiner has pointed out that it is the most creative people in art and poetry who resist ascribing meaninglessness to the world and history.[48] They 'wager' on the meaningfulness of the world. Bauckham and Hart suggest that this in fact is a wager on God, for it is only through faith in a transcendent God that you actually get meaning or ending. The Christian is able to wager on God of the resurrection, which at the same time affirms the physical creation, disrupts the pessimism of the world and offers hope of a new beginning. They conclude:

> In faith we shall see duly, our imagination is engaged, stretched and enabled to accommodate a vision of a meaningful and hopeful future for the world, a meaning which could never be had by extrapolating the circumstances of the tragic drama of history itself.[49]

Neither the despair of Weinberg or the confidence in human progress of Dyson and Tipler give the hope that faith in a transcendent God gives.

Does this search for hope concerning the end of the universe fall into the revised natural theology so popular in terms of the beginning of the universe in anthropic balances and intelligibility? There, scientists on the basis of the science see pointers towards transcendence. The futility of the end of the universe may be another pointer to the hope that only a transcendent God gives. Polkinghorne has rightly pointed out that even suggestions in quantum

---

48. G Steiner, *Real Presences: Is There Anything in What We Say?* (London: Faber, 1989), 227.
49. Bauckham and Hart, *op cit*, 51.

cosmologies of inflationary universes bubbling up all of the time can be seen as the hope of endless fertility.[50]

What does the end of the universe mean for ethics?
There are ethical questions about the future, which seem irrelevant at this point, but are already being mentioned by scientists and philosophers. It would seem that within the next century, human beings will have the technological and financial ability to live beyond the atmosphere of the earth. Cities in space or 'terraforming' on planets such as Mars are theoretical possibilities.

The ethical questions concerning these possibilities are very real. Terraforming has been considered as a way out of the ecological crisis. Put bluntly, you do not have to worry about global pollution or using up all the resources, because you can simply move on to another planet. However, it seems likely that the only ones who will 'move on' will be the rich and powerful, leaving the rest to the polluted, overpopulated and exploited planet earth.

Yet in terms of the end of the universe, even terraforming or cities in space are limited. Does this long-term end of the universe have any bearing on ethical questions?

Bridger makes an interesting comment on this in the context of ecology. Noting that most ecological ethics stem from some understanding of creation in terms of its beginning alone, he argues that eschatology should not be neglected:

> The primary argument for ecological responsibility lies in the connection between old and new creation. We are called to be stewards of the earth by virtue of our orientation to the Edenic command of the Creator and also because of our orientation to the future. In acting to preserve and enhance the created order, we are pointing to the coming rule of God in Christ. Ecological ethics are not, therefore,

---

50. CJ Isham, 'Quantum Theories of the Creation of the Universe', in *Quantum Cosmology and the Laws of Nature: Scientific Perspectives on Divine Action*, edited by RJ Russell *et al* (Berkley: Center for Theology and the Natural Sciences, 1993), 49–89.

anthropocentric; they testify to the vindicating acts of God in creation and redemption. Paradoxically, the fact that it is God who will bring about a new order of creation at the end, and that we are merely erecting signposts to that future need not act as a disincentive. Rather it frees us from the burden of ethical and technological autonomy and makes it clear that human claims to sovereignty are relative. The knowledge that it is God's world, that our efforts are not directed toward the construction of an ideal utopia, but that we are (under God) building bridgeheads of the kingdom, serves to humble us and to bring us to the place of ethical obedience.[51]

In the integration of the scientific and theological pictures, does the holding together of creation and eschatology give a stronger basis for ethics?

Hardy has pointed out that in earlier times moral patterns as well as the physical conditions of the world suggested 'the fundamental shape of the eschata'.[52] He suggests that apocalyptic accounts identify the moral issues taken into account in final times, and show how they will be resolved. Does the scientific view of the end of the universe itself pose a moral question that has to be taken into account in any understanding of how God relates to the last things?

Conclusion

Einstein once wrote to a child anxious about the fate of the world, 'As for the question of the end of it I advise: Wait and see!' It may be wise advice but sometimes Christian theology may be taking it too literally. We may need to be tentative in our theological speculation about the future. Yet the God of the future who reveals himself in the

---

51. F Bridger, 'Ecology and Eschatology: A Neglected Dimension', *Tyndale Bulletin*, 41.2 (1990): 290–301.
52. DW Hardy, *God's Ways with the World* (Edinburgh: T&T Clark, 1996), 155.

death and resurrection of Jesus gives us a basis for considering the future now.

The questions I have attempted to outline above may provide a link from the scientific picture to the theological picture, helping in some way a fruitful integration or at least interaction. In some cases I have made some suggestions on how these questions might be addressed. In other cases I have simply raised questions for further work. In some cases, the scientific picture of the end of the universe may have no theological significance at all. However, it is difficult to be confident of such a conclusion when so little work that takes seriously both the science and theology has been done in this area.

In particular, I suggest the resurrection of Christ needs more consideration in this integration. It provides some basis for the relationship of creation and new creation, it raises questions for providence, becomes the foundation of hope and has been argued to be the ground for Christian ethics.[53] In the face of those who view the futility of the future of the universe with great despair, it is in the words of Moltmann not only 'a consolation in a life . . . doomed to die, but it is God's contradiction of suffering and death'.[54]

53. O O'Donovan, *Resurrection and Moral Order: An Outline for Evangelical Ethics* (Leicester: IVP, 1986).
54. J Moltmann, *Theology of Hope* (London: SCM, 1967), 21.

Index

A

B